Axis Consultation

754-8500

754-9

Also by Wesley J. Smith

The Lawyer Book
The Doctor Book
The Senior Citizens' Handbook

With Ralph Nader

No Contest: Corporate Lawyers and the Perversion of Justice in America
Collision Course: The Truth About Airline Safety
The Frugal Shopper
Winning the Insurance Game

Forced Exit

FORCED EXIT

The SLIPPERY SLOPE *from*
ASSISTED SUICIDE
to LEGALIZED MURDER

WESLEY J. SMITH

TIMES 𝕿 BOOKS

RANDOM HOUSE

Grateful acknowledgment is made to Larry Johnson for permission to reprint excerpts from letters and an editorial from the December 9, 1994, issue of *The Vancouver Sun* written by his son, Teague Johnson, which appear on pages 186 and 187 of this book, and excerpts from letters from Larry Johnson to the author. All material copyright © by Larry Johnson. Used by permission.

Library of Congress Cataloging-in-Publication Data

Smith, Wesley J.
Forced exit : the slippery slope from assisted suicide to
legalized murder / Wesley J. Smith.
p.   cm.
Includes index.
ISBN 0-8129-2790-7 (alk. paper)
1. Assisted suicide.   I. Title.
R726.S576   1997
179.7–dc21   96-46723

Random House website address: http://www.randomhouse.com/

Printed in the United States of America on acid-free paper

24689753

First Edition

To my father, Wesley L. Smith, who faced his own death with such courage and fortitude, and to my mother, Leona Smith, who loved him, and loves me, so well

ACKNOWLEDGMENTS

The creation of this book would literally have been impossible without the active assistance of so many people who freely shared their feelings, knowledge, attitudes, and opinions with me, including Pieter Admiraal, M.D.; Dr. William S. Andereck; Dan Avila, attorney-at-law; Robert Bernhoft, M.D.; James Bopp, attorney-at-law; William Burke, M.D.; Ira R. Byock, M.D.; Daniel Callahan; Charles L. Cavalier II; Eric Chevlen, M.D.; Dana Cody, attorney-at-law; Diane Coleman; Mathew E. Conolly, M.D.; Yeates Conwell, M.D.; Paul Corrao, M.D.; E. J. Dionne; Richard Doerflinger; Ljubisa J. Dragovic, M.D.; Beth Roney Drennan, attorney-at-law; Vincent Fortanasce, M.D.; Michael J. Franzblau, M.D.; Cheryl Eckstein, M.D.; Hugh Gallagher; Carol Gill; K. F. Gunning, M.D.; Jacqulyn Hall, attorney-at-law; Herbert Hendin, M.D.; Nat Hentoff; Larry Johnson, Melanie Zdan, and Cara Elrod; Professor Yale Kamisar; Evan J. Kemp, Jr.; W.C.M. Klijn; Dr. Gerald (Chip) Klooster II and Mary Klooster; Charles Krauthammer; Madelaine Lawrence; Gary Lee, M.D.; Paul Longmore; Tom Lorentzen; Tom Marzen, attorney-at-law; Ginny McKibben; Steven H. Miles, M.D.; Donald Murphy, M.D.; Fr. Richard Neuhaus; Mark O'Brien; Timothy Quill, M.D.; Harvey Rosenfield; Matthew Rothschild; Daniel P. Salmasy, O.F.M., M.D.; Dame Cicely Saunders; Randolph Schiffer, M.D.; Janie Hickock Siess, attorney-at-law; Lonny Shavelson; Elizabeth Skoglund; Beverly Sloane; William Stothers; Eugene Sutorius; W. Russell Van Camp, attorney-at-law; Teri Van Camp; Terry Stimpson; William F. Stone, attorney-at-law; I. van der Sluis, M.D.; Dr. Maurice Victor; Nancy Valco; Richard Vigilante; Rebekah Vinson; Kathy Weaver; Jos V. M. Welie; Jim Werth; Kathi Wolfe; and Jessica Yu.

Special thanks to special friends and colleagues who do such good and important work with the International Anti-Euthanasia Task Force: Rita Marker, Mike Marker, Kathi Hamlon, John Hamlon, Robert Hiltner, Nancy Minto, and Tom Murray.

I thank everyone at Times Books for their encouragement, commitment, and steadfast belief in this work, including (but not limited to) Peter Smith, Betsy Rapoport, Mary Beth Roche, Benjamin Dreyer, and Kate Scott.

Finally, my deep appreciation and love for all of my friends and family, who have put up with me during the writing of this book with such patience, good cheer, and affection, especially Ralph Nader; my Brotherman, Arthur Cribbs; Bub; the entire Saunders family, Florida, Connecticut, and Rhode Island branches; Jerry, Barbara, Jim, Vickie, Jennifer, Jeremiah, Stephen, Leslie, Rebecca, Eric, and Joshua; Chloë Barrett; M. B. Smith; Mom; and, most of all, my wife and total sweetheart, Debra J. Saunders.

Contents

INTRODUCTION

The seeds for this book, and my efforts as an anti-euthanasia activist, were sown on November 1, 1992. On that day, a Sunday, my friend Frances went to a hotel, checked in, got into bed, took some sleeping pills, pulled a plastic bag over her head, and died.

Frances's suicide was not an act born of impulse or momentary despair. She had been planning it for years. Indeed, almost from the moment I met her in Los Angeles in 1988, she had spoken enthusiastically about how empowering and ennobling it would be for her to take her own life. In her mind's eye, she saw herself beginning to suffer the debilitations of age. Rather than endure a slow decline and become a "burden" to her friends, Frances would say, "I'm going to hold a going-away party," where she hoped her many friends would surround her as she lay on a couch, tell her how much she meant to them, hold her hands and stroke her brow as she swallowed the drugs from her "horde of pills," and where she would slowly and quietly transform from living friend to deeply treasured memory.

Most of us who were among Frances's closest friends were appalled by her suicide fixation, and each, in our own way, tried to convince her not to do it. We told her repeatedly that we valued her presence among us. We tried to assure her that growing old did not make one less valuable as a human being, and that illness or disability did not make one a burden. We urged her to seek counseling, hoping that if she put as much energy and effort into living as she seemed to be putting into plans for dying, she could find renewed meaning and joy from a life that clearly did not satisfy her. We worried about her continually and wondered where on earth she had come up with the idea that self-destruction was a positive thing. Who had coined all of the euphemisms for self-destruction that sprinkled her vocabulary, such as "deliverance" and "final passage"?

It is important to note that in the first two years of our friendship, as Frances fantasized about her future death, she was not ill. She was, however, very unhappy. She had divorced years before, and her husband had remarried a younger woman, a fact of Frances's life that deeply humiliated and embittered her. The divorce had also hit her hard in the pocketbook, removing her from a thoroughly enjoyed life of upper-middle-class ease and gentility and forcing her to count pennies from her rent-controlled one-bedroom apartment. Meanwhile, the fact that her successor and her ex (who was ill with Alzheimer's) continued to live well was a constant wound that ate at Frances with every sparse alimony check she cashed, money she genuinely needed and at the same time deeply resented.

Frances had other emotional burdens. She said that one of her two sons was cognitively and emotionally disabled from injuries sustained in an auto accident. The accident had come just as the young man was making a big breakthrough in the screenwriting trade, and had cut him off from a dream come true. Frances never stopped worrying about him, and she despaired about his future once she was gone. Even more painful, Frances was so estranged from her other son that it would be an exaggeration to call their interaction a relationship.

Frances's talk about her suicide would wax during her more unhappy times and wane during the times she felt productive and useful—surely no coincidence. She was very active in local community clubs and was always thinking about how she could help those she loved to "get ahead." For example, Frances often helped her friends with business ideas, introducing them to others in her stable of associates and acquaintances who she felt could provide sage advice, opportunity, or help with ideas. Her female friends told me that hers was a great shoulder to cry on, especially for pals who had relationship difficulties. She definitely helped me and she knew it. She took great pride in being the inspiration for my book *The Senior Citizens' Handbook: A Nuts and Bolts Guide to More Comfortable Living*.[1]

Unfortunately, Frances's happy times were generally short-lived, and thoughts about suicide would again tug at her as relentlessly as gravity. It was like some perverse dance. She would plan the thing, we would change her mind, and then, for no apparent reason, she would announce she was planning it again.

At one point we all became convinced that Frances wasn't just talking anymore, that she was about to do it. Interventions were held. We pleaded and cajoled, doing everything we could think of to help her keep a firm grip on life—all to no avail. It would take a miracle, it seemed, to dissuade her.

Then, a miracle of sorts did happen. But it was nothing supernatural: Her alimony was cut off. Suddenly, Frances had a cause! The suicide was forgotten as Frances headed for court under a full head of steam, acting as her own attorney to force a resumption of her payments, and she succeeded. Clearly, here was a woman who, despite all her romanticized talk of her warm and fuzzy "deliverance," desperately needed a reason to live. But her triumph did not satisfy her for long. As the glow of her court victory wore off, Frances again spoke of suicide. At about this time she was diagnosed with lymphatic leukemia, which was treatable but certainly upsetting. She developed a neuropathy (a degenerative state of the nervous system), from which she experienced a distressing burning sensation on her skin. (Frances would complain bitterly that her H.M.O. doctors did not take her pain seriously, but she also refused to take the pain medication prescribed to help her.) While she had no visible limp, she was also a candidate for a hip replacement. And underneath it all was the abiding sadness about her life's many disappointments.

By this time, I had moved to San Francisco, so I had less personal contact with Frances than in previous years, although we kept up a lively interaction over the phone. Then, one day, one of her friends called, very upset, telling me, "Frances is planning to die next week, on her birthday." I called Frances immediately. I implored her at least to see a psychiatrist before doing it. She refused, saying, "He might give me a pill that would make me not want to kill myself."

I was later told that she invited her friends in Los Angeles to her long-planned going-away party. All of her friends refused to attend. They loved her. They did not want her to kill herself. They would not support this chosen action.

Frances then told everyone the suicide was off. She even called my mother, who had also become her friend, and said that a "divine intervention" had saved her life. We all breathed a sigh of relief.

Frances was lying. Secretly she paid a distant cousin five thousand dollars to go with her to a hotel, where her only luggage was a stash of pills and a plastic bag. Two days afterward I and her other friends received her photocopied suicide note (the return address was simply "Frances"); in it she spoke of herself as being "in control" and stated that the "act is not one of 'suicide'—I consider that it [is] my final passage."

Frances's death was not noble and uplifting as she had fantasized. We miss Frances and mourn her loss, but she has not left behind the sweet garden of memory she fervently believed her death would create. None of her friends appreciated the morbid experience of receiving photocopies of her suicide letter in the mail after she was gone, and most of us felt angry, betrayed, and empty in the wake of her self-destruction.

With her death, Frances took her place among suicide statistics. More than thirty thousand people die by their own hand each year in the United States, more than are murdered and only about ten thousand fewer than are killed in auto accidents.[2] Suicide is the second leading cause of death among college students and the third leading cause of death among young people ages 15 to 24. The suicide rate for children ages 10 to 14 has more than doubled in the last ten years.[3] The elderly, like Frances, are particularly susceptible to self-destruction: Rates among that group rose 9 percent between 1980 and 1992.[4]

Usually, after a suicide, those who were close to the deceased person wonder why, grieve, and finally go on with their lives. But I had a queasy feeling that there was more to Frances's death than appeared on the surface. It was as if she had somehow been encouraged to pursue death. Yet I knew her friends had all tried to persuade her to embrace life. I tried to set this feeling aside but it would not go away. My unease was abstract, yet it was very real. I reminded myself of a character in a Stephen King novel who can sense, yet cannot see, the darkness that lurks behind a façade of normalcy.

I decided to investigate. Frances was one of the most organized women I have ever met. She kept a file for everything. I called the executrix of her will and asked her to look through Frances's papers to see whether she had kept a suicide file and, if so, to please send it to me.

A week later it arrived. It wasn't very thick. There were some news clippings that put a positive spin on suicide and a smattering of poetry. But most of the material was from an organization I had paid scant attention to before, the Hemlock Society. Specifically, Frances had collected several issues of the organization's newsletter, the *Hemlock Quarterly*. That these writings had a major influence on Frances there can be little doubt. She had highlighted much of the text with a yellow marking pen. Several issues were dog-eared from frequent reading.

As I read the material, my jaw literally dropped. I could not believe my eyes. The documents seemed scurrilous to me—nothing less than pro-suicide propaganda extolling self-destruction as a morally correct and an empowering experience. Most of the newsletters had stories in them—allegedly letters from satisfied readers—of warm and successful suicides, and/or advocacy pieces by euthanasia proponents. The articles had an almost religious tone to them that made me feel as if I were reading tracts from some bizarre death cult.

The January 1988 issue of the *Hemlock Quarterly* caught my eye because it was especially worn from frequent reading.[5] One of the stories inside, entitled "A Peaceful Passing," signed by "A New Member in California" (supposedly a grief counselor), told in glowing terms of the suicide of Sam, allegedly a terminal cancer patient. Frances had underscored these words from the story:

> *Believe it or not, we laughed and giggled and [Sam] seemed to relish the experience. I think for Sam it was finally taking control again after ten years of being at the mercy of a disease and medical protocols demanded by that disease.*

Suicide promoted as uplifting, enjoyable fun sickened me.

This wasn't the only disturbing passage. Sam's suicide was described as peaceful and calm, and the reader was assured that "all went smoothly" through the suicide, funeral, and burial. The writer even extolled the act of assisting the death as "very profound in my life," one that "has changed me and grown me."[6] In other words, the author depicted suicide as empowering and beneficial, not only for the deceased but for the "helper."

Another story in the newsletter, called "Planning Made Death Peaceful," written by "a loving family member," described the author's "instant" agreement to assist the "self-deliverance" of a relative with an "uncurable [*sic*], debilitating and hideous illness." The story described how the author collected the drugs to be used over time (just as Frances had done) and how the relative died "in complete peace within 15 or 20 minutes at most." The last paragraph had caught Frances's attention, as evidenced by the yellow highlighting:

> *It was indeed a good deliverance; much of it was due to foresight and planning. We had the necessary medications and the necessary knowledge. But I will always believe that most of it was due to the steadfast will and soul of my family member, who made a decision for self-deliverance and fully accepted it.*[7]

In other words, this "good deliverance" occurred because the ill person had the moral fortitude to go through with it, seeming to imply that those who don't have such courage are somehow not "steadfast" or lack "soul."

Other articles in the issue explained how to commit suicide. One provided a listing of the drugs that were good for suicide, describing the relative toxicity and the amount of each drug required to constitute a lethal
dose ("Drug Dosage Table").[8] Frances had underscored the names of the
drugs with the highest toxicity levels.

In "Self-Deliverance with Certainty," the reader was instructed on the
proper use of a plastic bag, described as a death method that is "less than
perfect but . . . not very much less than perfect."[9] Chills ran up my spine. It
was as if I were reading an exact description of Frances's death, so closely
had she followed these instructions.

There was a disclaimer of sorts in the article on drug dosages that read,
"Only for information of members of the National Hemlock Society for
possible self-deliverance from a future terminal illness and used in con-
junction with the material found in the book, *Let Me Die Before I Wake.*"[10]
That was just not credible to me. The entire message of the newsletter was
so positive and supportive of suicide as an answer to life's difficulties that
this caveat seemed to be less than veneer, in the end meaning absolutely
nothing. Frances, who was *not* terminally ill, had not underscored the
warning passage.

The more I thought about the Hemlock Society propaganda and its direct connection with Frances's death, the angrier I grew. Who were these
people to push a pro-suicide message on the depressed and vulnerable,
people looking desperately for some way to be in control of their unhappy
lives? They didn't even know Frances. Yet they had given her the moral
support to kill herself and had taught her how to do it. Although Frances
was without question responsible for her own self-destruction, I felt that
the Hemlock Society had fostered in her a romanticism about suicide that
helped her move to consummation. As I saw it, morally they had much to
answer for.

I am not alone in believing that the euthanasia movement, in which the
Hemlock Society plays an active part, has influenced the rise in our country's suicide rates, at least among the elderly. For example, Barbara Haight,
who directs a program at the University of South Carolina College of
Nursing to prevent suicide among the elderly, believes that the rise in euthanasia advocacy over the last ten years, the publicity surrounding Jack
Kevorkian, and other related events have "made suicide more acceptable
to people who once would not have considered it because of religious and
family concerns. They see it as a solution to their problems."[11] Frances is a
case in point.

One of the benefits of being a writer is that the word processor provides a productive outlet for painful feelings. In my anger, I wrote an article for the "My Turn" section of *Newsweek* called "The Whispers of Strangers," which was meant as a wake-up call about the dangers of the euthanasia movement and the message it sends to weak and vulnerable people.[12] My article touched people emotionally, but not in the way I had expected. I received about 150 letters. A few were very supportive, thanking me for warning about the euthanasia movement and commiserating about the pain that suicide causes survivors. But the vast majority of my correspondents were outraged that I criticized euthanasia. They did not believe it can destroy vital moral concepts, that "the preservation of human life is our highest moral ideal," that "a principal purpose of government" is to protect human life, that "those who fight to stay alive in the face of terminal illness," such as the actor Michael Landon, are "powerful uplifters of the human experience."[13]

These sentiments enraged my detractors. I was lectured that the idea of human life as "sacred . . . is no longer tenable."[14] I was accused of wanting "the pleasure of seeing her [Frances] as an incontinent living corpse ravaged by pain and drugs."[15] My thoughts about protecting life were seen as proof that "Wesley Smith lacks genuine compassion."[16] Another writer accused me of "self-righteous arrogance" because I disapproved of Frances's act to "advance slightly the date on which . . . she must inevitably shuffle off this mortal coil."[17] An especially harsh critic compared me to "Torquiemada [sic] of the Spanish Inquisition who devised fiendish tortures because our highest moral ideal was to get infidels to adapt [sic] Christianity."[18] And more than one correspondent echoed the hope expressed by "M.B." that "you live a long and suffering life."[19] Many correspondents expressed views that can only be described as pro-suicide. "This is the 90's, and suicide IS an alternative to life," one letter writer advised me.[20] "I congratulate Frances," another reader wrote, "on her decision to end her life when and how she wanted."[21] "R.K." thought that "we as a society will come to see the day we view suicide (and euthanasia) as acceptable and even good."[22] "L.M.S." was moved to proclaim that "suicide, as the act is called—for a person without responsibilities, or with a chronic disease—*is* a noble act" (italics in original).[23]

I was genuinely surprised. Were my correspondents outside the cultural mainstream, I wondered, or was I? If I was, when had the values that not so long ago were deemed self-evident truths by most of society changed so dramatically? And where was I when this change occurred?

The next paragraph in my article also attracted attention and criticism. I wrote:

> *Of greater concern to me is the moral trickledown effect that could result should society ever come to agree with Frances. Life is action and reaction, the proverbial pebble thrown into the pond. We don't get to Brave New World in one giant leap. Rather, the descent to depravity is reached by small steps. First, suicide is promoted as a virtue. Vulnerable people like Frances become early casualties. Then follows mercy killing of the terminally ill. From there, it is a hop, skip and a jump to killing people who don't have a good "quality" of life, perhaps with the prospect of organ harvesting thrown in as a plum to society.*[24]

Every reader who commented on this passage, both supporters and detractors of my point of view, was convinced I was overreacting. Each believed that such a progression was unthinkable in the United States, that as a humane people we would never allow ourselves to engage in such inhumane conduct. I was advised earnestly to have a bit more faith in people.

Would that my correspondents were correct. Unfortunately, I wasn't paranoid or alarmist; I was prescient. As this book will detail, my fears about the "moral trickledown" (the "slippery slope" I will frequently refer to)—and more—are justified either by events already happening or by proposals put forward seriously by mainstream opinion setters, by the medical intelligentsia, and by public policy makers. For example:

- In the United States, several courts have ruled that laws prohibiting assisted suicide are unconstitutional. One state, Oregon, has passed a law (Measure 16) that would specifically permit doctors to prescribe lethal drugs to patients diagnosed as having six months or less to live.

- Advocacy in favor of assisted suicide "only" for the terminally ill is already passé among euthanasia advocates. Legalizing hastened death is now promoted for the "hopelessly ill" or "desperately ill," as well as the dying. The "hopelessly ill" are disabled people, those with chronic illness, the frail elderly. Some "rational suicide" proponents advocate including those with severe mental or emotional problems who have no physical illness.

- Ann Landers has endorsed the establishment of death clinics where the elderly could go to be put to death rather than receive long-term care, calling the notion "a sane, sensible, civilized alternative to existing in a nursing home, draining family resources, and hoping the end will come soon. Too bad it's against the law. . . ."[25]

- Some people are already being killed on the basis of quality-of-life considerations, specifically the cognitively disabled, both unconscious and conscious, by having their feeding tubes removed in order to cause their deaths. Tube feeding has in fact been classified as a medical procedure, to permit the process of withholding it in such cases.

- The American Medical Association Council on Ethics and Judicial Affairs for a short period of time advocated that organs be harvested from anencephalic babies (babies born with parts of their brains missing) while they are still alive. The council was forced by A.M.A. opposition to retract this opinion, pending further study. But it is highly likely that the issue will return in the near future. If ever implemented, this would mark the first time in the United States since the end of slavery that the bodies of living human beings could be legally exploited as a natural resource.

And these items represent just the tip of the iceberg.

As the great United States Supreme Court justice Benjamin Cardozo once wrote about an earlier drive to legalize euthanasia, "Just as a life may not be shortened, so its value must be held as equal to that of any other, the mightiest or the lowliest."[26] Cardozo's point is that legalized euthanasia, which would permit the killing of certain categories of people by doctors (and perhaps others), is fundamentally incompatible with the traditional Western ethic, which I like to call the *equality-of-human-life ethic.*

The equality-of-human-life ethic requires that each of us be considered of equal inherent moral worth, and it makes the preservation and protection of human life society's first priority. Accepting euthanasia would replace the equality-of-human-life ethic with a utilitarian and nihilistic "death culture" that views the intentional ending of certain human lives as an appropriate and necessary answer to life's most difficult challenges. As I hope to demonstrate in this book, the dire consequences that would flow from such a radical shift in morality are profound and disturbing.

Frances always used to say that her forte was helping people find their proper place in life. Ironically, her suicide has done that for me. Since her death—largely because of the way she died—I have immersed myself in the euthanasia issue, reading volumes of material both pro and con, writing, and speaking out about the issue in the print and electronic media and in public speeches as often as I can. I have worked in close association with the International Anti-Euthanasia Task Force, an organization dedicated to raising awareness of the dangers inherent in legitimizing and legalizing euthanasia and assisted suicide. I have become acquainted with an international network of concerned people who share my views and who help me in my work as I help them. In short, I have become an activist. It is not an overstatement to say that I consider this the most profound endeavor in which I have ever engaged.

During these last few years, as I have immersed myself in euthanasia and related health-care issues, I have pondered, explored, and learned. It has not been easy. Euthanasia is an emotional and controversial subject, one that has confronted me with my fears about my own mortality, about growing old or becoming disabled. It has torn at my heart as I have been moved to tears in compassion for the ill, the dying, the discouraged, those in unrelieved pain, and the abandoned among us.

I have not come to my conclusions easily or glibly. I worry about whether my views are correct, my concern justified, my insights valid. But the more I think it through—the more I observe the trends, the more I learn, the more I ponder, the more I understand context—the more convinced I become that euthanasia is unwise, unethical, and just plain wrong, a social experiment that if implemented will lead to cultural and ethical catastrophe.

In this book I share what I have learned and trace how I have come to my conclusions. Or, as one of my friends described this project, I hope the book will help readers "connect the dots" about what the euthanasia path will do to our culture, our health-care system, our morality, and the way we view and treat ill and vulnerable people.

Finally, it is not enough to be a naysayer. The euthanasia issue did not arise in a vacuum. In my view, it has been driven by the despair caused by too many people watching helplessly as their loved ones writhe in pain because they received inadequate medical care. It has been fueled by the very reasonable fear of being victimized by our money-driven, dehumanizing, and increasingly impersonal health-care system. It is also a symptom of malaise, caused by the unraveling of community ties and the breakdown of families. But the death culture is not the answer to these abiding problems. Rather, it is a surrender to them.

There is another way. Humane and effective alternatives to euthanasia exist, alternatives that receive far too little attention in our national discourse. I will close this book by exploring some of these options in the firm belief that we can effectively meet the challenges of death, dying, and human suffering without losing our own humanity.

We know the way. The only question is, can we find the will?

WESLEY J. SMITH
OAKLAND, CALIFORNIA

A Word About Terminology

Before we begin our discussion of euthanasia, I would like to clarify the terminology utilized in this book. Many different terms are used by different sources for the acts of killing that will be discussed within these pages: *active voluntary euthanasia, nonvoluntary euthanasia, involuntary euthanasia, passive euthanasia, good death, planned death, assisted death,* etc. These terms and phrases, which may have great meaning in the ivory tower of academia, are of little use in a book designed for a general audience; in this context, they would only be confusing.

I will generally use the terms *kill, euthanasia,* and/or *assisted suicide.* I use the word *kill* because it is accurate and descriptive of what euthanasia and assisted suicide are about: "to deprive of . . . or put an end to life." Some may object to the use of this word because it elicits a strong emotional reaction—and well it should. Killing is what we are discussing here. The subject is too serious, in my view, to accept the fuzzy words and euphemisms preferred by euthanasia advocates as the spoonful of sugar that helps the hemlock go down.

By *euthanasia* I mean the killing of one person by another (usually but not always a doctor) because the person killed has a serious disease or injury, is disabled, is emotionally or mentally disturbed, is anguished, or is elderly. *Euthanasia* means, literally, "good death." (I do not believe that being injected with or swallowing poison is a "good death." But the term is so much a part of the language that no usable alternative exists.) *Assisted suicide,* for my purposes, means self-killing for the same reasons that euthanasia is undertaken. It differs from suicide in that it is not a solitary action but rather a joint effort. Another person actively participates, assists in, and/or facilitates the termination of life. Thus, if a doctor injects a patient with a sedative followed by curare (a lethal poison)—the usual practice in the Netherlands—that is euthanasia. If a doctor knowingly prescribes drugs for use in a suicide, or someone mixes a lethal dose of drugs in liquid form for another knowingly to drink, those are examples of assisted suicide.

In my view, the practical distinctions between euthanasia and assisted suicide are about as substantial as the differences between the actions of the left and right leg while walking; one step naturally follows the other.

Forced Exit

CHAPTER 1

Death Fundamentalism

On October 23, 1991, fifty-eight-year-old Marjorie Wantz and forty-three-year-old Sherry Miller kept their appointment at a cabin in a park near Detroit with an unemployed pathologist named Jack Kevorkian. Kevorkian was then still relatively unknown, although over a year before he had made headlines after hooking up Janet Adkins, who had early-stage Alzheimer's disease, to a suicide machine of his own design that killed her by way of intravenously administered barbiturates and poison when she flipped a switch. (Adkins died well before her disease became debilitating, a good ten years prior to the point when it could have been expected to end her life.) Now Wantz and Miller wanted to die.

Neither was terminally ill. According to later court testimony, both were suffering from depression. Miller was disabled by multiple sclerosis. A few years prior to her death, just when Miller's disease had begun to worsen and restrict her activities, her husband left her, taking custody of their children. Miller was forced by the divorce to live with her elderly parents, and she worried about being a burden to them.[1] She claimed that her self-disgust with her disabilities was her reason for wanting to die. Yet Miller, forty-three, might eventually have adapted to her disability—as so many people disabled later in life do—as well as to the loss of her family, and might have created a new life for herself.

After benign growths had been removed from Wantz's vagina, she began to complain bitterly of severe pelvic pain. Many doctors tried to discover the cause through various means, including surgery. None was found. Indeed, her autopsy would show that she had no organic disease whatsoever. Not coincidentally, Wantz suffered from a depressive disorder, had been treated in mental hospitals, and, according to an article in the *Detroit News,* had been using a sleep aid called Halcion in higher-than-recommended doses because of difficulties sleeping.[2] (Halcion, if abused, can cause the side effect of suicidal impulse.)

Entering the cabin, the women lay down on cots. Kevorkian hooked Wantz up to his suicide machine, and soon she was no more. But he couldn't find a vein in Miller's emaciated arms. Always a tinkerer, he improvised. He rushed out and obtained a canister of carbon monoxide and a face mask and jury-rigged another suicide machine. Soon Miller was dead too. Their bodies would later be found amid dozens of burning candles.

On May 10, 1996, a jury acquitted Kevorkian of the common-law crime of assisting the suicides of Wantz and Miller, despite its being undisputed that he had done just that.* (At this writing, he has not been charged in the Adkins case.) Much ado was made in the media about the jury's swallowing Kevorkian's specious claim that he did not intend for the women to die and merely wanted to alleviate suffering. In all of the commentary, perhaps the most important point was missed: the statement by some jury members to reporters after the trial that it did not matter to them that Miller and Wantz were not terminally ill. That incontrovertible aspect of the case simply was not significant in their decision-making processes.

Kevorkian's acquittal in the deaths of Wantz and Miller was a watershed event in the history of euthanasia in the United States. The proposal to give doctors the legal right to kill certain patients in the United States was no longer unthinkable but, rather, distinctly possible.

The acquittals also exposed the often avoided truth about the so-called "right to die" movement. The shrug of the shoulders by the jury and nation over the tragic deaths of Wantz and Miller—one disabled, the other deeply emotionally disturbed—demonstrates that euthanasia is not about allowing the "terminally ill" who are in "unrelievable pain" and on the brink of death to "die with dignity," as the issue is usually described in the media. Rather, as the more candid proponents of euthanasia acknowledge, it is about creating a culture and medical system

---

* At the time of the Wantz and Miller killings, Michigan did not prohibit assisted suicide by statute. On the basis of previous court rulings, the Michigan Supreme Court later ruled that assisted suicide was a crime.

that accepts assisted suicide not only for the terminally ill but for anyone suffering a "hopeless illness" (a term that I will define in a few pages), both as a beneficence for suffering individuals and a good for society as a whole that will reduce health-care costs and the burdens of care on society and families.

This is a truly radical idea. If accepted, we will have moved away from being a society that promotes improved medical and psychological care and emotional support as the proper and humane response to a patient's desire to die to being one that accepts killing as both appropriate and somehow compassionate. To state it dramatically but accurately, if euthanasia is legalized, doctors will be given a license to kill some of their patients and these patients will be given a legally enforceable right to be killed.

What makes this proposition so extraordinary is that protecting human life has been viewed as the central purpose of organized society. Consequently, intentional killing by private persons is profoundly disfavored and severely restricted, being legally allowed only in exceptionally limited circumstances: acts of legitimate self-defense or defense of others, and even then only when deadly force is reasonably necessary to protect human life. The state, too, has severe restrictions on killing. Police may kill only when necessary to protect themselves, other officers, or the public. A soldier can kill if following legal orders in a combat situation. The death penalty is permitted, but only after the condemned is accorded due process of law, a process often taking many years.

Legalized euthanasia would dismantle this venerable tradition. Allowing killing in the commonplace circumstances of terminal illness, chronic illness and pain, disability, and prolonged mental illness, including depression, as is currently advocated by many in the euthanasia movement, would render the ethical and legal foundations of society unrecognizable. Legalization would shake the physician-patient relationship to its core. For one thing, the essential bond of trust between doctor and patient would likely be torn asunder. A recent survey of cancer patients found that if their doctor were to raise the issue of assisted suicide with them, they would lose trust in their physician. Moreover, the cancer patients stated they would change doctors if they discovered that their physician had helped kill another patient.[3] Add the changing economics of health care to the distrust equation, in which doctors actually lose money if they provide patients with "too much" care (doctors' conflicts of interest are discussed in Chapter 6), and the potential for estrangement between patient and doctor is made manifest.

Losing Our Way

What is driving people to abandon traditional moral standards and embrace the death culture? The Canadian newspaper columnist Andrew Coyne, reacting to the widespread public support of Robert Latimer, who killed his twelve-year-old daughter because she was disabled by cerebral palsy (discussed further in Chapter 7), said it most eloquently and succinctly when he wrote: "A society that believes in nothing can offer no argument even against death. A culture that has lost its faith in life cannot comprehend why it should be endured."[4]

Seen in this light, support for euthanasia is not a cause but rather a symptom of the broad breakdown of community and the ongoing unraveling of our mutual interconnectedness. The consequences of this moral Balkanization can be seen all around us: in the disintegration of family cohesiveness; in the growing nihilism among young people leading to a rise in suicides, drug use, and other destructive behaviors; in the growing belief that the lives of sick, disabled, and dying people are so meaningless, unimportant, and without value that killing them—or helping them kill themselves—can be countenanced and even encouraged.

But there is more to this story than passive cultural decay. There are several interrelated and interconnected cultural themes that have combined to produce the euthanasia juggernaut. The most visible is a new and radical notion of individualism that elevates personal autonomy above all other cultural values. Not that there is anything wrong with a broad and healthy respect for the rights of individual expression and freedom of conduct. Individualism is an inherent American trait, as natural to us as building dams is to beavers. But unbridled, near-absolute individualism leads to social anarchy that asphyxiates true freedom. That is why self-determination, while very important, is but one of several equally important and sometimes conflicting values that add up to the dynamic concept the Founders called "ordered liberty." One such competing value, communitarianism, promotes mutual interpersonal care, concern, and support. Communitarianism mandates that the state prevent harm to the weak and vulnerable—for example, by stopping suicides—not as some loathsome act of paternalism but as our human obligation to protect and care for one another.

Ordered liberty protects and defends both the forest and the trees, the society as well as the individual. Individual freedom is certainly valued and encouraged, but in order to protect the greater good, it is not absolute: It is properly limited when individual acts are unduly harmful to self, others, or to the whole, even if the harm is indirect. Thus, the community prevents individuals from injecting heroin, because drug addiction harms both the person who is abusing the drug and the overall society. People are not allowed to sell their vital organs, even if they want to, in order to prevent individual harm and to ensure that the poor will not be exploited. Likewise, the law absolutely prohibits adult siblings from marrying, even if they are deeply in romantic love, because of the adverse societal consequences that would follow from allowing open sexuality between close blood relatives. In these and many other examples that could be given, individual self-expression and fulfillment are subordinated to other vital community concerns.

This mix of competing and complementary values has created a nuanced public policy around issues of death, dying, and suicide. On the one hand, it criminalizes euthanasia and assisted suicide in order to protect the suffering individual, by reducing the danger that the dying and chronically ill will be exploited or coerced into an early death, and in order to protect society from the moral harm that would result should the killing of the dying, the sick, and the disabled become routine. At the same time, we properly allow people to refuse unwanted medical treatment, even if that choice might lead to death. (The vital distinctions between being killed and refusing medical treatment are discussed in later chapters.) Suicide, however, is not considered a crime in any state, the attempt at self-killing being viewed as a cry for help rather than a violation of law. But even though suicide itself is not a crime, there has heretofore never been a "right" to self-destruction. Police generally are empowered to use non-deadly force to prevent a suicide and are authorized, if necessary, to bring the self-destructive person to a psychiatric facility for observation. Moreover, if the patient is found beyond a reasonable doubt to present a danger to his or her own safety, he or she can be hospitalized for treatment until the threat passes. A multitude of once-suicidal people are glad to be alive today who would have been dead had "society" not cared enough to protect them from themselves during their time of despair.

Euthanasia proponents scorn such policies as paternalistic, at least as they relate to ill, disabled, and chronically mentally distraught individuals. They urge us to accept a relatively new concept known as "rational suicide," which views self-destruction as the result of a rational decision and thus appropriate when one's personal circumstances become particularly difficult. According to proponents of this view, if suicide is a rational choice, as opposed to an irrational urge, then it should be not only accepted but also facilitated upon repeated request. To many of these advocates, committing physician-facilitated rational suicide is, in the words of the Hemlock Society's cofounder Derek Humphry, the "ultimate civil liberty."[5]

Who should have the right to such a hastened death? Early on in euthanasia advocacy, proponents swore that it was to be reserved only for those who were terminally ill when nothing else could be done to relieve pain and suffering. But once entered upon, the slippery slope grows progressively steep. Now, even before euthanasia has been legalized, many advocates have upped the ante, arguing that euthanasia should be available for those suffering from "desperate," "incurable," or "hopeless" illness.

These terms are cleverly designed to fool the listener into believing that the reference is still to terminal disease. In reality, rational-suicide advocates are opening the door for physician-assisted suicide for almost anyone who has a sustained desire to die. For example, *hopeless illness,* the preferred term of the moment, is generally defined in psychiatric literature as including but not being limited to people with

> *terminal illnesses, [maladies causing] severe physical and/or psychological pain, physically or mentally debilitating and/or deteriorating conditions, and circumstances where [the] quality of life [is] no longer acceptable to the individual.*[6]

This definition is wide enough to drive a hearse through. A condition causing severe physical or psychological pain could be virtually any illness, injury, or emotional malady, from incontinence to migraine headache, from clinical depression to diabetes, from arthritis to cancer. Moreover, by definition, a person only wants to commit suicide because, at the time, he or she thinks that "life is no longer acceptable." Thus, the concept of "hopeless illness" is a prescription for abandoning depressed and suffering people to a policy of death on demand.

Legalized euthanasia would not occur in a vacuum. The anticommunitarian values it represents would undoubtedly ripple throughout our culture and be adopted by the many structures of society and would likely usher in a new era in which exercising personal autonomy and maximizing self-determination would become the culture's overriding purpose, rather than an important *part* of a broad mix of values that make up a healthy, balanced, and free society. Our duties and responsibilities to community and each other would be eclipsed, sacrificed on the altar of individual fulfill-

ment. We would become so many rocks and islands, interacting but isolated, individuals placed side by side with few mutual commitments. Woe
betide the unfortunates who "can't keep up," even if they self-destruct.
They can do with their bodies what they want, we will shrug, as an increasing number of despairing individuals "choose" to end their lives.

The bioethicist Arthur Caplan fears we may already be on the
precipice of this runaway self-determinism. He writes of the sad case of
Thomas W. Passmore, a man with a history of mental illness, who, thinking he saw the sign of the devil on his right hand, cut it off with a circular
saw. He was taken to a hospital, where, according to Caplan, things took
a "crazy turn." Upon being told by the surgeon that his hand could be
saved, Passmore refused treatment, still believing that his hand carried
the sign of evil. A psychiatrist interviewed Passmore; lawyers were consulted; a judge refused to intervene. In the end, no one would decide that
Passmore was incompetent to make his own medical decisions, and his
hand was permanently lost.

This was a profound abandonment of a mentally ill, self-destructive
man in desperate need of help from his community. Thanks to the increasingly extreme view of self-determination, those who should have assisted Passmore were instead morally paralyzed. So distorted were their
perceptions of their responsibility to Passmore, so stunted were their facilities to engage in critical thinking, that they allowed a hallucinating man
to dismember himself because of a sign of evil that wasn't really there. As
Caplan so aptly put it, "A nation that has created a health-care system in
which doctors, nurses and administrators are not sure whether it is the
right thing to do to sew a mentally ill man's severed hand back onto his
arm is a society gone over the edge regarding autonomy."[7]

What happened to Passmore's hand will happen to people's lives if this
trend continues. Euthanasia and assisted suicide represent the ultimate
abandonment of people made vulnerable by physical or mental illness, inadequate medical care, and depression. Legalization would lead to a
moral and ethical catastrophe in which those least able to defend themselves would be victimized.

It is also interesting to observe that the most vocal people pushing the
death agenda seem to be those least likely to be victimized by it. Jack
Kevorkian aside, most leaders of the euthanasia movement, such as the author Betty Rollin and the physician Dr. Timothy Quill, are people of the
"overclass": well-off whites with a strong and supportive family or social
structure who never believe they could be victimized or pressured into

choosing an early death. They want what they want (to be able to die) when and how they want it. They downplay the harm that will follow for the poor, the uneducated, those without access to medical care, or the disabled, many of whom see themselves as being in the crosshairs on this issue. Not to worry, these leaders breezily assert, "protective guidelines" will fix everything.

Euthanasia is being promoted by its advocates through a very sophisticated political campaign. Proponents use all the tools of the political trade. Focus groups and polls have told them that people respond negatively to words such as *euthanasia,* and so they resort to euphemisms such as *deliverance* and *gentle landing* to describe killing. Their research also shows that arguments appealing to traditional notions of freedom resonate with people. Thus, like a boxer repeatedly jabbing at an open cut on an opponent's face, they pepper their advocacy with the lexicon of freedom and elicit an emotional response in the listener, especially with that sound bite of all sound bites, "choice." They argue that legalizing physician-assisted suicide is about personal autonomy, the right to be left alone. Appealing to our traditional distrust of government, advocates self-righteously assert that legalization of physician-hastened death would deny the state "any right to compel innocent, competent adults to needlessly suffer," as if laws prohibiting killing were some fiendish authorization for torture.[8] Some even compare the campaign to create a "right to die" with the great civil rights movement. Martin Luther King, Jr., must be turning over in his grave.

Claiming the civil-liberties high ground for the idea of "choosing the manner and timing of one's death" serves another purpose. It keeps the discussion on a theoretical level and allows suicide proponents to avoid an in-depth analysis of the dysfunctional *context* within which the "choices to die" would be exercised. But successfully deflecting discussion of these context issues does not make them any less important. As Matthew Rothschild, the editor of *Progressive* magazine and a strong civil libertarian, puts it, "I think a lot of people are persuaded by the civil liberties cloak that has falsely been placed around this issue. But the reality is quite the opposite. Euthanasia is not a 'choice' issue at all. Rather, choices to die would be made by others for people who are powerless and who are weak, whose right to live would be taken out of their own hands."[9]

Another driving force behind the euthanasia movement is the issue of "control." At the same time that they hoist high the banner of hastened death as a liberty, proponents exploit people's fear of death and the suffering that can accompany the dying process, promising that choosing the time and manner of death will somehow tame the Grim Reaper. In this atmosphere, dying naturally is increasingly promoted as a "bad death" if it involves discomfort or time, and hastened death is presented as empowering, courageous, and somehow noble.

For some suicide advocates, controlling death has become a fixation. One cannot seriously engage the issue for long without hearing the terms *good death, planned death, assisted death, death with dignity, rational death, deliverance, gentle landing, soft landing,* etc.–the list goes on and on.

The Dutch physician Dr. I. van der Sluis, who has opposed his country's slide down euthanasia's slippery slope for more than twenty years, has observed the same phenomenon in the Netherlands. "I have studied [euthanasia proponents'] mentality," he told me. "They are like a little church, a cult of death. They are fascinated by the subject. They are always obsessing on dying and the suffering that may be a part of dying."[10] The disability rights activist and college professor Paul Longmore, who resists legalized euthanasia as a form of bigotry against the disabled, agrees. "Some of these people can only be described as 'death fundamentalists,' " he says. "They are so fixated on death and their ideology, that the facts of the debate have little meaning for them."[11]

Death fundamentalism, an apt description, may be contagious. My friend Frances was a death fundamentalist; so fixated was she on her own self-destruction, even before she became ill, that no appeal to reason or emotion could dissuade her from her chosen course or convince her to search for a different answer to her problems. When the suicide guru Derek Humphry published his how-to-commit-suicide book, *Final Exit,* in August 1991, it made the *New York Times* best-seller list. A few years ago, 175 people attended a "self-deliverance" course taught by Humphry, in which people were instructed on how to commit suicide by using a plastic bag. For those who missed the course, Humphry's current organization, ERGO (Euthanasia Research and Guidance Organization), sells illustrated instructions for five dollars (ingredients: a plastic bag, two elastic bands, a paper painter's mask, and an ice bag).[12] On the Internet, Death-Net brings web surfers daily doses of news from the euthanasia front, as well as DeathTALK, a chat room for discussing euthanasia; the Garden of Remembrance, an on-line obituary service where home pages of the deceased can be created; and Life'sEnd, an on-line shopping center for "end-of-life needs." One product advertised through DeathNet is the "customized Exit Bag," a trademarked device to be used in combination with sleeping pills or other drugs; it "takes the guesswork out of the use of plastic bags" in suicide, says the cheery sales pitch.[13] Even more disturbing, if one is a member of a right-to-die organization, explicit information on how to commit suicide is also available on the Net. Meanwhile, in Australia, a pro-euthanasia physician has topped Jack Kevorkian's suicide machine by creating a computer program to allow people to commit assisted suicide at the push of a button; the program has been posted on the Internet. (The first PC-facilitated death occurred on September 26, 1996.) There is even a group on the Internet called the Church of Euthanasia.

Jack Kevorkian is a high priest of death fundamentalism. According to *Newsweek,* Kevorkian, while in medical school in the 1950s, "made regular visits to terminally ill patients and peered deeply into their eyes. His objective was to pinpoint when the precise moment of death occurred."[14] Kevorkian is a ghoulish artist who paints grotesque pictures, such as one "of a child eating the flesh off a decomposing corpse."[15] He has long been fascinated with the mechanics of capital punishment.[16] He even transfused blood from corpses into living human beings without testing the procedure on animals to make sure it was safe.[17]

Kevorkian is so death-obsessed that he proposes the nauseating prospect of performing live human experiments on people being killed in order to learn more about human death. He calls this "obitiatry." He used to call assisted suicide "medicide" but now labels it "patholysis." In his own words, from his book *Prescription Medicide:*

> *If we are ever to penetrate the mystery of death—even superficially— it will have to be through obitiatry. Research using cultured cells and tissues and live animals may yield objective biological data . . . but knowledge about the essence of human death will of necessity require insight into the nature of the unique awareness or consciousness that characterizes human* life. *That is possible only through obiatric [sic] research on living human bodies [emphasis as in original].*[18]

Indeed, the primary motivation behind Kevorkian's death crusade is to pave the way for live human experiments on those being killed, not to ease suffering. Again, from *Prescription Medicide:*

> *[Assisted suicide] is not simply to help doomed persons kill themselves—that is merely the first step, an early distasteful professional*

obligation. . . . [W]hat I find most satisfying is the prospect of making possible the performance of invaluable experiments or other beneficial medical acts under conditions that this first unpleasant step can help establish.[19]

The increase in the popularity of legalized euthanasia is also a vote of no confidence in the medical profession. Many supporters are afraid—nay, terrified—at the prospect of being victimized at the hands of an out-of-control doctor who, they fear, will hook them up to a machine and force them to suffer as cash cows lingering in an agonizing limbo until they die or their health insurance runs out—whichever comes first. Thus, euthanasia is sold as a guarantee of sorts against both suffering and financial difficulty.

While the ongoing changes in health-care financing make it more likely that patients will receive too little care rather than too much, terror of being forced into a lingering death is not irrational. Too many people have seen their loved ones writhing in pain that could have been relieved, too many have had their own suffering ignored, too many have been treated impersonally and dismissively by health-care professionals. As one study into the euthanasia issue put it, "Public perceptions about . . . assisted suicide and euthanasia are determined by many issues, including fears of intolerable suffering at the end of life, and a perception that the healing professions have paid inadequate attention to relieving suffering when a cure is not possible. This perception may well be right."[20]

Paradoxically, the very people who support euthanasia because they don't trust the medical profession, who fear they will be victimized by unwanted care or medical neglect of their suffering, accept the idea that doctors should be relied on to engage in medicalized killing. Yet these same doctors, it is widely recognized, are generally undertrained in treating pain and do a terrible job of diagnosing clinical depression in their chronically ill and dying patients.

Then there is the issue of compassion, which euthanasia advocates claim as their primary motivation. Some speak as if they have a monopoly on the virtue, while casting euthanasia opponents as people who care more about legalism than about relieving suffering. It's not true, of course. Dignified, compassionate, and effective means exist today to reduce or eliminate pain and suffering without eliminating the patient, such as pain control, treatment for depression, independent-living assistance for people with disabilities, hospice, and other care opportunities. Unfortunately, these measures receive only a fraction of the media visibility and publicity of that for the drive to legalize killing. For example, most people don't even know what hospice care is, much less how to obtain it. This is tragic, because these underutilized and underfunded programs can make all the difference in the lives of people who are suffering, and often can change a desire to die into a drive to live.

Euthanasia advocates' compassion argument also overlooks the prospect that legalizing euthanasia would lead to more suffering rather than less. Think about what could happen to funding for AIDS research and efforts to improve the care and long-term prospects for people suffering from that horrible disease. Some with little sympathy for AIDS victims might say that with a quick and painless death available, money now spent on curative research could be better invested elsewhere. And what about improving pain-control education and increasing access to hospice care? Chances are they would wither on the vine. And what about the desperate need to improve access to medical care? Dr. Joanne Lynn, professor of medicine at Dartmouth Medical School, has said, "If we choose to kill [those] with limited life prospects [rather than] trying to serve them, we will have foreclosed the possibility of reforming our dysfunctional care systems," which cause feelings of "isolation, meaninglessness, and abandonment," emotions that often lead the ill to want to kill themselves.[21]

Finally, there is a less visible but perhaps ultimately the most influential and dangerous force driving the euthanasia juggernaut: money. Our healthcare system is quickly being transformed from a fee-for-service system, where medical professionals earn money by treating people, to a system dominated by for-profit health maintenance organizations (H.M.O.s), in which money is made by health insurance companies primarily by reducing costs. In an H.M.O., a penny saved is literally a penny earned. That is why legalized euthanasia would be especially profitable to the fast-growing for-profit H.M.O. industry. Just imagine the money that can be saved—and thus earned—by *not treating* AIDS patients because their deaths have been hastened by euthanasia, in *not treating* cancer patients because their deaths have been hastened through euthanasia, in *not treating* people with physical disabilities because their lives were ended by euthanasia. To put it bluntly, the day doctors are legally allowed to kill patients, Wall Street investors in for-profit H.M.O.s will be dancing in the streets.

Money imperatives often help shape our values and ethics. If promoting certain behavior can make fortunes, rationalizations to justify the conduct will soon be found, even if it is inherently immoral. One reason that slavery became so entrenched in the Old South was that the peculiarities of the Southern economy made human bondage profitable for those in power. Similarly, the genocide of Native Americans was often stimulated by the expectation that there was money to be made from taking their lands. For a modern equivalent of putting dollars ahead of the lives of people, just look at the activities of the tobacco industry, which has been accused, among other moral wrongs, of promoting tobacco use by young people despite knowing tobacco's profound health dangers.

It may not be a coincidence, then, that the ethics regarding end-of-life medical care are changing just as the money imperative in medical practice has reversed itself. When the system was primarily fee-for-service, the prevailing medical ethic was to keep patients alive at all costs, or at least until the health insurance ran out. But now that managed care is supplanting fee-for-service, we hear much talk about "good death" and "death with dignity," about how patients should be more willing to give up the ghost and refuse end-of-life medical treatment.

It is thus worth noting that health-care foundations are among the primary financers of the many bioethics think tanks and "researchers" who without notoriety or notice "educate" the medical establishment, hospital ethics committees, physicians and nurses associations, etc., about euthanasia, assisted suicide, and related death issues. More than half the members of the board of directors of the new bioethics umbrella organization, the American Association of Bioethics, openly advocate euthanasia and/or health-care rationing. The A.A.B. has received substantial financial support from the FHP Foundation, a charity with strong connections to FHP, Inc., a for-profit H.M.O. located in California. The FHP Foundation also helps fund Choice in Dying, originally known as the Euthanasia Society of America.

Legitimizing the Euthanasia Consciousness

Of course, most people don't think about public policy in such philosophical terms. More often, public attitudes and perceptions are a product of cultural currents driven by television, music, movies, magazines, talk shows, and the manner in which news events are reported, as well as the general moral beliefs of the citizenry. So, too, with euthanasia.

Most people are not activists either for or against euthanasia, paying little attention to the issue except in passing. Consequently, what many think they know and what they believe about the issue is often the result of attitudes seeping unnoticed into their consciousness from the society around them. It is here, among the uninvolved, that organs of the popular culture have for years been quietly altering public perceptions about death and dying without people's conscious awareness that it is happening.

The popular culture is dominated by people with certain mind-sets. These attitudes are reflected in our entertainment, particularly Hollywood-made movies, where euthanasia is deemed politically correct. Television shows often deal with the issue, almost always presenting hastened deaths in a sympathetic light as the "only" choice available to alleviate a desperate patient's suffering. Popular television series such as *ER, Homicide, Chicago Hope, Star Trek: Deep Space Nine, Star Trek Voyager* (in which we learn that Vulcans like Mr. Spock practice ritual suicide in old age), and *Law and Order,* just to name a few, have all aired episodes dealing positively with the theme of hastened death. At the same time, magazines we subscribe to or pick up in a doctor's waiting room present the same message, typified by an article in *The New Yorker* in which the writer extols his mother's assisted suicide. He concludes, "Having seen the simple logic of euthanasia in action and witnessed the comfort of that control, what astonishes me is how many people die by other means."[22] Similarly, the January 1997 *Ladies' Home Journal* had a "special report" on assisted suicide consisting of a "round table" discussion. Amazingly, there were *no opponents* of legalization presented in the entire article.

This is powerful stuff. When a popular television program depicts a courageous and handsome doctor killing a patient as the "only way" to relieve unremitting suffering, or the sympathetic and beautiful homicide inspector winks at a mercy killing because she would have done the same thing in the suspect's place, the audience gives no thought to the false premises that underlie the drama or to the systemic consequences of making such acts routine. When famous talk-show hosts bring families on television to justify the hastened deaths of their loved ones, it is difficult to see past our sympathy for the plight of the deceased or the grief of his or her family to the broader issues; consequently, viewers tend to come away from these programs and reports thinking favorably of "the right to die." When popular magazines and newspaper stories deal with the issue, they invariably concentrate with laserlike intensity on a suffering individual who "just wants to die," while failing to train an equally penetrating light on the many ways of relieving suffering without killing or on the potential for coercion or abuse that, are inherent in legitimized euthanasia. Thus, it is not surprising that viewers and readers develop pro-euthanasia attitudes.

The news media, increasingly driven by ratings and circulation concerns, cannot be relied upon to plumb the depths of the issue: To an increasing degree, a "good story" is short on depth and long on emotionalism. If an ill person is assisted in suicide by a doctor or family member, "news" coverage focuses intently on the reasons the person wanted to die. Friends speak of his or her great suffering. With few exceptions, little investigation, if any, is undertaken to discover whether the deceased was receiving adequate medical care, proper pain control, or treatment for depression. Even if doubts are raised in the story about the propriety of the hastened death, right-to-die advocates will inevitably be shown cluck-clucking about how abuses wouldn't happen if assisted death were legalized.

Most of the stories written about the Jack Kevorkian assisted killings are cases in point. The reporting about the September 3, 1996, death of Jack Leatherman, seventy-three, who had pancreatic cancer, is just one example. The newspaper story carried in *The Boston Globe* was typical: It told about the man's death and the nature of his illness and reported the allegation by one of Kevorkian's representatives that "no amount of pain relief could control the pain that he was suffering."[23] That assertion was not questioned or investigated. Had it been, reporters would have discovered that morphine pills are very effective in controlling the pain associated with pancreatic cancer. Moreover, according to the board-certified oncologist and pain-control specialist Dr. Eric Chevlen, in the rare event in which opioids are insufficient to adequately control pancreatic cancer pain, a medical procedure can be performed to numb the nerve that transmits pain stimuli from the abdomen to the spinal cord and the brain, thereby eliminating all pain caused by the cancer.[24] Yet that story, which would have given cancer victims and their families so much hope, was never reported.

With a few exceptions, stories that highlight the reasons to oppose legalization of euthanasia generally do not receive equivalent coverage. If reported, these stories generally are not presented with the same level of emotional intensity or drama. A story of hospice care helping someone die a dignified, natural death in comfort and surrounded by a loving family won't make the news at all unless the person is famous. It is no big deal if a cancer patient is no longer suicidal because he received effective pain control. It's the proverbial dog-bites-man story—happens every day. Conversely, it rarely becomes a public matter when a patient is somehow coerced into an early death, since the abuser will not be anxious for public exposure.

This is not to assert that Hollywood and the news media have joined in some vast conspiracy to legalize euthanasia. It's just that their treatment of the subject follows from the nature of our popular culture. Entertainment and the news both require conflict to grab the audience and hold its interest. Euthanasia fits the bill. What could be more dramatic than the television doctor risking his license and a jail sentence to "selflessly" help end the life of an irremediably suffering patient on the brink of death? Then, stay tuned for the eleven o'clock news report that Jack Kevorkian has assisted in his umpteenth suicide; truth and fiction merge.

With the media and the various organs of popular culture playing the same tune, with opposition voices generally muted to a discordant note in the deep background, the awesome power of repetition, like ocean waves breaking against a rock, contributes individually and collectively to the gradual erosion of the equality-of-life ethic, to an accepting and sympathetic attitude toward euthanasia.

Also contributing mightily to the growing acceptance of euthanasia is a form of pervasive cultural decay that I call "terminal nonjudgmentalism" (T.N.J.). Our society has become so steeped in relativism, so unable to distinguish right from wrong, that it increasingly fails to react to or to criticize truly reprehensible concepts or conduct. When destructive ideas and practices are not condemned, it is a form of praise. That which is not seen as wrong must be right. As the winds of the death culture blow with increasing velocity, the vitality of the equality-of-life ethic recedes like a green valley slowly turning into desert. Where one year there was life, in the next there is only sand. Soon, the lushness that once was is forgotten and the barren landscape seems the norm.

A good example of T.N.J. in action—or, better, inaction—can be seen in the book *A Chosen Death,* by Lonny Shavelson, and the reaction of critics to its contents.[25] Shavelson, described on the book jacket as an emergency-room physician and a photojournalist, writes about five assisted suicides he observed and/or participated in during the book's preparation. One case, that of "Gene," stands out in its brutality.

As depicted by Shavelson, Gene is a depressed, lonely widower with a pronounced alcohol problem. Twice previously he has tried to commit suicide. The first attempt occurred before he had two strokes that left him moderately impaired—but definitely not terminally ill.

Gene wants to end it all. He contacts an undisclosed chapter of the Hemlock Society and asks its head, a woman given the pseudonym "Sarah," to assist in his death. According to Shavelson, Sarah has experience in this dark business, having previously assisted a close friend to com-

mit suicide. Sarah found her first killing experience tremendously satisfying and powerful, "the most intimate experience you can share with a
person. . . . More than sex. More than birth . . . more than anything," including being present for "the deliveries of my four grandchildren."[26] A
committed death fundamentalist, Sarah wants again to enjoy the intense
rush she experienced facilitating her friend's death, and so she jumps at
the chance to help kill Gene.

Gene hems and haws, avoiding suicide and seemingly relishing the newfound companionship of Sarah and Shavelson that his suicide wish has
provided him. Then, one night, he decides the time has come to die. He
calls Shavelson and Sarah to his home for his suicide. Shavelson watches as
Sarah mixes Gene a poisonous brew and gives it to him, saying, "O.K.,
toots, here you go," as if she were handing him a beer.[27]

Gene drinks the liquid and begins to fall asleep, with Sarah holding his
head on her lap. As he begins to snore, Sarah places a plastic bag over his
head and begins to croon, "See the light. Go to the light."[28] (Sarah apparently had seen the movie *Poltergeist* once too often.)

But then, suddenly, faced with the prospect of immediate death, Gene
changes his mind. He screams out "I'm cold!" and tries to rip the bag off
his face. But Sarah won't allow it. From Shavelson's account:

> *His good hand flew up to tear off the plastic bag. Sarah's hand
> caught Gene's wrist and held it. His body thrust upwards. She pulled
> his arm away and lay across Gene's shoulders. Sarah rocked back
> and forth, pinning him down, her fingers twisting the bag to seal it
> tight at his neck as she repeated, "the light, Gene, go toward the light."
> Gene's body pushed against Sarah's. Then he stopped moving.*[29]

If Shavelson's depiction of the event is accurate, there is a word that describes what happened to Gene, and that word is *murder*.

The right, proper, and ethical thing for Shavelson to have done as he
watched Sarah asphyxiate Gene would have been to knock Sarah off the
helpless man and then quickly dial 911 for an ambulance and the police.
But Shavelson did not do anything, so paralyzed was he by his own self-
described T.N.J. as he watched the Sarah-Gene tableau, just before the old
man tried to rip the bag off his face:

> *"Stop, Sarah" raced through my mind. For whose sake, I thought—
> Gene's, so intent on killing himself? The weight of unanswered ques-
> tions kept me glued to my corner. Was this a suicide, Gene's right*

finally to succeed and die? Or was this a needless death encouraged by Sarah's desire to act? Had Gene's decision to have me there, to tell me his story, given me the right to stop what was happening—or, equally powerful, the responsibility not to interfere? Or was I obliged by my very presence as a fellow human being, to jump up and stop the craziness? Was it craziness?[30]

Suddenly, Sarah is holding Gene down, preventing him from tearing off the plastic bag. But Shavelson's T.N.J. continues. Unable to decide on the right thing, he simply watches as Sarah kills Gene.

I interviewed Lonny Shavelson about all this. When asked whether he agreed that Gene's death was a murder, Shavelson said that his answer was too complex for a "sound bite response."[31] How could he watch a woman snuff the life out of a man clearly struggling to stay alive?, I asked. I reminded Shavelson that when he and I had met previously, in a radio station greenroom before a debate, I had asked him why he hadn't tried to stop Sarah. His response at the time was "I am a journalist."[32] Shavelson now acknowledged saying this, but he correctly noted that our conversation about the issue at that time was brief and not conducive to a more detailed response. (Nor, in fairness to Shavelson, was it a conversation geared toward inclusion in a book, although I did mention I would want to interview him about the issue for this one.) So I asked him to clarify his statement or comment further. Shavelson demurred, citing the "complexity" of his answer and worries about the "sound bite" nature of any quote that I might use. He did, however, point out the section in his book where he is about to describe Gene's asphyxiation as containing the reason why he did not act. In that section Shavelson wrote, "Events suddenly moved faster than my thoughts."[33] In other words, Shavelson is claiming that it all happened too fast. Yet Shavelson is an emergency-room physician. Surely he should be equipped to deal with fast-moving events.

I then asked Shavelson whether he thought Gene's death fell within the guidelines that are being proposed to regulate and limit legalized assisted suicide. He said that he believed Gene's condition to be "outside" the acceptable reasons for assisted suicide of any guidelines he knew of or supported, and added that regulating assisted suicide would mean that such deaths as Gene's could be prevented because legalization would "clarify what is and is not acceptable."[34] However, he agreed that nothing in any guidelines would prevent a death cultist like Sarah from acting outside the guidelines, just as her killing Gene was clearly outside any acceptable conduct under the law as it exists today. In fact, I contend that Gene could easily have been labeled "hopelessly ill," and thus would have fallen within some proposed "guidelines."

The point that Shavelson and other death fundamentalists miss is that so-called protective guidelines are meaningless; they provide only a veneer of respectability. They don't close the door to deaths outside their parameters. Rather, they break the doors of hastened death wide open by destroying the existing locks. Once killing is deemed an appropriate response to suffering, the threshold dividing "acceptable" killing from "unacceptable" killing will be continually under siege. But the fiction of control, essential to the public's acceptance of euthanasia, will have to be maintained, so the definition of what will be seen as "legitimate" killing will be expanded continually. Jack Kevorkian is living proof. Many of his subjects were no more terminally ill than Gene.

What about the reviewers of Shavelson's book? Surely they shared my horror at Gene's murder and Shavelson's passivity in the face of it. Not a chance. None I read materially criticized Gene's killing. The *San Francisco Chronicle* review is typical of the attitude. The reviewer, Steve Heilig, coeditor of the *Cambridge Quarterly of Healthcare Ethics,* didn't condemn Shavelson for allowing a murder to take place, unimpeded, under his very nose. Nor did he demand that Shavelson reveal the identity of Sarah and Gene so that the death could be appropriately subjected to a criminal inquiry. Rather, the review merely recounts that Shavelson is "appalled" at Sarah's "unregulated secretive approach" (not appalled enough to protect Gene, however) and opines that "the book superbly tackles this most difficult of ethical issues." What we don't condemn, we allow.

Another recent pro-euthanasia book that has been praised with faint condemnation is *Rethinking Life and Death: The Collapse of Our Traditional Ethics,* by Peter Singer.[35] *Rethinking Life and Death* can fairly be called the *Mein Kampf* of the euthanasia movement, in that it drops many of the euphemisms common to pro-euthanasia writing and acknowledges euthanasia for what it is: killing. Indeed, Singer is straightforward about how pervasive these death practices have become in our society and, unlike his fellow death fundamentalists, is quite candid about their destructiveness to the concept that all human life is inherently equal, a degeneration he celebrates and I condemn. Indeed, what makes Singer's book noteworthy is that he takes the step that most euthanasia proponents avoid for tactical reasons: He specifically advocates the outright destruction of the equality-of-human-life ethic that has undergirded Western civilization for two thousand years.

Singer advocates what he calls a "quality-of-life ethic." Under the quality-of-life ethic, being a human being is not a crucial determinant of one's inherent rights, since, Singer believes, all human lives do not have an inherently equal moral value. Rather, being a *person* is what counts to Singer, and only persons enjoy the right to life.

Most of us think *person* and *human* are synonymous. Not Singer. He elevates some "nonhuman animals" (such as dogs, elephants, and pigs) to the status of persons, on the basis of his contention that they are self-aware. At the same time, he strips some human beings of personhood, specifically those with cognitive disabilities and all newborn infants, because of their lack of the "relevant characteristics" of self-awareness over time and the ability to reason.

The practical application of these theories? Singer specifically embraces infanticide. Since, according to the author, an infant has no inherent right to life, a baby can be killed ethically if parents and doctors decide this is for the best. Speaking specifically of Down syndrome babies, Singer writes:

> *We may not want a child to start on life's uncertain voyage if the prospects are clouded. When this can be known at a very early stage in the voyage, we may still have a chance to make a fresh start. This means detaching ourselves from the infant who has been born, cutting ourselves free before the ties that have already begun to bind us to our child have become irresistible. Instead of going forward and putting all our efforts into making the best of the situation, we can still say no, and start again from the beginning.*[36]

In other words, according to Singer an acceptable answer to the difficulties of having a baby born with Down syndrome or another birth defect is to kill the child, an option that Singer muses should be available to parents for the first twenty-eight days of an infant's life.

Singer has been making such Nazi-like proposals for years. That he is nevertheless *respected* internationally as a "philosopher" and "bioethicist" is proof enough of rampant T.N.J. Further proof is the book review in *The New York Times,* May 7, 1995, by Daniel J. Kevles, of the California Institute of Technology. The closest Kevles comes to criticizing Singer's thesis is to suggest that some of his opinions are "highly debatable." Indeed, the review states that *Rethinking Life and Death* "is analytically rich on the moral rights of newborns compared with those of unborn fetuses, and how we treat anyone who is so physically or cerebrally degraded that they have no chance of a life of reasonable fulfillment."[37] In other words, that the right to live often depends on the values and attitudes of those who possess the power to kill is of no serious concern.

The death fundamentalist community expressed nothing but kudos for the book. A book review in *Hemlock TimeLines,* the successor to the *Hemlock Quarterly* as the official newsletter of the Hemlock Society, applauds, "The true message of this book is one of reason and responsibility."[38] The comments of Ralph Mero, former director of Compassion in Dying, an offshoot of Hemlock created to actively assist the suicides of the terminally ill, reveals a similar death cult mind-set: "*Rethinking Life and Death* . . . should be required reading for physicians, legislators, and judges. The new medical ethics being forged today will revolutionize our attitudes toward everything from fertilized zygotes to comatose bodies. Out of it should come a heightened respect for *persons and personhood* and just in time" (italics in original).[39] Derck Humphry, cofounder of the Hemlock Society, donated a book-jacket blurb that states in part, "Brilliantly debunks old concepts and introduces honesty to modern medical ethics."[40]

It is a sad and frightening day when a noted author writes a book advocating infanticide and involuntary euthanasia of the cognitively disabled, when it is published by a major New York publishing company, and when it is received to the sound of general applause. (Singer has, however, been severely criticized and demonstrated against in Germany, a country with an acute memory of the horrors that can result from adopting such values as his. See Chapter 3.) Singer is not on the fringe. Rather, he is widely respected with an international following. Incredibly, despite his advocacy of the right of parents and doctors to kill unwanted babies, he wrote the major article on ethics in the current *Encyclopaedia Britannica.*

Finally, let us look once again at some of the dark activities of Jack Kevorkian, who has been praised by faint damnation by juries, by the media, and, indeed, by much of the population. The acceptance of Jack Kevorkian is evidence of the progressive decay of the American culture. This failed pathologist

- has written that his ultimate goal is to conduct live human medical experiments on dying people, including infants and children[41]

- wants to create suicide centers "for all those who need or desire it"[42]

That such a man is tolerated, much less respected, by millions of people speaks volumes about how far we have already fallen down the death culture's slippery slope.

Let us remind ourselves why Jack Kevorkian must be stopped. There were at least forty-five of them, at last count, forty-five dead people. A minority of them were dying, but few would have been likely to succumb soon (approximately 20 percent were diagnosed with a terminal illness).[43] As Stephanie Gutmann pointed out in *The New Republic,* more than two thirds were women, most of whom were "not complaining of severe or constant pain"; rather, "most [were] worried about the disease's impact on others."[44] In other words, many of the women willing to allow Kevorkian to hook them up to his carbon monoxide canister or other suicide machine were doing so to relieve other people as much as themselves. Others who were "Kevorkianed" were disabled, depressed, afraid of future suffering, were receiving inadequate pain-control medication or refusing to take pain medication, had been abandoned by their own doctors and/or families, or were affected by a combination of these and other factors.

Whether dying, chronically ill, disabled, or depressed, each one of Kevorkian's "subjects" (his term) deserved better than to end life as a showcase in Kevorkian's one-man death circus.[45] For example, recall Janet Adkins, Kevorkian's first subject. Many don't know it, but it was not Adkins who contacted Kevorkian after she was diagnosed with early Alzheimer's disease. Rather, it was her husband who took care of the arrangements. (Both Adkinses were members of the Hemlock Society.) It is also important to note that Janet Adkins was not in pain or in the least frail. Actually, she had beaten her son in tennis the week before her death. The original death date, November 30, 1989, was set so she "wouldn't spoil Christmas for the kids."[46] She actually died on June 4, 1990.

Marjorie Wantz's tragic death also deserves recounting. According to her autopsy report, Marjorie Wantz was in good health on the day she flipped a switch, and poison from Jack Kevorkian's suicide machine poured into her veins. Jack Kevorkian helped kill this poor woman anyway, presumably without examining her, verifying the presence of any physical illness, or determining Wantz's psychiatric condition.

One of Kevorkian's most disturbing deaths—they are all disturbing—is that of Margaret Garrish. She had several serious maladies, and had endured amputations, but she turned to Kevorkian because she was in terrible pain from rheumatoid arthritis that her family doctor was apparently not adept at relieving. Prior to her assisted death, one of Kevorkian's representatives held a press conference and played a videotape of a woman whose identity was disguised (but who was Mrs. Garrish), who stated that unless she received control for her pain, she would go to Kevorkian.[47] At least seven pain-control experts responded, offering to assist the woman without charge.[48] Unfortunately for Garrish, she was never put in touch with the physicians who might have controlled her pain and helped restore her desire to live. In the end she took the Kevorkian way out: death by carbon monoxide poisoning. When asked why Garrish was not given access to the pain relief that might have saved her life, one of Kevorkian's lawyers sneered that the doctors were nothing but "publicity seekers."[49]

More than 2.1 million Americans have been diagnosed with rheumatoid arthritis. Imagine the toll if only 1 percent of them were to decide to be euthanized. Perhaps that is why, in response to Margaret Garrish's death, the Michigan chapter of the Arthritis Foundation issued a press release that stated in part: "The Arthritis Foundation does not view planned death as an appropriate option for people with arthritis. Rheumatoid arthritis is regarded as a nonfatal disease. . . . There are many actions that can make life with arthritis easier and less painful."[50]

Then there is the case of Esther Cohan, forty-six, who had multiple sclerosis. She was disabled but not terminally ill. After her death, Cohan's sister told reporters that her sister's body was covered with bedsores. Yet according to Dr. Randolph B. Schiffer, an adviser to the National Multiple Sclerosis Society, "If a patient with multiple sclerosis has bedsores, it means by definition, that for whatever reason, he or she is not receiving adequate medical care."[51]

The circumstances of these and other deaths facilitated by Jack Kevorkian and the seeming public acceptance of them illustrate the same pattern that has already overtaken the Netherlands, which, as will be discussed in Chapter 4, has accepted euthanasia for more than twenty years: Once euthanasia and assisted suicide are legitimized (whether or not by formal laws), it doesn't matter much why people "choose" to die. Standing back and letting them do it becomes the prevailing ethic. Soon, the dying, chronically ill, disabled, depressed, people receiving inadequate medical care, those worried about becoming a burden, and even infants born with birth defects are abandoned to the death culture.

Exploring Hidden Premises:
"There's No Such Thing as a Simple Suicide"

The abuse and exploitation inherent in the euthanasia consciousness are rarely discussed explicitly but are often readily apparent, even in pieces that promote the practice. A prominent article published in a major magazine typifies the kind of euthanasia promotion that is so depressingly common throughout the media.

On November 14, 1993, the cover story of *The New York Times Magazine* was "There's No Such Thing as a Simple Suicide."[52] The story details the sad saga of a dying woman, "Louise," who killed herself with the active assistance and moral support of Ralph Mero, a Unitarian minister and the cofounder of the pro-euthanasia group Compassion in Dying.

An offshoot of the Hemlock Society, Compassion in Dying actively counsels dying people who express a desire to commit suicide and assists in their self-killing. Its founder and former director, Ralph Mero, insists that he eschews publicity and is acting only out of selfless compassion. Yet he and his "work" have somehow managed to be featured in an Ann Landers advice column, complete with mailing address, in the major article in *The New York Times Magazine,* and in many national print and television newsmagazine pieces and documentaries.[53]

The "No Simple Suicide" story was written by Lisa Belkin, a former *New York Times* reporter and author of the book *First Do No Harm,* about medicine and ethics. This excellently written piece presents Louise's story as melodrama, taking the reader on an emotionally wrenching roller-coaster ride of her assisted suicide, complete with a cast of heroes and villains and a gripping life-and-death plot. To make matters more compelling, we are told that the tale is true, with only the dying woman's name changed to protect her family's privacy.

The Story

"No Simple Suicide" chronicles the last few months of Louise's life. We learn early on that Louise suffers from an unidentified degenerative brain condition. Her doctor, described as "a warm, down-to-earth woman," informs Louise that she has only months, perhaps weeks, to live. Louise is afraid of dying in a hospital, hospice, or other "facility," a scenario her doctor bluntly tells her is quite likely to occur.

Louise tells her doctor that rather than die in a cold, impersonal facility, she would rather kill herself. The doctor almost leaps at the chance to prescribe the drugs for Louise to take.

We are told that the doctor had previously "cooperated" with another patient's suicide, but that there had been difficulties, so she contacts Ralph Mero at Compassion in Dying to solicit his help and active assistance in facilitating Louise's death. The doctor later tells Belkin, "I was ecstatic to find someone who's doing what [Mero is] doing. I loved the fact that there were guidelines. It made so much sense. This was a human being who could help, not some book."[54]

A few days later Mero visits Louise, who lives with her mother. Mero tells Belkin that Louise appeared relieved when he didn't flinch or judge her desire to kill herself and that she asked Mero to be with her when she died. He agreed, stating that the decision was hers.

Louise has asked her friends to attend her suicide, but none will. When a medical assistant of one of her doctors hears that Louise's "trusted friends" have backed away, she befriends the ill woman and supports her in her self-destruction.

Mero, the medical assistant, Louise, and Louise's mother become a cohesive group with one goal: Louise's assisted suicide. They meet to discuss how the self-termination will be performed. The deadly drugs will be mixed with a small amount of food and antinausea medication so that they can be kept down. Louise is to be monitored as she dies, and the assistant is to administer antipain medication if Louise seems to be suffering. After the death, the doctor will report to the authorities that the deceased was terminally ill and that the death was from natural causes after a prolonged illness, so no autopsy will be conducted. The doctor is also to falsify the death certificate as to the actual cause of death.

Weeks pass. Louise grows ever weaker. Yet the frail woman does not kill herself. Mero becomes alarmed. He calls Belkin to inform her that he and the group have been told by the doctor that Louise is running out of time within which to kill herself. It is feared that the disease may soon render Louise mentally incompetent. Mero worries that Louise's "window of opportunity will slam shut" because Compassion in Dying will assist suicides only for persons who are mentally competent. He also worries that if Louise waits much longer she will be unable to self-administer the deadly drugs.

Lisa Belkin drops everything and flies to Seattle to speak with Louise, who tells the reporter that she wishes to conclude some business and spend some more time with her mother before killing herself. This upsets Belkin, who blurts out the doctor's prognosis: Louise does not have much time within which she will be capable of killing herself.

Yet, for all of her stated desire to commit assisted suicide, Louise still does not act. Some time later, the medical assistant–turned–friend tells the group she will talk to Louise to see if she can get the suicide back on track. She asks the dying woman, "I kind of want to get an idea of what your time line is. Where do we stand?" Louise's eyes brim with tears and she tells the medical assistant that she does not want to talk about it. The woman apologizes. Louise justifies her delay by saying that she wants to wait until Mero returns from out of town to get his opinion of her condition. The medical assistant replies that is a "bad idea" because Mero might not notice subtle changes in her condition.

Still Louise does not kill herself. Mero withdraws, checking in by phone but keeping the conversations short. He tells Belkin that he wants to remain in the background so as not to influence the outcome.

Then Mero gets a message. Louise is finally ready. The group assembles. Louise eats poisoned ice cream and applesauce that has been prepared pursuant to Mero's previous instructions and immediately falls asleep on the couch clutching a teddy bear. Hours pass as Louise sleeps. The group waits for her to die. She does not. Mero worries that he might have to help the process with a plastic bag. Finally, Louise's breathing slows and she expires. Mero contacts the funeral director and leaves.

As the article concludes, we are informed that Louise's death was not listed as a suicide and that her friends and relatives were told that she "died in her sleep with her mother at her side, as she had wanted."

The Propaganda

Every drama is supposed to elicit a response from the audience. "No Simple Suicide" is no exception. On its face, the article appears to be an objective piece of journalism: Belkin does not praise or criticize the people involved or the events, nor does she give her personal opinion on the merits of Mero's cause. Scratch the surface, however, and the piece can be seen as an advertisement for legalizing and legitimizing assisted suicide and euthanasia.

What leads to this conclusion? First is the manner in which the article came to be written. Belkin didn't find the story, the story found her. As Belkin appropriately reveals, she was contacted by the board of directors of Compassion in Dying, who invited her to observe their usually secret suicide-assistance activities.

There is nothing illegal, immoral, or unusual about a reporter being contacted about a story. Stories are often found in this manner. However, it is safe to assume that Mero and the board had more in mind than merely illustrating the emotional difficulties surrounding terminal illness. Surely they hoped to further their cause through the article. That being so, it is likely they would carefully choose a writer in the hope of finding one who could be expected to take a positive view of their work. In fact, in her story Belkin exhibits an uncritical acceptance of the methods and motives of Mero, the doctor, and the friend.

Whether or not Belkin approached her work with a pro–assisted suicide bias, a more important matter is the powerful message communicated by "No Simple Suicide." Bluntly stated, whether Belkin intended it or not, the article promotes the euthanasia cause by seeking to persuade the reader that assisted suicide is an acceptable act. Proponents of legalizing assisted suicide and euthanasia are ever about the task of proselytizing the public, seeking converts to their cause. The more we are exposed to depictions of assisted suicide, the more commonplace it will seem and, then, the more acceptable. Through this process we become desensitized. Practices that we once found abhorrent begin to seem like a normal part of life—or, more precisely, death. "No Simple Suicide" serves this purpose in several ways:

"No Simple Suicide" Implements the Either/Or Strategy.

One of the tools used by pro-euthanasia advocates when arguing for legalization is to create a false premise: Either we provide "deliverance" to suffering people, or they will be forced into cruel and unnecessary anguish. Either they die peacefully and painlessly now, or in agony later.

"No Simple Suicide" similarly casts Louise's plight as a forced choice between two horrible options: assisted suicide or an out-of-control death at a "facility." Not once is the reader (or Louise, as far as we know) informed that hospice and palliative care could probably have mitigated most if not all of her pain and discomfort. As reported, not once is the reader told that the hospice experience is designed to provide love, comfort, and support for the patient and the family, supplied by medical and mental health professionals and volunteers. Not once is the reader told that hospice care can be supplied *in the home*—clearly a major issue for the dying woman. Not once is the reader told that the very purpose of hospice care is to facilitate a gentle and peaceful transition from life to whatever comes next. The fact that the truly compassionate option, from what is reported, was virtually unexplored speaks volumes about the doctor's agenda, and that of Mero and perhaps the friend.

It is also notable that Louise's doctor treats her patient's suicidal desire as expected, rather than as a cry for help. Yet studies prove that the vast majority of dying people do not exhibit suicidal tendencies. When dying patients do ask for suicide, they are almost always clinically depressed, just as are suicidal people who are not terminally ill. Depression is a treatable condition. Unfortunately, most doctors are not adept at recognizing depression in their dying patients. Thus, whether through ignorance or arrogance, Louise's doctor probably abandoned her patient to the throes of depression, which could well have been overcome.

"No Simple Suicide" Creates the Impression That Euthanasia Is a Loving Rather Than a Violent Act.

The suspicion that there was an unspoken agenda behind "No Simple Suicide" is supported by the striking artwork that illustrates many of the scenes described in the text. While Belkin undoubtedly had little or nothing to do with their creation, the pictures, which appear to be oil or watercolor paintings, are powerful and moving. The article doesn't tell us Louise's actual age or what she looked like, but the pictures depict Louise as a woman in her late twenties, her youth and delicate beauty adding to the tragedy of her condition. In one picture, Louise is curled up peacefully asleep on a couch after eating the poisoned ice cream. She is holding a teddy bear as her gray-haired mother sits beside her, the older woman's hand resting lightly upon her dying daughter's leg. In another picture, we see Louise and Mero in a counseling session. He is a strong presence, solid and dependable with his white beard and black suit, a striking contrast to the frail Louise, who has a blanket wrapped around her shoulders. In another picture, Louise's mother is pictured leaning over her daughter, who is so weak the older woman can barely hear her speak.

The paintings have been created in the warm colors of autumn so as to invite us in, to linger as if we were standing in front of a crackling fire, indeed, to enter and become intimate participants in the unfolding drama. The paintings grab our hearts and rivet our attention solely and exclusively and in extreme close-up on the suffering of the dying woman. In that way we are less likely to think critically, to look beyond Louise's personal tragedy to the broader implications of what is being done to her. Also, by making the scenes seem gentle and warm, we are far less likely to recoil in horror at the actual events.

"No Simple Suicide" Creates the Impression That Louise's Assisted Suicide Was a Necessary Choice.

The article supports the beneficence of Louise's assisted suicide on several levels. Belkin's prose creates the impression that Mero and the others are compassionate pioneers leading the country toward an enlightened view of facing and overcoming the ravages of terminal illness. In fact, according to Belkin, that is how the group viewed themselves, writing that each saw Louise's pending assisted suicide as a "poetic expression of control, a triumph over the indignities of disease." That is a typical view held by death fundamentalists and no doubt is the view Mero hoped would be accepted by the reader.

Belkin came to a less romantic but equally erroneous conclusion about the affair. The only time she expresses a personal opinion in the article, she describes Louise's assisted suicide as a "second choice" to not being sick, and as the "most acceptable" of the dying woman's "unacceptable options." But that is a distinction without a difference. Whether euthanasia is pushed as a heroic statement of control or a rational choice between the lesser of two evils, the result is the same: legitimization of that which is ultimately profoundly destructive to individuals, the health-care system, and society.

Whether motivated by the death-fundamentalist notions of Mero, the "pragmatic choice" view of Belkin, the participants' genuine desire to serve Louise, or a combination of these factors, Louise was pushed by those around her into suicide because that was the death *they* wanted her to have. As the psychiatrist Dr. Herbert Hendin, director of the American Foundation for Suicide Prevention, has written about the case: "Like many people in extreme situations, Louise . . . expressed two conflicting wishes—to live and to die—and found support only for the latter."[55] One wonders what the outcome would have been had someone—*anyone*—supported Louise's oft-expressed desire to live and had stayed with her to the natural end of her life. Perhaps, then, she would have been surrounded by her friends in her final days. Perhaps Louise and her mother would have had a more meaningful time together, spared the undignified and excruciating dilemma over when and whether Louise would kill herself. Perhaps Louise could have really and truly died in peace.

"No Simple Suicide" Suggests That It Should Be Easier to Help People Die.

Louise's assisted suicide took place in the underground, amid the shadows of people who lied and broke the law in order to facilitate her so-called death with dignity. The attitude of the article is implicitly critical of the fact that this subterfuge was necessary. The reader is given a subliminal message, often voiced out loud by assisted-suicide advocates, that goes something like this: Unreasonable people who refuse to allow others to control their own destiny are insensitive, thoughtless, and cruel. They force dying people to endure unnecessary suffering. Such judgmental attitudes caused Louise's friends to abandon her when all she wanted to do was control the time and place of her own death. Her caring doctor was prevented from actively participating in her patient's final "treatment" because euthanasia by lethal injection is forbidden. Mero, a compassionate clergyman, was forced to risk imprisonment in his pursuit of providing care and comfort to the suffering.

The Other Side of the Story

The bitter irony is that the members of the little group surrounding Louise and their pro-euthanasia agenda were the ones who were thoughtless, insensitive, and cruel, for they took from Louise, in Dr. Hendin's words, "her own death."[56]

Louise Was Unable to Give Informed Consent to Her Suicide Because She Was Denied Information About Hospice Care.

According to what is revealed in the story, both the doctor and Mero allowed Louise to believe the either/or scenario: that she would have to die in a "facility" or kill herself at home. Apparently, neither discussed the option of hospice care with Louise or described the palliative care that could have reduced her discomfort. Thus, it appears that Louise was presented with a false premise from which to choose how to proceed.

The Medical Assistant Pushed Louise into Going Forward with the Assisted Suicide.

The medical assistant who suddenly embraced Louise as a friend is suspect. Was she part of a pro-euthanasia group? Did she have an agenda? We are not told. Wasn't Belkin even a little curious about this? Regardless of her motives, the assistant is a powerful actor throughout the drama, urging Louise on to self-destruction. Recall that when it became clear that Louise was delaying her self-destruction and appeared not to want to go forward, the medical assistant grew impatient and confronted the ill woman, saying, "I kind of want to get an idea of what your time line is. Where do we stand?"[57] When Louise says she doesn't want to talk about it but would rather wait for Mero to return to give his opinion of her medical condition, the friend tells her it is a "bad idea," and urges her not to wait because Mero may not be able to notice "subtle changes" in Louise's temperament and thus might give the wrong advice.[58] That is pressure disguised as advice.

Ralph Mero's "Compassion" Was Available to Louise Only If She Carried Out Her Designated Role.

This is the most insidious part of the story. It is important to remember how emotionally vulnerable most terminally ill people are as the end of life approaches. Louise was certainly no exception. Then, along comes "compassionate" Ralph Mero—a minister, no less—who tells Louise, "I'll be with you and I'll support you." From that point on it is quite clear that Louise has become dependent on the moral judgment and emotional support of Mero, to the extent that she even wanted to rely on him for *medical advice* as to how far her decline had progressed.

Note that throughout the early part of the process, Mero was there for Louise. He held her hand. He patiently and gently went over the guidelines for the assisted suicide. He presented himself as a source of strength, a nonjudgmental rock to lean on in this difficult and emotional time. But when Louise hesitated and refused to be pressured into suicide, what did this altruistic man of compassion do? Did he hold her hand and discuss alternatives to killing, such as hospice care? Did he pray with Louise so that together they could seek God's guidance? He is a minister, after all. Did he assure her that whatever her choice might be, he was her friend and would be there to the end? No. He withdrew!

> *Over the next few days, Mero checked in with Louise and her mother by telephone, but kept the conversation short. "I was measuring my phone calls," he says. He wanted to remain in the background and allow Louise to control the timing and pace. Her growing dependence on him was making him uncomfortable, and he needed to keep it clear in her mind, and his, that she was the driver and he was just along for the ride.*[59]

Mero was along for the ride, all right, but only if the ride took Louise down Suicide Lane. When she seemed to be choosing a different course, his absence made it clear that Louise was on her own if she chose to die a natural death.

Imagine how painful it must have been for Louise when her minister, the man she was leaning on for strength and guidance, was suddenly holding her at arm's length, especially after being so intensely a part of her life over the previous weeks. This certainly looks like emotional manipulation on Mero's part, communicating a harsh and powerful message to the dying woman: Kill yourself and I am your man; stick it out to the end and I am out of here. That wasn't compassion. That was cruelty.

The Reporter Also Pushed Louise Toward Killing Herself.
As if all of that isn't disturbing enough, what are we to make of the reporter, Lisa Belkin, and her participation in these sad events? Recall when the doctor informed Mero and the reporter that Louise was likely to slip quickly and become mentally incompetent and therefore become unable to kill herself or receive Mero's assistance, Belkin immediately flew to Seattle, unaware that Louise has not been told of this prognosis. During an interview on that occasion, Louise tells Belkin that she wants to wait a week or so before killing herself. Belkin is appalled. From the article:

> *I was surprised, confused and extremely uncomfortable. . . . Without thinking, I blurted out a question: "Your doctor feels that if you don't act by this weekend, you may not be able to . . ."*
>
> *My words were met with a wrenching silence. Louise blanched, her pale skin turned even paler. I was horrified with myself. . . .*
>
> *"She didn't . . . she never . . . I didn't know that," Louise said, sharply looking at her mother.*
>
> *"That's what she told me," her mother offered gently.*
>
> *Louise became silent. . . .*
>
> *"It's O.K. to be afraid," her mother said.*
>
> *"I'm not afraid. I just feel as if everyone is ganging up on me, pressuring me," Louise said. "I just want some time."*[60]

Indeed, Louise was being pressured, now even by the reporter who at that point crossed the line from an observer and chronicler of events to a participant in them.

There Is No Compassionate Voice of Opposition.
"No Simple Suicide" presents a one-sided version of assisted suicide. Except for one brief passage, people who resist legalizing euthanasia are not heard from, nor are the many reasons given why opponents of the death culture are so devoted in their resistance. That brief passage reads as follows:

> *That view [Louise's extolling Mero for "being there" for her] impels a harsh reaction from people like Ned Dolesjsi, executive director of the Washington State Catholic Conference. " 'I am God, I control life and death,' that's what they're saying. God is God, and we're not. It's that simple."*[61]

Notice that the one quote selected for use in the article by Belkin, presumably from a longer interview, describes opponents to euthanasia as "harsh," reinforces the false stereotype that opposition is based primarily on religion, and does not express any concern for the well-being of Louise.

Such short shrift was not accorded proponents of assisted suicide. At one point in the article, Mero describes his work for Compassion in Dying as an experiment to "show, demonstrate, prove, that when people make a claim for humane treatment, it can be provided in a way that does not jeopardize vulnerable people or pose a threat to the social fabric."[62] Leaving aside the perversion of the word *treatment* in that sentence, we can assume that Mero hoped that by inviting Belkin to observe his work, his vision of a world where the ill can be routinely euthanized would be accepted by readers.

But as this analysis of "No Simple Suicide," an article typical of this genre, demonstrates, what actually happened to Louise was just the opposite of the impression the story sought to convey. Instead of receiving compassion (literally, "suffering with") from those she trusted, a sick and vulnerable woman *was pushed* by them into suicide in order to further their agendas. In Dr. Hendin's words, Louise's "death was virtually clocked by their [Mero's, the doctor's, her mother's, the medical assistant's, Belkin's] anxiety that she might want to live. Mero and the doctor influence the feelings of the mother and the friend so that the issue is not their warm leave-taking . . . but whether they can get her to die according to the time requirements of Mero, the doctor, the reporter, and the disease. . . . Individually and collectively, those involved in [Louise's assisted suicide] engender a terror in Louise with which she must struggle alone, while they reassure each other that they are gratifying her last wishes."[63]

Dr. Hendin has it exactly right. What happened to Louise was not merely a "threat to the social fabric." It was, in fact, a rending.

Ralph Mero was unavailable for comment about my criticisms.[64]

CHAPTER 2

Creating a Caste of Disposable People

Nearly fifteen years ago I was an attorney working on behalf of a sixteen-year-old girl whom I will call Sally. Several years earlier Sally had had surgery to correct a progressive case of scoliosis, a back problem commonly known as curvature of the spine. At the time of her operation Sally was a bright, alert twelve-year-old with long blond hair. Her mother said she had a ready laugh, and photographs showed a smile to knock your socks off.

As Sally was wheeled out of her room on a gurney for her surgery, she turned to wave to her parents, a half-fearful smile on her face. *Click/flash.* Her parents took the last picture ever taken of that Sally. Less than an hour later her heart stopped, owing to the negligence of her anesthesiologist. C.P.R. was successful within a minute. Surgery continued until Sally had a second cardiac arrest. This time her heart was still for twelve minutes before resuscitation succeeded in saving her life.

Sally's brain, starved of oxygen, was severely damaged. She was now a quadriplegic and had a profound cognitive disability. She could not feed herself, speak, or, some said, interact meaningfully with others. The hospital doctors did what they could for her; then Sally was transferred to a state hospital where she lived in what used to be called "the basket ward."

This was as difficult and tragic a case as I had ever seen in my legal career. A young girl's life was ruined, her family destroyed by grief and self-recriminations, which contributed mightily to her parents' subsequent divorce. Four years after her injury, Sally's father rarely spoke her name, and her mother had put her own life on hold so that she could devote herself almost entirely to her disabled daughter's care.

Early on I decided that it was my professional duty to visit with my client, even though she would not know who I was or why I was there. But month after month I found excuse after excuse to put it off. I was busy, after all. Many clients required my attention. Besides, I worked hard. I deserved that fishing trip.

These were all rationalizations, of course. I wasn't so busy and in demand that I couldn't spare a few hours for the drive to the hospital and back. And even if the hectic pace of an active civil litigation practice kept me tied to my desk or in courtrooms, there were always the weekends. Finally I faced the hard fact: The real reason I hadn't visited Sally was that I was afraid.

It isn't easy seeing the Sallys of this world. They remind us too much of our own mortality, of life's caprice, of the chance that we or a loved one could, like Sally, lose the ability to control our body, the ability to speak, perhaps even to think. Is it any wonder, then, that many of us ignore such people and, when confronted with the reality of the severely disabled (and sometimes even the not-so-severely disabled), wish they would just go away?

As time passed and the case moved closer to trial, my guilt finally overcame my fear. One day the unexpected settlement of a case opened up a block of free time. I found myself phoning Sally's mother to arrange the visit. Twenty-four hours later I was driving into the parking lot next to the state hospital building in which Sally now resided.

I sighed nervously as I got out of the car. I did not want to do this! I still remember my heart pounding as I opened the door, walked to the elevator, and pushed the UP button. My hands were sweating. Please, God, I thought as I entered the elevator, don't let it happen to me.

Ding. The elevator door opened. I walked down a hall and entered Sally's ward. On my right was a long, narrow room filled with profoundly disabled people: dwarfs with heads enlarged by hydrocephaly; people of all ages apparently in comas; one unconscious or sleeping young woman, her face half covered with small tumors while the other half was as clear as the skin of a magazine cover girl. A nurse later told me that she had one of the most rare conditions known to medical science.

Then, quietly, almost imperceptibly, my fear evaporated and was replaced by feelings of comfort, then warmth, and then, much to my amazement, joy. Here was a very human place. Curtains were hung, and bright colors were painted throughout. There were plants around. Window shades were open to admit sunlight. The place smelled clean, not antiseptic. The nurses were deeply caring toward, indeed, loving of their patients. The mood was relaxed and gentle. I realized this was a home in the truest sense.

Then the nurses wheeled Sally to me. She was lying in a bed, seemingly unaware and unable to focus on her surroundings. I would not have recognized her. The pretty, optimistic face I knew from her presurgery photographs was gone, obliterated and distorted by her antiseizure medication. Many of her teeth were now missing. Her hair was short and stringy.

Yet none of that mattered. Sally was profoundly disabled, but that did not prevent her humanity from shining brightly through the veneer of difference. I experienced her as a sublime, even beautiful presence. My heart opened like a blossom unfolding.

I held her hand and began to sing to her. For some reason, I chose Dean Martin's theme song: "Everybody loves somebody sometime. Everybody loves someone somehow."

As I sang, Sally's eyes focused and she looked up at me. She smiled and lifted her head. She liked my singing. The nurses gathered around. Sally began to "sing" too, although it sounded more like a moan because she could not form words. Still, there was no doubting the happiness in her eyes and the smile on her face. Tears were in all our eyes (except Sally's) as we all joined in singing together. It was a precious moment that will remain with me for the rest of my life. I spent an hour with Sally, holding her hand, singing to her. She was no longer an abstraction but a client and, I felt, a friend.

I came away from that experience a better man, unalterably convinced of two things: Sally had bad taste in music, and she was fully and completely a human being, worthy of the same love, care, and respect as all of us.

(Sally's case ultimately was settled for a very large sum, enough to assure her the best of medical care for the rest of her life.)

A Changed World

Before the euthanasia consciousness seeped into America's cultural bloodstream, society expected the Sallys among us to receive proper and humane care. The equality-of-human-life ethic demanded it. They, like those who were not cognitively disabled, were human beings, equally endowed with the inherent human right to live.

The actual practice of caring for disabled people did not always come up to the ideal, of course. Some of our most vulnerable citizens were subjected to horrible conditions and truly terrible abuse. That did not mean, however, that the equality-of-human-life ethic itself was compromised. Quite the opposite. It was the belief that each of us has inherent equal worth that caused us to demand reform and improved care whenever such gross misconduct was exposed.

Times change, and not always for the better. People like Sally are for the most part viewed differently today. "In a short time, we have gone from the attitude that all of our patients are human who deserve care—no matter what their level of functioning—to believing that some people aren't people anymore," says Sharon S. Orr, a registered nurse who has spent a career caring for profoundly brain-damaged people.[1] One of her charges was a young woman named Nancy Cruzan, who was the subject of a lawsuit that made legal history (see page 45). The once-broad consensus in favor of the equality-of-human-life ethic for all has been substantially undermined. Not that we don't decry physical and mental abuse of the physically and mentally disabled. Of course we do. But a growing number of people no longer believe that cognitively disabled people possess the same inherent human worth and right to live as those of us who are able-bodied, "productive," and generally pleasing to look at. Indeed, to a disturbing degree many in the legal and medical communities, in academia, within religious institutions, and among the general public view these helpless people as pointless and useless burdens to themselves, their families, to society. Some have always believed this, of course. What has changed is that such beliefs have become respectable and mainstream.

When a value as fundamental as the equality-of-human-life ethic is weakened, it changes our attitudes toward each other, our behavior, our concept of what constitutes a humane and compassionate society. We no longer speak much of people such as Sally and Nancy as possessing an inherent right to live. Instead, we proclaim their inalienable "right to die."

Robert Wendland

"Wife requesting transfer [of Robert] to discontinue tube feeding for euthanasia," the concerned nurse wrote in the nursing notes that became a part of Robert Wendland's medical records. "Caloric needs have increased . . . [due to] his hard work in therapies. The shock of this decision and committee approval! Is very difficult for obvious reason of his progression."[2]

A few years ago, Robert Wendland, then forty-two, came home from an all-night drunk and was confronted by his wife, Rose, and his brother, Mike. An argument ensued. Rose told him that if he continued drinking and driving he would end up dead, kill someone else, or spend the rest of his life in a hospital, and that the family would all have to suffer for it.[3]

Robert dismissed her concerns, replying that if such a thing happened, if he could not live as a full man, he would rather be dead.

One week later, Rose's worst fears came to pass. After a terrible auto accident, Robert was in a coma.

Robert remained unconscious for sixteen months. Then, in January 1995, he unexpectedly began to stir. At first the changes were almost imperceptible; a grimace here, a hand movement there. Soon, however, there was no doubt: Robert was conscious.

According to court testimony by his nurses and therapists, confirmed by the medical records, after he awakened, Robert's condition continually improved. He learned to maneuver a motorized wheelchair on command and avoid obstacles, and at least once he even wheeled himself out of the hospital. Just a few months after waking up, he was able to respond to requests such as "Hand me the ball" 80 to 100 percent of the time. As proved by a videotape taken of one of Robert's therapy sessions, he was able to retrieve and return colored pegs from a tray when asked to do so by a therapist,[4] evidence of sophisticated neurological function.[5] He was able to support up to 110 pounds on one of his legs, which meant his muscle tone was returning.[6] Although unable to communicate, he showed emotional responses to his environment by, for example, kissing his mother's hand.[7]

By every measure Robert's cognition level and physical abilities are far above what Sally's were. Yet while she benefited from kind and loving care in a health-care world where no one seriously would have proposed taking action to end her life, Robert's doctors and his wife, Rose, want to take away Robert's tube-supplied food and fluids so that he dehydrates to death. Even more disturbing, their decision has received the unanimous approval of the Lodi Memorial Hospital Ethics Committee. (Ethics committees, as the name states, advise family members and health-care professionals on ethical questions that may arise in the course of medical treatment. Most hospitals have such groups, made up of doctors, nurses, members of the clergy, community leaders, and members of the general public. The membership of the committees is generally confidential, as are the details of the committee's deliberative processes.) Robert would be dead today but for an anonymous nurse who risked being fired by blowing the whistle to one of Robert's sisters.

When Robert's mother, Florence Wendland, and one of his sisters, Rebekah Vinson, asked the Stockton, California, attorneys John McKinley and Janie Hickock Siess to represent them in a court case to save Robert's life, both were shocked. "I was flabbergasted when the case came in," recalls Siess. "I knew from my studies in law school about the Cruzan case [discussed later in this chapter] that unconscious people could have their food and fluids terminated, but I had no idea that anyone would ever consider dehydrating a conscious human being. But, here it was. The plans to end Robert's life had already been made. He was to be discharged from the hospital, picked up by an ambulance, brought to a skilled nursing facility, where he would be starved to death. I couldn't believe it. I thought, this can't be legal. What sane person would want to do this?"[8]

McKinley quickly obtained an injunction prohibiting the dehydration, setting the stage for a momentous court battle between Rose on one side and her mother-in-law and sister-in-law on the other.[9] San Joaquin County Superior Court Judge Bob McNatt ultimately will decide whether Robert lives or dies, and a court of appeals or the California Supreme Court may eventually decide whether the lives of conscious disabled people who cannot make their own medical decisions can be intentionally ended. To put it another way, the Wendland case may decide whether all or only some Californians possess the inherent human right to live.

That Rose's request wasn't rejected out of hand by Robert's doctors, the Lodi Memorial Hospital Ethics Committee, and Judge McNatt shows the extent to which the equality-of-human-life ethic has already been undermined in this country. This is amply illustrated by the conduct of the ethics committee. Rather than giving all benefit of the doubt to life, committee members seem to have done just the opposite. As far as is known, no one argued on behalf of saving Robert's life. The nurses and therapists who spent the most time with Robert, many of whom were extremely upset by Rose's decision, were never asked their opinions. Indeed, Robert's sisters and mother, who would have argued against his killing, were not even told that it was being contemplated. (Robert's brother, Mike, who supported Rose, was aware of her decision.) There were probably no disabled people on the committee who might have better defended Robert's right to life. Moreover, the county ombudsman, whose specific job it is to advocate on Robert's behalf, supported Rose's decision without taking the time to learn that Robert could maneuver a wheelchair.[10] The ombudsman testified in court that her primary concern was to determine whether Rose's decision was made in haste. Once she believed that it was not, the ombudsman had no problem with the dehydration.[11]

It is important to emphasize that Robert was not terminally ill. His own doctor admitted on the witness stand that there was no medical reason to withhold food and fluids.[12] His life was and is endangered solely because it is not viewed as worth living, a view Rose claims Robert would have shared before he was injured, and thus his death is promoted as a means of protecting his personal autonomy. Yet, whatever Robert's previous feelings about profound disability, postinjury he has cooperated with his therapy, at least implying that he wants to live. And he has slowly improved. "Robert has now been taught successfully to push 'yes' or 'no' buttons when requested," attorney Siess says. "And he gets it right most of the time."[13]

The case is pending as of February 1997. Rose remains Robert's guardian, in charge of all health-care decisions, but has been ordered to continue Robert's nutrition support pending trial. For various reasons, the ultimate decision has been repeatedly put off. The bitterly fought case has already gone to the California Supreme Court, where John McKinley and Janie Siess successfully obtained a ruling requiring Judge McNatt to appoint an independent lawyer to act on Robert's behalf. (If Robert dies, Rose will collect on a life insurance policy;[14] Florence and Rebekah claim that represents at least the appearance of a conflict of interest. Thus, they wanted an independent voice to speak on behalf of Robert.) The independent lawyer subsequently obtained a court order from Judge McNatt for an independent medical examination by a neurologist and other experts.

In order to understand the radical changes in medical ethics that have occurred since the day I met Sally in the early eighties, one must grasp two related but distinct concepts: The first is the absolute right of all patients, no matter what their condition, to receive humane care. The other is the right of patients or their surrogate decision makers to refuse or discontinue unwanted medical treatment.

Humane care consists of basic nonmedical services that each human being is absolutely entitled to receive in a medical setting: warmth, shelter, cleanliness, etc. No matter how ill a patient, no matter the level of his or her disability, humane care can never be withdrawn ethically—even if the patient would prefer it. For example, if a patient wanted to be denied humane care so as to die by hypothermia by being left uncovered in front of an open window during a blizzard, medical personnel would have to refuse the request.

Medical treatment consists of action taken by doctors or other health-care professionals whose purpose is to provide a medical benefit to the patient. Obvious examples of medical treatment are surgery, prescribed medications, diagnostic tests, etc. Unlike the case with humane care, the patient must consent to receive medical treatment and may at any time refuse or discontinue such care. This right exists even if the refusal of treatment will likely result in death. Thus, a cancer patient is entitled to refuse chemotherapy and the heart disease patient can refuse bypass surgery.

The differences between warmth and chemotherapy as examples of humane care and medical treatment are clear. It wasn't too many years ago that food and fluids were considered humane care. That is no longer true, at least for food and water supplied through a feeding tube. Such care has been redefined as medical treatment, creating a vehicle to intentionally end the lives of cognitively disabled people while retaining the pretense of ethical medical practice.

This did not just happen. It resulted from a deliberate campaign. As bioethicists and others among the medical intelligentsia began to worry about the cost of caring for dependent people and the growing number of our elderly, and as personal autonomy increasingly became a driving force in medical ethics, some looked for a way to hasten the deaths of the most marginal people without seeming to be actually killing the patient, and thereby arouse hostility and opposition among the public.

Removing food and fluids provided by tube was seen as the answer. After all, it was rationalized, use of a feeding tube (whether in the stomach or through the nasal passage) requires a minor medical procedure. Moreover, the nutrition supplied by tube is not steak and potatoes but a liquid formula prepared under medical auspices so as to ease digestion. The term *artificial nutrition* was coined, making it appear that what was being withheld or withdrawn was not food and water but medicine, i.e., medical treatment.

From such small beginnings—changes in definitions and terminology—have come profound consequences. The "food and fluid" cases have rippled through traditional medical ethics and public morality, undermining one of the primary purposes for which our government has been instituted: the protection of the lives of all of its citizens.

Destination: Euthanasia

The theologian and philosopher Richard John Neuhaus has written: "Thousands of ethicists and bioethicists, as they are called, professionally guide the unthinkable on its passage through the debatable on its way to becoming the justifiable until it is finally established as the unexceptional."[15] Neuhaus's point is that the loosening of ethical guidelines generally occurs first among self-described health-care "bioethicists," theorists, philosophers, physicians, academics, and others, long before entering the realm of public attention. These ivory-tower types argue behind the scenes in the medical literature, within professional organizations, in universities, at conventions, etc., about the alleged need to "reform" existing standards of morality, ethics, health-care protocols, and public policy. The debates, which receive little if any media attention, rage for a few years and eventually culminate in a rough consensus that gives both "liberals" and "conservatives" something of what they want: an agreement that policies should change, tempered by "guidelines" to prevent abuse.

The next step is usually a series of legal test cases in which the judges generally lean on the testimony of expert witnesses—often the very doctors and bioethicists pushing the new agenda—who assure the judge that the health-care profession has worked it all through and reached an ethical consensus. Most judges decide the case along the lines of this so-called consensus. After all, he or she will reason, I am trained in law, not medicine. If doctors and professional ethicists think it is right, who am I, a mere judge, to determine otherwise? The judge's own prejudices and fears about disability or dying may also play a part in the decision.

The court's imprimatur in turn legitimizes the new ethic among the public. The media pick up the baton, running sympathetic stories that play on the emotions of the moment rather than the likely consequences. Soon, public opinion polls reflect the public's increasing acceptance of policies they would once have disdained, which stimulates politicians to frame the policy as statutory law or at least deters them from leading any opposition. In the end, as Neuhaus wrote, what once was unthinkable policy becomes the starting point for the slide down the next section of the slope.

This general pattern can be seen at work in the dehydration cases. The fundamental moral consensus that required the cognitively disabled to receive humane care, including nutrition and fluids for the duration of their natural lives, was attacked in this manner and eventually broken in the 1980s.[16] In March 1986, the first concrete step was taken to legitimize the intentional dehydration of unconscious, nonterminally ill patients. The American Medical Association Council on Ethical and Judicial Affairs, responsible for deliberating upon and issuing ethics advisories for the A.M.A., issued the following opinion: Although a physician "should never intentionally cause death," it was ethical to terminate life-support treatment, even if

> *death is not imminent but a patient's coma is* beyond doubt irreversible *and there are adequate safeguards to confirm the accuracy of the diagnosis and with the concurrence of those who have responsibility for the care of the patient. . . . Life-prolonging medical treatment includes medication and artificially or technologically supplied respiration, nutrition and hydration [emphasis added].*[17]

There it was. For the first time, food and fluids provided by a feeding tube were "officially" deemed a medical treatment that could be withdrawn ethically, the same as turning off a respirator or stopping kidney dialysis.

The opinion, written in passive prose, appears very narrowly drawn. Only those who "beyond doubt" were permanently unconscious were supposed to be eligible for terminating the "treatment." And protective guidelines were supposed to protect against abuses.

Nancy Cruzan

Once "consensus" was reached that dehydration was allowable, at least in some situations, the issue was ripe for adjudication. Lawsuits soon appeared in which judges were requested to permit a disabled patient to be made to die by dehydration. The case of Nancy Cruzan, the most famous and significant, had the greatest impact on that issue and has materially affected the entire debate on assisted suicide.

On January 11, 1983, Nancy lost control of her car on an icy road in Missouri and crashed. She was thrown from her car and landed face-down in a water-filled ditch. Nancy's heart stopped, but she was revived by paramedics.

Nancy's injuries included profound cognitive disability. In the media and in books about her case she is usually described as unconscious from the time of the accident, but that does not appear to be true.[18] For a period of time after the accident, Nancy was able to chew and swallow food and drink fluids. Indeed, she was first put on a feeding tube to make her long-term care easier. There was also evidence that she could hear and see; she smiled at amusing stories and sometimes cried when visitors left.[19]

While the actual level of her abilities was (and still is) in some dispute, no one contends that Nancy required intensive-care hospitalization or skilled nursing care. She was not on a respirator, nor did she receive dialysis. She was not terminally ill. All she required to maintain her life was humane care: nutrition, fluids, warmth, cleaning, and turning to prevent bedsores or pneumonia.

If Nancy was unconscious, as her parents and proponents of cutting off her food and fluids claimed, then she was in no pain. The same cannot be said of her mother and father. None can doubt that seeing a loved child so profoundly disabled over many years was an agonizing experience for the Cruzans, a deep psychic wound that never scabbed or healed. Perhaps the depth of their pain was why they began consulting with the Society for the Right to Die about ways to end Nancy's life. (The Society for the Right to Die, formerly known as the Euthanasia Society of America, has since merged with another euthanasia advocacy organization to form the group Choice in Dying.)[20]

The year after the A.M.A. ethics council's opinion was published, in May 1987, the Cruzans filed a lawsuit seeking to force hospital employees where Nancy was living to remove their daughter's food and fluids. Hospital administrators and especially the nurses who cared for Nancy, who saw her as a living, breathing human being deserving of respect and proper care, resisted. They wanted not to kill their patient but to continue to care for her. However, they were unable to persuade Jasper County Circuit Court Judge Charles E. Teel to let Nancy live. He ordered the hospital to do as the Cruzans requested.

The Missouri Department of Health appealed the decision. On November 16, 1988, the Missouri Supreme Court reversed the trial court. The court found, "This is not a case in which we are asked to let someone die. . . . This is a case in which we are asked to allow the medical profession *to make Nancy die* by starvation and dehydration" (emphasis added).[21]

Next, it was on to the United States Supreme Court. The Court's decision in *Cruzan v. Director, Missouri Department of Health* dealt primarily with the evidentiary standard established in Missouri law, which was that life support could be withdrawn from an incompetent patient only if there was "clear and convincing evidence" that the person would have wanted the treatment terminated. The Court upheld this requirement as constitutional, ruling that such a strict standard was properly in keeping with the state's obligation to protect the lives of its citizens. Since no clear and convincing evidence had been offered in the trial that removing food and fluids was what Nancy would have wanted—as opposed to what her parents desired for her—Missouri could thus require that Nancy's life support continue.[22] (Unfortunately, the Court also accepted by implication that tube-supplied food and fluids is a form of medical treatment that can be withdrawn ethically. Pro-euthanasia advocates misconstrue this aspect of the case as an argument for recognition of a new "right to die.")

What at first appeared to be a resounding victory for those who believed that the interests of cognitively disabled persons were best served by providing proper care for them rather than causing their death by dehydration soon turned sour. The Cruzans went back to court. This time, two of Nancy's former coworkers came forward to describe a conversation that, they testified, had occurred many years before, while the participants were engaged in their work activities. The details were sketchy, but the gist of the testimony was that Nancy had indicated she would not want to live in a coma. Nancy's exact words could not be described, nor whether she had made the statement or simply agreed to a statement made by another. But that was all Judge Teel (who had originally determined that Nancy could be dehydrated) required to rule that the Cruzans had provided clear and convincing evidence that Nancy would want her treatment ceased.

There was no appeal. By this time, the Missouri Department of Health had abandoned the case, deciding to allow Nancy's parents to have their way. Those who opposed the ruling were not parties to the case and thus were powerless to intervene. Nancy's foods and fluids were withdrawn on December 14, 1990. She died twelve days later. The cause of death listed on her death certificate: "dehydration."

(It is worth noting that opponents of dehydrating the cognitively disabled who comment on such killings are often depicted in the media as uncompassionate interlopers who are interfering with the most intimate of private family matters. Yet few media commentators objected to the Cruzans having film crews record Nancy's saga, from their first meeting with their attorney until Nancy's death. The film was later shown on the PBS program *Frontline*.)

Postscript: In August 1996, the Cruzan family suffered another tragedy when Nancy's father, Joe Cruzan, hanged himself in the family home. Joe was characterized by family and friends as unable to recover emotionally from his daughter's death. Dr. Ronald Cranford, a neurologist and euthanasia advocate who often testifies as an expert witness in favor of dehydrating cognitively disabled patients (including Nancy Cruzan and Robert Wendland, as well as Christine Busalacchi and Michael Martin, whose cases are discussed below), was a friend of Joe Cruzan's. Cranford characterized Cruzan's tragic death as a "rational suicide" because, despite treatment, "He was never going to get better."[23] Joe Cruzan left behind a wife and two children.

Christine Busalacchi

Since Nancy Cruzan's death, the starving and dehydration of cognitively disabled patients has become almost routine in hospitals and nursing homes all around the country. Moreover, such killings have definitely *not* been limited to people who, in the words of the A.M.A. ethics council opinion, are "beyond doubt" permanently unconscious. When the parents of Christine Busalacchi, a twenty-year-old auto accident victim, sought permission to end their daughter's life, doctors described her condition as a persistent vegetative state (P.V.S.). In P.V.S. the patient has sleep and wake cycles but lacks reflex response and does not interact with his or her environment. The patient's eyes may be open, but he or she is believed to be unaware. This is distinct from a coma, where the patient's eyes are closed. Christine's father, Pete Busalacchi, believed that his daughter was "one hundred percent gone."[24] Dr. Ronald Cranford, testifying in favor of dehydrating Christine, dehumanized her by saying, "She's got a shell of a body, lying there with a brain stem."[25]

Yet nurses and medical personnel who had close interaction with Christine told a different story. Their descriptions do not fit the P.V.S. label. Some testified they had heard her grunt to indicate her choice of soap opera on television. They told of her smiling and interacting with favorite nurses. Nurse Sharon Orr recalls, "Christine was awake and alert. She would push buttons to call us. She would eat a bite and push a button, saying another bite please. We fed her with a spoon."[26] A videotape of Christine released to the media showed that she could indeed eat food by mouth, press a switch to ask for food, and obey simple requests. Thus, while there is no doubt Christine was profoundly disabled, it is highly unlikely that she was permanently unconscious.[27]

Christine's father strongly objected to the release of the videotape, claiming it was a violation of his daughter's privacy. But perhaps he was more upset because, as the old saying goes, a picture is worth a thousand words. The same objections and arguments were made by Rose Wendland and the Lodi Memorial Hospital in the Wendland case after KRON-TV in San Francisco aired a video of Robert performing simple tasks[28] and I wrote an opinion article in the *San Francisco Chronicle* publicizing concerns about the quality of Robert's medical care.[29] Rose, supported by a friend of the court brief filed by the Lodi Memorial Hospital, went so far as to seek a court order from Judge McNatt imposing secrecy; he rejected the request.[30] As to the observations of Christine's nurses, Dr. Cranford discounted them, claiming that the nurses were too emotionally involved to see the truth about Christine's condition. This conforms to a pattern common in these cases, whereby nurses' opinions and observations are often discounted by judges in food and fluid cases, even though they have the closest relations with patients. By contrast, testifying doctors, whose word has greater sway, may only have spent a few minutes examining the person.

Compelling evidence of her consciousness was not enough to save Christine's life. Nancy Cruzan had broken the ice. A new public-policy paradigm was in play. It wasn't the presence or absence of consciousness that mattered. What counted was the view that death was the answer to profound cognitive disability. Since dehydration was considered appropriate for the unconscious, why not also the conscious who required a feeding tube? Christine soon followed Nancy into death by means of intentional dehydration.

The slide down the slippery slope from killing the unconscious (assuming for the sake of argument that Cruzan was unconscious) to killing the conscious but cognitively disabled (Busalacchi and other conscious cognitively disabled people who have met a similar fate) belies the argument that policies permitting the killing of patients can be strictly controlled. The carefully shaded moral distinctions in which the health-care intelligentsia and policymakers take so much pride are of little actual consequence in the real world of cost-controlled medical practice, in busy hospital settings, and among families suffering the emotional trauma and bearing the financial costs of caring for a severely brain-damaged relative. Once killing is seen as an appropriate answer in a few cases, the ground quickly gives way, and it becomes the answer in many cases.

This slide down the slope has dragged the A.M.A. along with it. In 1994, a brief eight years after its first ethics opinion reclassifying tube feeding as medical instead of humane treatment, the A.M.A. Council on Ethics and Judicial Affairs made a crucial revision. Where once the patient had to be "beyond doubt" permanently unconscious to permit withdrawing food and fluids, now

> Even if the patient is not terminally ill or permanently unconscious, *it is not unethical to discontinue all means of life-sustaining medical*

treatment [including food and fluids] in accordance with a proper
substituted judgment or best interests analysis.[31]

This is a classic example of the slippery slope phenomenon. Once the
killing of one group, the unconscious, was permitted, those killed in actual practice included another group, the conscious. When it became
clear that the guidelines were not being adhered to, the guidelines were
expanded rather than enforced more rigorously, which formally legitimized practices that a few years before had been deemed completely unacceptable.

That conscious people are now being commonly dehydrated is particularly disturbing when the realities of this type of death are understood.
Proponents of dehydration contend that such deaths are peaceful. Yet Dr.
William Burke, who opposes the practice, describes death by dehydration
as painful:

A conscious person would feel it [dehydration] just as you or I
would. They will go into seizures. Their skin cracks, their tongue
cracks, their lips crack. They may have nosebleeds because of the dry-
ing of the mucus membranes, and heaving and vomiting might ensue
because of the drying out of the stomach lining. They feel the pangs of
hunger and thirst. Imagine going one day without a glass of water!
Death by dehydration takes ten to fourteen days. It is an extremely ag-
onizing death.[32]

Even Jack Kevorkian finds death by dehydration inhumane.

To counter worries about inducing an agonizing death, doctors generally
prescribe morphine or other narcotics. But who knows whether this pre-
caution truly masks the agony of dehydration. For example, when the lawyer
Janie Hickock Siess asked what level of morphine would have to be given to
Robert Wendland to prevent him from suffering the agonies of dehydration,
Dr. Ronald Cranford testified that the dose would be "arbitrary" because
"you don't know how much he's suffering, you don't know how much aware
he is. . . . You're guessing at the dose. . . ."[33] Thus, even according to dehydration advocate Cranford, it is quite possible that dehydrated conscious
people die in a prolonged and perhaps excruciating manner. We wouldn't
execute the most heinous murderer this way. It is a crime to do this to a dog
or horse. Yet virtually every day, fellow humans are being deprived of the
mere basics required for life just because they are disabled.

The attitude that it is better to die than to become cognitively disabled has so pervaded the culture of health care that some doctors are beginning to worry about a rush to write off newly unconscious patients and consign them to death by cutting off life support before they have a chance to recover. According to Dr. Vincent Fortanasce, a board-certified neurologist and psychiatrist, too many doctors are making diagnoses of permanent unconsciousness after a few days or a week, when it takes at least three to six months before a firm diagnosis can be made.[34] "Eighty to ninety percent of the cases I see have been improperly diagnosed," Fortanasce says, "often by doctors who are not qualified to make the determination. Unfortunately, that's the real practice in medicine today."[35]

Dr. Fortanasce recounts one example of this rush to write off unconscious patients from his own practice. A sixty-year-old patient collapsed and was diagnosed as P.V.S. by his internist, who strongly urged the family to discontinue all life support, including nutrition. The family was reluctant and so they sought a second opinion from Dr. Fortanasce. "I came in, took the appropriate tests. The patient wasn't P.V.S. He had experienced a severe brain seizure. I prescribed continued life support and medication. A week later, the patient walked out of the hospital in full possession of his faculties. Had the family listened to the internist, the man would be dead today."[36]

The frequency of such cases is unknown. (So far, no studies have been done.) In most cases the withdrawal of food and fluids is done with the consent of the families, so no notice is taken. Unless someone objects to the dehydration or the premature withholding of life support, the patients are killed and no one is the wiser.

Decisions of Life and Death

The legality of dehydrating the cognitively disabled has not yet been set completely in concrete, although not for lack of trying. Many relatives of the unconscious and cognitively disabled refuse to permit their loved ones to be killed. A few courageous judges, such as Alabama's Pamela Willis Beschab, still hold the legal line against these killings. When relatives of Correan Salter, a stroke patient, wanted a court ruling permitting her dehydration, Judge Beschab refused, writing, "Once the state accepts a policy that some lives are not worthy to be lived and some people would be better off dead, it takes the first step on a long and slippery slope from which there can be no turning back."[37] Unfortunately, most judges and family members are swept along by the prevailing cultural tide.

The following recent cases illustrate the acute danger to the weakest and most helpless among us.

Ronald Comeau

On June 21, 1993, Ronald Comeau, a thirty-year-old drifter, was arrested in Bennington, Vermont, accused of robbing another homeless man. Comeau grew despondent. Alone, his freedom forfeited, he had no one to turn to. It had been a very long time since he had had any contact with his father, and their relationship had never been good. His mother had no phone. He hadn't seen his brothers for nearly seven years. He was without a future, without hope. Not even the police cared enough to watch him in the station holding cell. Soon after Comeau was put in the cell, a police officer found him hanging from a noose apparently made from the trim of a cheap jail blanket.

Unconscious, Comeau was cut down. No pulse. He didn't appear to be breathing. C.P.R. was administered, after which he seemed to have a weak pulse.

The paramedics arrived and performed more C.P.R. A wailing ambulance ride in the dead of night to the Southwestern Vermont Medical Center followed. In the emergency room, the doctors could once again find no heartbeat. Comeau received advanced life support: an injection of atropine and two pulses of electricity to restart his heart. It worked. After about fifteen minutes without a pulse, Comeau was alive.[38]

Nothing unusual here. Go to any big city hospital or small-town medical center and sooner or later you will see the unwashed and unwanted who are helped as much as possible and then soon forgotten. But few would ever forget Ronald Comeau.

The hospital was able to locate Comeau's father, Renald Dupois of Maine, who was contacted within hours of his son's near death. Amy Swisher, the director of community relations for Southwestern Vermont Medical Center, says that the doctors and hospital personnel followed procedures that are standard in cases such as Comeau's: They advised Dupois that his son was severely injured and might die, requested permission for HIV testing, and asked about the possibility of organ donation, should he die.[39] There is some dispute as to the accuracy of this account. However, it is not disputed that Dupois failed to come to his son's bedside and that soon his phone was disconnected.

Decisions needed to be made about Comeau's health care. Without family available to make them, he needed a court-appointed guardian to make decisions on his behalf. Enter Joseph Schaaf, well known in the local legal community because of his volunteer work as a guardian *ad litem* (a temporary representative during a court case) in local child custody matters. He agreed to serve as Comeau's permanent guardian without pay and was so appointed by Judge Doris Buchanan of Bennington Probate Court, on July 23, 1993.

Schaaf took his responsibilities to Ronald Comeau seriously, visiting at least five days a week and discussing the case with doctors and staff as he contemplated what would be best for his ward. By mid-August Schaaf had come to a difficult decision. Comeau had been diagnosed as being in an irreversible persistent vegetative state (P.V.S.). He was awake, he had reflexes, but he was not aware. There appeared to be no cognitive ability whatsoever. Schaaf instructed Stephen Saltonstall, his pro bono attorney in the Comeau matter, to seek permission from the probate court to remove the ventilator that aided Comeau's breathing, an act expected to lead to the young man's death.

On August 17, Judge Buchanan held a hearing. On the basis of the testimony of the attending physician, Dr. Michael Algus, and a consulting neurologist, Dr. Keith Edwards, she ruled that Comeau was a "blind quadriplegic" who was "unaware" of what was happening "around him and to him" and that there was "no reasonable possibility of recovery or improvement." Convinced it was in Comeau's best interests, she signed the order permitting the ventilator to be withdrawn.[40]

But Comeau didn't die. In fact, he began to improve.

By the middle of September, Comeau was no longer P.V.S.; he was awake and aware. But this was not viewed as a cause for joy. Joe Schaaf was horrified by Comeau's condition. "I saw a person who could register some feelings but those feelings were pain, agony and fear," he recalls. "His hands were bent in toward his wrists. It appeared he was trying to remove his feeding tube. Whether it was a conscious act, I couldn't tell."[41]

On occasion, others saw a different Ronald Comeau. The speech-language pathologist Juanita J. Cook noted:

> *Seems to recognize personnel—favorite nurses. On 9/21, definitely responded with recognition today when I went in and said my name, reminding him that I was the person who came in to talk—not to do any direct care, etc.—Big smile, with overall body movement. Very different from the grimace at having hands restrained.*[42]

Other notes in Comeau's medical file show a man who was aware—sometimes grimacing, seemingly in pain; at other times intently concentrated on discussions about his future care.[43]

Despite Comeau's cognitive improvements, Joe Schaaf began to discuss the issue of removing his feeding tube with doctors and other medical personnel. He says of his thinking at that time, "I thought that if it were me there, lying helpless in a bed, I hope to God that someone would help me move on from my misery to whatever comes next, because whatever comes next can't be worse than that."[44] On the basis of these personal fears, Schaaf decided to pursue the option of having Comeau's food and fluids withheld.

Not everyone approved of the proposal. Dr. Edwards, the consulting neurologist, wrote a report stating in part, "Although I would have no ethical or moral problems in letting . . . a medical complication go untreated, it is difficult to support withdrawing nutrition in a patient who is demonstrating some neurological function. . . . [I] would continue comfort care and nutritional care as currently undertaken."[45]

The psychiatrist Dr. Peter Zorach was the chairman of the Southwestern Medical Center Ethics Committee. In October 1993 Joe Schaaf asked the committee for its formal opinion on his plan to starve and dehydrate Ron Comeau to death. Comeau was neither terminally ill nor in an irreversible coma. He was awake and aware, if profoundly brain-damaged and disabled. At the time, the 1986 A.M.A. Council on Ethics and Judicial Affairs opinion was in effect. Indeed, it had been reiterated in 1992. Had its guidelines been followed, Comeau would not have been a candidate for dehydration. But if the guidelines concerned the ethics committee, it was not apparent. Dr. Zorach described the subjective nature of the committee deliberations as follows:

> We had a discussion. We weren't going to take a vote but Mr. Schaaf felt it would be helpful to him if he knew whether people would support his position. There were people in the discussion who had taken part in Mr. Comeau's care and who were able to express observations about what could be done. We imagined that his being in a hospital bed not able to move, might be a frustrating experience. If being in jail made him so unhappy that he wanted to kill himself, then being in a hospital partially paralyzed would also make him unhappy. People felt that he was not happy and that there was not much likelihood that he would ever be happy. His emotions usually looked like fear, anger, rage and sometimes sadness.[46]

The vote was 10–3 to support whatever decision Joe Schaaf might make on behalf of his ward—including completing Ronald Comeau's suicide attempt for him by withdrawing his food and fluids.

On November 9, Stephen Saltonstall and Joe Schaaf appeared before Judge Buchanan for the purpose of determining whether Comeau's feeding tube should be removed. Drs. Algus and Zorach testified in support of removing nutritional care. No one argued against removal. Dr. Edwards's report recommending against this course was not mentioned to the judge. Saltonstall says he was unaware of Dr. Edwards's opinion.[47] It was disclosed that Comeau was no longer P.V.S. and that he had improved in the weeks since the previous hearing seeking permission to remove the ventilator, but the judge seems not to have grasped the implications of the fact that those who argued for killing Comeau at that earlier time were *mistaken* when they assured her that he would not improve beyond P.V.S. Perhaps that was because now the information presented to her was couched in graphic terms of unbearable suffering, once again with assurances that there was no hope of further improvement. Still, her apparent lack of curiosity about the accuracy of Comeau's initial prognosis is puzzling.

Judge Buchanan granted the motion, ruling that Comeau was "helpless and debilitated," and that he appeared to be experiencing "pain, terror, suffering, and horror." She further ruled that Comeau would "beyond any reasonable doubt . . . ask that artificial nutrition and hydration be terminated."[48] Food and fluids were immediately withdrawn.

If all had gone as planned, Ronald Comeau would have been dead within two weeks. But a hitch developed in the person of Reverend Mike McHugh, the minister of Grace Christian Church in Essex Junction, Vermont. A committed pro-life activist and founder of the Vermont chapter of Operation Rescue, McHugh sees it as his Christian duty to seek to preserve life, primarily the life of what he terms "preborn children." Reverend McHugh is a controversial figure in Vermont. He is not known for his tact.

Two days after Judge Buchanan ruled that Ronald Comeau's food and fluids could be withdrawn, McHugh received a phone call from someone who had heard a radio report that a young man was being legally starved to death. Was there anything Mike McHugh could do?

McHugh obtained a copy of the *Bennington Banner* issue that had run a story on the case. He was appalled. This is euthanasia, he thought, no different from a murder orchestrated by the government, especially since the decision was being made by a court-appointed guardian.[49] He knew he had to stop it and called on his network of pro-life attorneys to discuss what he could do. He then went to a prayer meeting of local pastors and sought their counsel. He came away from these discussions and his prayers having decided to be bold.

McHugh called Judge Buchanan at her home and told her he wanted a hearing so that he could petition the court to become Ronald Comeau's guardian. (Vermont law permits the clergy to intervene in guardianship cases under certain circumstances.) She agreed to convene one immediately. McHugh then decided to go high-profile. He issued a press release on the case announcing that he was going to fight to save Ronald Comeau's life. A hearing was held at 8:00 P.M. on November 11, 1993. Among those present were Joe Schaaf, Stephen Saltonstall, and Mike McHugh. Also present: representatives of much of Vermont's local media. The Comeau case was about to become an event.

McHugh asked for a stay of the order removing Ron's feeding tube and asked to intervene in the guardianship case. Under cross-examination he admitted to having willfully violated a federal judge's restraining order to desist from blocking access to abortion clinics and to having been arrested twenty times in connection with his anti-abortion activities. He also admitted that he had never met Ronald Comeau and that Comeau was not part of his congregation. Judge Buchanan ruled that she could not stay her own order. Moreover, she ruled that under Vermont law, McHugh had no legal standing to enter the case. In other words, it was assumed that he had nothing at stake. Consequently, he had no legal right to intervene.

McHugh was undaunted. The next day, along with a less controversial pastor named John Goyette, he filed an appeal in the Bennington Superior Court seeking to reverse Judge Buchanan's ruling. This judge agreed with Judge Buchanan, finding that the clergymen had no direct interest in the case.

But McHugh was not done yet. He asked an attorney, Norman C. Smith, to get actively involved in the case. Smith immediately prepared and presented an emergency motion to the chief justice of the Vermont Supreme Court requesting a stay of Judge Buchanan's order removing Comeau's nutrition. On November 12 the request for a stay was granted, pending a hearing to be held the following Tuesday, November 16. The order was served on the hospital and Ronald Comeau's food and fluids were restored.

McHugh viewed the stay as a temporary reprieve of execution. When the emergency hearing started on November 16, he and Smith believed they would lose because of the issue of legal standing. After that, nothing could be done to save Ronald Comeau's life. Dejected and growing desperate, feeling the burden of Comeau's life on his own shoulders, McHugh had one last card to play. He decided to appeal to Comeau's father, Renald Dupois, even though the media had depicted the man as uncaring about his son's fate. To try to locate Dupois he made some phone calls to police contacts he knew, and headed north toward Maine.

Later, he called one of the police contacts whom he had asked to assist him. "We found Renald Dupois," the policeman told him. "He is willing to meet you. He doesn't want his son to die."[50] For the first time since he had determined to save Comeau's life, Mike McHugh felt hope.

McHugh met Renald Dupois and his brother, Raymond Dupois. The men were not well educated. They wanted to know what was going on. McHugh showed them news clippings and said to Renald Dupois, "I am told you don't have an interest in this."

"That's not true," Renald Dupois insisted. He had been confused by the hospital's brief contact with him and didn't understand Ron's status. Raymond Dupois thought that the hospital had told his brother that Ron was going to die. He was shocked that his nephew was still alive.

McHugh offered to pay all expenses if the two men would go back to Vermont with him and appear at the November 16 hearing. They agreed. With the help of McHugh's personal finances and contributions of other pro-life supporters, the Dupois brothers were soon in a hotel in Bennington.

If Mike McHugh's primary motive was to gain publicity for himself, as some accused, he got what he wanted. With the dramatic surprise appearance of Renald and Raymond Dupois at the Tuesday hearing, Ronald Comeau's case became a local front-page media sensation. The court continued the hearing until the Dupois brothers could visit Comeau and determine whether he was indeed their son and nephew, at which point McHugh held a news conference that quickly descended into an ugly shouting match between him and reporters when he excluded one paper from the gathering and refused to allow the brothers to be questioned directly by reporters.

An angry debate was on. Most people were glad that Ron Comeau's family was involved, but many resented McHugh's intrusion and the transformation of the young man's tragedy into a media circus. McHugh wasn't pulling any punches either, stating at one point that those who advocated for Comeau's death were no better than "executioners." Schaaf's attorney, Stephen Saltonstall, says, "I particularly resented this allegation, since I had been one of the lawyers who had convinced the Supreme Court of Massachusetts to throw out that state's death penalty law."[51]

Each day's paper and TV news reports heralded the unfolding events of the case. Editorials were flying. Strangely, the actions of Mike McHugh seemed to be as big an issue as the life or death of Ron Comeau. A *Rutland Herald* editorial admitted that Comeau's future should be a central issue but opined, "It is too bad that the sanctity of life should have as its defender a religious freebooter such as McHugh," and worried that "those involved in Comeau's case fear McHugh will succeed in manipulating Comeau's father . . . to his own ends."[52] A newspaper commentator named Jack Hoffman was furious that the press had allowed "Michael McHugh, the anti-abortion fanatic," to dictate "the terms for staging his own publicity stunts," further grousing that "the media got jerked around."[53] Meanwhile, an anonymous hospital official fretted to a reporter that Comeau's family had come under the influence of "confrontational individuals with an agenda."[54]

Amid the media uproar, indications appeared that Comeau had a higher level of cognitive ability than had been previously described. After visiting his son, Renald Dupois told the press, "I said, 'This is Dad.' When he heard that, he had a smile on his face and started to move all over the place. That made me happy." Comeau's uncle, Raymond, added, "If he's in a coma, it's the funniest coma I ever saw."[55]

The case was about to take another twist. In Worcester, Massachusetts, Renald Comeau, Ron's brother, heard a news report about the brouhaha going on in Vermont and suddenly realized, "That's my brother!" He and his wife, Patricia, immediately left for Bennington. There they were joined by the Comeau boys' half brother, Robert DesRosiers.

The family assembled at Comeau's bedside, the first such gathering in a very long time. More evidence appeared that Comeau's condition was not as bad as had been previously described. When Ron Comeau was reunited with his brothers, he delighted at being shown a shirt with the Harley-Davidson logo on it. He and his brothers laughingly compared tattoos.[56]

It was clear that Comeau was able to react and communicate feelings. The brothers came away from the reunion quite upset at what had almost happened to him. "Can you imagine, they were going to kill this guy?" DesRosiers said to reporters after the reunion. "There's a lot of life there."[57]

After that, things moved quickly. Joe Schaaf met with Renald Comeau, and it was agreed that Renald would take over as his brother's guardian. Any thought of dehydrating Ron to death was abandoned.

According to his family, in the years since Comeau's plight divided a community, his condition has significantly improved. Like all of us, he has his bad days as well as his good, sometimes becoming quite frustrated by the limitations caused by his disability. But for the most part, the news is good. He recognizes family members, enjoys listening to music, can sit up or roll over, use the television remote control, and clumsily push himself in a wheelchair. His personality has reemerged. "He's a real flirt," Ron's sister-in-law, Patricia Comeau, says with a laugh. "He makes eyes at the nurses all the time." Moreover, Patricia Comeau reports that "Ron can communicate quite well now. He speaks one-syllable words. His reading comprehension is good, and he loves to draw using an Etch-a-Sketch." The family hopes someday to get him a computer system to aid his speech.[58]

Despite Comeau's improved condition, Joe Schaaf still believes he acted appropriately. "I have no regrets," he says, adding, "Crystal balls are hard to come by. I have thought it over many times. We did what we thought was right at the time."[59]

No doubt that is true. But why did so many well-meaning people give every benefit of the doubt to inducing Ron Comeau's death rather than protecting his life? Why were the neurologist's report opposing dehydration for Comeau and the therapist's reports about his ability to respond to stimuli not mentioned in court, even by his own temporary guardian? Why did the hospital downplay Comeau's capacities? And why were so many people so upset with Mike McHugh for trying to save Ron's life?

Once we accept the idea that some lives are not worth living, once we come to see the intentional ending of lives of the profoundly disabled as proper, once we claim the right to judge who should live and die on the basis of subjective standards such as happiness, quality of life, or dignity, we have created a disposable caste: fellow humans who can be killed without legal consequence, whose intentional deaths do not disturb a good night's sleep.

Being an honorable and compassionate people, it is painful and difficult to admit that, so we are forced into pretense. We invent new terms and definitions to govern our actions: Intentional dehydration is labeled "allowing to die"—it sounds nicer that way. We twist the basic meaning of terms and concepts: Abandonment of the helpless is called "beneficence," an end to suffering. We create slogans such as "death with dignity" to help us rationalize the appropriateness of the once unacceptable. Under these circumstances, it is easy to understand why the opponents of these practices cause so much consternation. They refuse to let us deceive ourselves about what we are doing. When, like McHugh, they are not gentle in their approach or circumspect in their language, they outrage.

Shortly after Ron Comeau's life was saved, Renald Comeau, reflecting on how close he came to losing his brother, asked, "How many other Ronnie Comeaus are there?"[60] The answer, it appears, is quite a few.

Michael Martin

"A-F-R-A-I-D," Michael Martin, a brain-damaged forty-one-year-old man, spelled out on the alphabet board.

"Are you afraid of somebody?" asked the speech pathologist at the Michigan hospital where Michael was being cared for.

Michael shook his head no.

"Are you afraid for somebody?"

Michael nodded his head yes.

The speech pathologist asked if he was afraid for the nurses, aides, or his roommate, David.

No.

"Are you afraid for yourself?"

Yes.[61]

Michael Martin, a profoundly disabled man, didn't know it, but he too was about to be the center of a bitter dispute over whether his life would be ended by dehydration. Unlike the Comeau case, where previously estranged relatives united as a family to save Ron Comeau's life, the Martin case deeply and bitterly divided a family. On one side was Mary Martin, Michael Martin's wife, who wanted Mike's life ended. Fighting to save him were Leeta Martin and Pat Major, Mike Martin's mother and sister.

"Do you like it here?" the pathologist continued.

Yes.

"Do you feel you get good care here?"

Yes.

"Are you afraid someone will take you from this facility?"

Yes.

The therapist then told Michael that he would be with them for "quite a while."

According to the chart notes, Michael then gave a big smile.[62] That hope was unduly optimistic. The judge of the Allegan County Probate Court, George A. Grieg, would soon issue a ruling allowing Mary Martin to order Michael's feeding tube removed in order that he die by dehydration.

What made the Michael Martin case significant was the relatively high level of Martin's functioning. Unlike Ron Comeau, when the court battle raged over Martin he was not only conscious but interactive. For example, in April 1992 he learned how to use a communication augmentation system in which he pointed to letters so as to communicate. Through the system he was able to say, "My name is Mike."[63] According to the therapist's report, when asked to spell a word,

> Mike spelled out the word [water]. When asked to find the character to clear this page, Mike was able to do it independently. Mike also indicated to us in response to a yes/no question, that the scanning device was too slow for him and he wanted it to be a little faster. When directed to the feelings page, Mike responded to the question of how he was feeling by indicating happy.[64]

Unfortunately, Mike's current feelings would not count for anything in the coming drama over his potential killing.

In October 1992, as part of the court case then ongoing, Michael Martin was evaluated by Dr. Robert K. Krietsch, a board-certified physician specializing in physical medicine and rehabilitation. Dr. Krietsch reported:

> When I first entered the room his radio was on and he agreed to allow it to be turned off. When asked if he is able to see television and follow some shows, he indicates with an affirmative and also again, with a "yes" head nod when asked if he likes certain types of shows. He brightened up with a large grin when asked if he liked cartoons. . . . When shown his poster with pictures of country western music stars, he again became quite animated with his expression, using a large grin, and was very cooperative in identifying by head nod and attempted to point with his right hand on questioning who were the different stars that I pointed to. . . . He was 100% accurate on identifying all of these.

In open court, Judge Grieg recalled a visit he had with Martin where he had seen for himself that Martin was conscious and interactive:

> I introduced who I was, that I was down—that we were having a hearing on whether or not he still needed a guardian. What did he think? Did he think he still needed a guardian? He shook his head yes.

*I mean it was a definite movement. It came at an appropriate time—
at the end of the question.*

Judge Grieg related how Martin would nod yes and no when asked various
questions about former coworkers and family members. He described
how he then asked Martin to show volitional movements:

> *I asked him, "Can you move your hand? . . . Is it your left one?"
> He shook his head no. I said "Is it your right one?" He said yes. I said,
> "Can you move it for me," and he raises it up and down.*[65]

Michael Martin became disabled on January 16, 1987, when the car in
which he and his entire family were driving was hit by a train. The accident not only disabled Michael but also killed the Martins' daughter,
Melanie, age seven. (Mary and the other two Martin children suffered injuries but fully recovered.) Michael Martin was unconscious for the first
several months following the accident. Then he began to improve. By
1990, his treating neurologist, Dr. Walter Zetusky, measured his I.Q. as
between 63 and 67.[66]

Almost since the accident, Mary had believed that it was best for her
husband to die. In August 1988, as Mike was slowly improving, she refused to permit antibiotics to be used to treat him for pneumonia. That,
and her refusal to share information about his condition with Pat Major,
his sister, and Leeta Martin, his mother, caused the two to seek Mary's
ouster as Mike's guardian. That dispute ended with an informal settlement, but the die creating two factions in the family had been cast.

Two years later Mike developed a bowel obstruction. Mary had him
transferred to Butterworth Hospital in Grand Rapids, Michigan. Unbe-
knownst to the rest of Mike's family, Mary asked hospital personnel to remove his feeding tube. That led to a meeting of the hospital ethics
committee, which issued a statement favoring the dehydration; it stated
in part:

> *While Mr. Martin is not in a persistent vegetative state, members of
> the Ethics Committee felt that the persistence of his condition and the
> level of his functioning were equivalent to a persistent vegetative state
> for purposes of considering the removal of nutritional support.*[67]

In defense of the hospital committee, Mike's abilities were significantly
reduced from what they had been only a few weeks before. Perhaps that

was because he was ill or because he was in an unfamiliar place. (Experts who work with the cognitively disabled report that they may become depressed in a new environment, leading to an apparent lowering of abilities.) Just as in the Wendland case, the committee was working with incomplete information. It made no effort to contact Mike's neurologist, Dr. Zetusky, or staff members of the New Medico Neurological Center (where Mike was cared for before coming to Butterworth), who knew Mike very well and could have told the committee that prior to his transfer he had interacted meaningfully with his environment and obtained enjoyment in life.[68] Nor were Pat Major and Leeta Martin permitted to give the committee their opinions. Thus, whether through willful ignorance, negligence, or a simple lack of facts, the committee issued a recommendation about Mike Martin's life and death without knowing the complete story.

Happily for Mike, a legal review of Mary's request had also been performed that would materially affect Mike's fate. Nervous about the previous legal scrap between Mary and her in-laws, in order to avoid litigation the lawyers recommended that the hospital should dehydrate Mike only if a court order permitted it to do so. That forced Mary to seek a judge's permission to end Mike's life, giving Pat Major and Leeta Martin the opportunity to stand up for Mike's right to live.

The case would take years. The first round went to Pat and Leeta when Judge Grieg ruled that Mike could not be dehydrated because he had not prepared a written advance medical directive (see page 240) indicating that that would be his desire.

Round 2 was Mary's: The Michigan Court of Appeals reversed Judge Grieg's decision, deciding that oral statements could constitute "clear and convincing evidence" (the standard of proof required in Michigan) of Mike's stated desires regarding his care if he were ever incapacitated. More worrisome was a ruling that pushed Michigan law down the slippery slope: The undisputed fact that Mike was conscious was not necessarily a bar to his dehydration. Rather, his medical condition and capabilities would be only one factor among many considered.[69]

Mary won the next two rounds also. Judge Grieg ignored plentiful evidence that Mike was currently happy, not in pain, and wanted to live. As if Mike were now a nonentity, the only thing that mattered in the decision was how Mike felt *before* he was injured. Relying on testimony by Mary concerning a private conversation she claimed to have had in which he allegedly said he would not want to live if he were incapacitated, Judge Grieg ruled that Mary could stop Mike's food and fluids. Judge Grieg did not take into account the admitted fact that Mary would lose a substantial amount of the settlement from the railroad if she divorced Mike but not if he died, nor Mary's admitted romantic involvements after Mike was injured. Despite these apparent conflicts of interest, Judge Grieg wouldn't even appoint a neutral attorney to look out for Mike's interests. The Michigan Court of Appeals agreed with Judge Grieg, affirming the trial court's ruling.

Mike's fate was ultimately decided in the Michigan Supreme Court, which ruled on August 22, 1995, that Mary's uncorroborated testimony was not sufficient to constitute clear and convincing evidence. Mary tried to take the case to the United States Supreme Court but was turned down.

But what if there had been clear and convincing evidence of Mike's desires before his injury? Indeed, what if he had signed a medical directive that his food should be withheld? Shouldn't the strong evidence that he is now happy, is not in pain, and enjoys his life count for something? Shouldn't the benefit of the doubt be given life, rather than death? And shouldn't the fact that Mike is awake, aware, and interactive by definition preclude dehydration?

Apparently not. Although the Michigan Supreme Court's ruling saved Mike's life, it is ominous that it did not prohibit ending the lives of *all* conscious but cognitively disabled people who rely on feeding tubes, although it certainly set a stringent level of proof required before such killings can take place. Indeed, Dr. Cranford groused that the Supreme Court's decision "shows how the clear and convincing evidence standard of proof can be manipulated to deny a person's liberty interest,"[70] which, he opined, should "frighten the people of Michigan."[71] In other words, according to Dr. Cranford it is wrong to give the benefit of the doubt to life.

Cut to Stockton, California, and the Robert Wendland case, where Dr. Cranford is expected once again to testify in favor of dehydrating to death a conscious, interactive, cognitively disabled man—despite the uncontested fact that he has improved enough to maneuver an electric wheelchair down a hospital corridor.

Truth in Advertising

These "food and fluids" cases, as they are usually called, were the opening salvo in the drive to legalize active euthanasia, that is, doctors killing patients by lethal injection. "It should be honestly recognized by all participants that . . . the right to forgo food and water is the first step toward recognizing a right to medically assisted, rational suicide," wrote Kenneth F. Schaffner, M.D., Ph.D., writing in favor of allowing food and fluids to be withdrawn from the permanently unconscious.[72] Speaking at the Fifth Biennial Conference of the World Federation of the Right to Die Society, Peter Singer's colleague Helga Kuhse, who also opposes the equality-of-human-life ethic, reportedly said in a similar vein that if people come to accept the removal of all treatment and care—especially the removal of food and fluids—they will see what a painful way this is to die, and then, in the patient's best interest, they will accept the lethal injection.[73]

That isn't how the concept has been sold, of course. And not every health-care professional who believes that it is ethical to dehydrate patients supports legalizing euthanasia. But whether legalization of euthanasia is intended or not, the change in medical ethics allowing the withdrawal of food and fluids from cognitively disabled people has prepared the way, as Kuhse and Schaffner said it would, for a far wider application of legalized killing through assisted suicide and/or euthanasia.

Many readers may consider my use of the word *kill* in this context to be provocative and hyperbolic. But is it? The euthanasia advocate and philosopher Peter Singer certainly wouldn't think so. Indeed, writing about the intentional dehydration of the profoundly cognitively disabled, Singer is quite candid on the significance of food withdrawal:

> *The lives of such [unconscious] patients are of no benefit to them, and so doctors may lawfully stop feeding them to end their lives. With this decision the law has ended its unthinking commitment to the preservation of human life that is a mere biological existence. . . . In doing so they have shifted the boundary between what is and what is not murder. . . . Now, conduct intended to end life is lawful [emphasis added].* [74]

"Conduct intended to end life"—in other words, killing. Singer is saying that we should recognize intentionally withdrawing nutrition for what it is. Calling it by some other name to make ourselves feel better does not change the nature of the act. What has changed, with Singer's approval, is the legality of these acts of killing, because to Singer, the lives of profoundly cognitively disabled persons, nonpersons in his view, are better off ended.

Some of the nation's highest courts have also seen through the semantics charade that dehydrating people is merely withdrawing "medical treatment" and "allowing" the patient to die. Indeed, the dehydration cases have become a major springboard for two federal courts of appeal to rule that laws prohibiting physician-assisted suicide are unconstitutional.

On March 3, 1996, in *Compassion in Dying v. The State of Washington*, the U.S. Court of Appeals for the Ninth Circuit (specifically citing the U.S. Supreme Court decision in *Cruzan*)[75] ruled in an 8–3 decision:

> *The Court majority clearly recognized that granting the request to remove the tubes through which Cruzan received artificial nutrition and hydration would lead inexorably to her death. Accordingly, we conclude that Cruzan, by recognizing a liberty interest that includes the refusal of artificial provision of life-sustaining food and water, necessarily recognizes a liberty interest in hastening one's own death.*[76]

The court is ruling that since dehydration and starvation are forms of intentionally ending life, and since they were approved by the United States Supreme Court (although, as clarified earlier, that's not what the Supreme Court actually ruled in *Cruzan*), then, logically, another form of medicalized killing, physician-assisted suicide, must also be legal.

On April 2, 1996, the U.S. Court of Appeals for the Second Circuit unanimous ruling in *Quill v. Dennis C. Vacco* was even more blunt:

> *Indeed, there is nothing "natural" about causing death by means other than the original illness or its complications. The withdrawal of nutrition brings on death by starvation, the withdrawal of hydration brings on death by dehydration. . . . By ordering the discontinuance of these artificial life-sustaining processes or refusing to accept them in the first place, a patient hastens his death by means that are not natural in any sense: It certainly cannot be said that the death that immediately ensues is the natural result of the progression of the disease or condition from which the patient suffers.*[77]

Because people who require nutritional medical treatment to stay alive can have their lives intentionally ended by intentional dehydration, then, according to the Second Circuit court's reasoning, terminally ill patients who don't require medical treatment to stay alive must also be given an unnatural method out of life; ergo, physicians must be permitted to prescribe a lethal overdose to terminally ill patients.

The food and fluids cases have desensitized and acclimated people to medicalized killing, leading to a wider application of induced death as the answer to serious maladies: Since the cognitively disabled have a "right to die," so too should the terminally ill. Once the terminally ill are seen to have this "right" and can be killed legally, the new "right" will be expanded to the disabled, the chronically ill, and the depressed.

Thus, from relatively small beginnings that concerned the approximately ten thousand people in the country who are permanently unconscious, the dehydration cases have been a springboard for legalizing euthanasia and assisted suicide for the many.

How this all would work—the details of the political proposals to legalize euthanasia and the current status of the court cases seeking to legalize euthanasia—is the subject of later chapters. But before we enter that discussion, it is important to take a step back, broaden our horizons, and explore the consequences for other societies that have accepted the death culture.

CHAPTER 3

Everything Old Is New Again

For more than two thousand years, mercy killing has been culturally disdained and illegal in the West and most of the rest of the world. Some euthanasia advocates claim that these life-affirming policies were instituted as part of some vast conspiracy by church leaders to impose religious hegemony on society and to promote suffering as a form of sacrament. While it is true that pragmatic concerns, humanitarian values, and religious tradition intertwined to create the particular cornerstone of Western civilization that I earlier labeled the equality-of-human-life ethic, this ethic is not in and of itself a religious belief. Indeed, the ethical precepts of modern medicine that prohibit killing date back well before the dawn of Christianity to the writings of Hippocrates, a Greek physician who lived in the fifth century B.C.E., who gave his name to the famous Hippocratic Oath, whereby doctors pledge, "First, do no harm."

That is not to say that the killing of the weak and ill has never been carried out. Some ancient Greek societies, Hippocrates notwithstanding, so disdained children born with birth defects that they found a convenient way around their legal proscription against killing by abandoning these unfortunate infants on hillsides. It is also true, as euthanasia advocates are fond of pointing out, that some hunter-gatherer societies traditionally expected the old and disabled to remain by the side of the trail when they couldn't keep up. Some of these cultures also routinely killed babies born with birth defects.

Unlike the reasoning behind today's advocacy to legalize euthanasia and assisted suicide, the purpose behind these acts of killing generally involved a perception of absolute necessity: a stark choice between maintaining the life of the individual and the continued existence of the society or tribe. Infanticide also often sprang from bigotry against children who were considered abnormal, a bigotry that, as this book demonstrates, alas, we have not outgrown to this day. These death practices targeting the weak and "abnormal" generally waned or ceased altogether as life became less harsh.

In the contemporary West we judge cultures as "advanced" or "civilized" in part by the manner in which the society cares for its weakest and most vulnerable members. Cultures that disrespect their dying, elderly, and disabled and refuse to protect and value their lives, or that do not provide for them in a caring and compassionate manner, generally are seen as backward, if not downright oppressive. Traditionally we have measured our own progress toward a genuinely humane and enlightened society against these same standards.

That may be changing. An ethical tug-of-war has emerged between those who continue to hold to the equality-of-human-life ethic and advocates who wish to replace it with a different, less egalitarian approach, sometimes described (euphemistically, in my opinion) as the "quality-of-life" ethic. I prefer to call it "the death culture." This wrestling match between what Abraham Lincoln once called "the better angels of our nature" and the utilitarian values of the death culture was described in September 1970 in a prescient editorial in *California Medicine,* published by the California Medical Association, whose members were familiar with the debates then ongoing among the medical intelligentsia. The editors saw radical change in the offing, writing:

> *The traditional Western ethic has always placed great emphasis on the intrinsic worth and equal value of every human life regardless of its stage or condition. . . . This traditional ethic is . . . being eroded at its core and may eventually be abandoned. . . . [H]ard choices will have to be made . . . that will of necessity violate and ultimately destroy the traditional Western ethic with all that portends. It will become necessary and acceptable to place relative rather than absolute values on such things as human lives. . . . One may anticipate . . . death selection and death control whether by the individual or by society.*[1]

In 1970, the very ideas of death control or death selection were beyond the pale for most people. After the destruction under the Third

Reich (the mother of all death cultures) and the lessons of the Holocaust, the equality-of-human-life ethic was at its zenith. "Never again!"

Now we exist in a confused state, no longer robust believers in the traditional Western ethic, feeling simultaneously compassionate and utilitarian. Thus, even as the Special Olympics celebrates the achievements of people with cognitive difficulties, and the Americans with Disabilities Act promotes equality for those among us with physical impairments, our society countenances the death by intentional neglect of infants born with Down syndrome and spina bifida, and blithely accepts the premise that suicide by the disabled is "rational."[2] Even as hospice is applauded for providing compassionate care, pain control, comfort, and emotional support for the dying and their families, juries exonerate Jack Kevorkian for assisting in the suicides of depressed, disabled, and/or dying people who could well have been helped to avoid wanting suicide by just such humane care.

Fortunately, we don't come to this crossroads without a road map. Others in this century have walked this way, with disastrous results: the Germans and the supporters of eugenics in England and the United States.

We are not they, of course. Those earlier proponents of the death culture were different people in a different time, many driven by intense bigotry and, in Germany at least, a fierce racial ideology that fueled the madness. Today's euthanasia advocates are generally not overtly racist. Nor do they claim to be creating a master race. Indeed, they are far more likely to wear the mantle of compassion than bigotry, and identify with libertarianism rather than with notions of totalitarianism embraced by the National Socialists.

These very real differences in motivation should not make us more receptive to the policies they advocate. Wicked ideas are hardest to detect in their own time, even when they are variations on a theme that has been tried before. For although there are many substantive differences between the values that drove the earlier German death culture and the ones emerging in our day, a careful analysis of the *actions* being advocated—rather than just the words used to promote those actions—leads to the uncomfortable inference that the differences are not as profound as many would like to believe.

Germany Abandons the Equality-of-Human-Life Ethic

In 1806, the German physician Christoph Wilhelm Hufeland wrote, "It is not up to [the doctor] whether . . . life is happy or unhappy, worthwhile or not, and should he incorporate these perspectives into his trade . . . the doctor could well become the most dangerous person in the state." Hufeland recognized the tremendous power society gives to physicians. Modern doctors are entitled to cut people with a scalpel, prescribe dangerous drugs, and learn the most intimate and private aspects of their patients' lives. So long as physicians exercise these powers strictly for the well-being of each patient, so long as they view the lives of all patients as inherently of equal worth, then the power is unlikely to be abused.

But if doctors were to practice medicine in a way that imposes their *own* values upon their patients, the potential for abuse would be enormous. People whose lives the doctor valued would likely receive appropriate care. Those whom the doctor disdained—whether on the basis of race, age, sexual orientation, disability, or emotional state—might receive shoddy care or even no care at all.

One hundred thirty-three years after Hufeland wrote those words, his worst fears about his profession came true in Germany. Between the years 1939 and 1945, the activity that is called euthanasia made the transition from being a theoretical idea that had been current for more than forty years to being practiced. During those years, German physicians participated willingly in a program specifically "designed to kill their most chronic patients."[3] Euthanasia, in turn, led directly to the death camps of Auschwitz, Treblinka, and Dachau, as, in the words of the psychiatrist and Holocaust historian Robert Jay Lifton, "the medicalization of killing" became "a crucial . . . terrible step [toward] systemic genocide."[4] During these six years, doctors and nurses intentionally killed more than 200,000 helpless people: the cognitively or physically disabled, people with mental disease, infants born with birth defects, the senile elderly, even severely wounded German soldiers. German euthanasia practices were the first movement of the symphony of slaughter that took the lives of millions of Jews, Gypsies, homosexuals, Communists, labor union members, Jehovah's Witnesses, Catholics, and other "undesirables" whose deaths we memorialize in the term *Holocaust.*

The medical professionals who killed their own patients did not act under duress, coercion, menace, or out of fear for their own lives. They were not drafted into performing euthanasia; they eagerly volunteered. "Those responsible believed in the necessity of what they were doing," writes Michael Burleigh of the London School of Economics.[5] The historian and author Hugh Gregory Gallagher, who has also written extensively about the subject of the German euthanasia program, agrees, stating, "German doctors were not coerced. In fact, it was doctors who went to the government and suggested it, not the other way around." Gallagher adds, in a point clearly relevant to today's euthanasia debates, "German doctors viewed their killing of certain patients as a final medical therapy."[6] Doctors and nurses, solemnly sworn to protect the lives and welfare of the people under their care, knowingly and willingly ended their most vulnerable patients' lives. In our policy dialogues today, in which many are urging that doctors be given the power to kill or assist in the suicide of patients, it is vital that we study the German example.

Many people mistakenly believe that German crimes against humanity were all Hitler's idea, purely a product of Nazi ideology. In actuality, doctors who later participated in mass killing had, in Lifton's term, developed a " 'euthanasia' consciousness," a value system that viewed some lives as unworthy of protection.[7] This unethical approach to the practice of medicine was already well developed in Germany by the time Hitler came to power in 1933. Indeed, euthanasia had been aggressively promoted as a proper and ethical public policy by the German medical, legal, and academic intelligentsia since the late nineteenth century, when Hitler was a child.

The first notable advocate of euthanasia was Adolf Jost, who publicized his ideas in *The Right to Death,* published in 1895. Jost considered the state to be a "social organism," a view later adopted by many Germans, Hitler included, and he argued that the life and death of each individual must ultimately belong to the collective. According to Lifton, Jost's thesis was "The state must own death—must kill—in order to keep the social organism alive and healthy."[8]

In 1913, euthanasia was popularized and legitimized in Germany through the publication of an open letter ("Euthanasie") written by Roland Gerkan, a man dying of lung disease. Reading Gerkan's text, one would think he was a contemporary euthanasia advocate: "Why, instead of permitting us to die gently, today, do you demand that we embark upon the long martyr's road, whose final goal is certainly the same death which you deny us today?"[9] Gerkan even penned a model law legalizing euthanasia for anyone with an incurable illness. He suggested that "protective guidelines" be enacted to protect against abuse, including the requirement that the person who wanted to be killed petition judicial authorities for permission, that the case be reviewed by two qualified physicians to determine the likely outcome of the disease, and that legal protection against liability be assured for "whosoever painlessly kills the patient as a result of the latter's express and unambiguous request."[10] The law would apply not just to the dying but also to the elderly and the "crippled."[11] Everything old is indeed new again.

Gerkan's thesis provoked much debate among German physicians, academics, lawyers, ethicists, and church leaders. However, the issue, then mainly seen as an intellectual exercise, was soon overshadowed by a more pressing matter for the German people: World War I.

The nation suffered terribly during the war, not only from the killing of its soldiers in battle but from the privations caused by shortages of food and other resources at home. During the war, lack of resources led to a harsh utilitarianism. Some Germans were considered expendable. Mental patients, for example, were deemed not worth feeding, which led to their intentional mass starvation.[12] It is no overstatement to say that the war and its consequences scarred the German soul.

At the end of the war, the country was reeling. Bitter in defeat, economically ruined, politically torn by factional fighting that would ultimately lead to the Nazi takeover, adjusting to the end of empire, the country was desperately searching for national meaning and a way to bind its wounds. Such was the social mood when, in 1920, two venerable German professors published a book on the subject of euthanasia: *Permitting the Destruction of Life Not Worthy of Life*.[13] The book consisted of two separate essays, one by each coauthor: Karl Binding, an intellectual star and one of Germany's premier legal experts, and the physician Alfred Hoche, then one of Germany's most prominent humanitarians.

The importance of the publication of *Permitting the Destruction of Life Not Worthy of Life*, a full frontal attack on the equality-of-human-life ethic and described by Lifton as "the crucial work," is difficult to overstate.[14] The respectability of its authors, their embrace of euthanasia as a proper and ethical medical procedure, their endorsement of legalizing the killing of weak and vulnerable Germans, deeply influenced the value system of the general public and the ethics of the medical and legal communities. One enthusiastic reader of *Permitting the Destruction of Life Not Worthy of Life* was a young army veteran and rabble-rouser named Adolf Hitler, who viewed the book as in step with his own value system. Hitler was so taken with Hoche's theories that he later allowed his name to be used in connection with advertising the doctor's books.[15] In myriad ways, Hoche and Binding's book became a cornerstone of the intellectual foundation upon which the coming euthanasia practices would be built.

Binding's and Hoche's theories mirror many of the concepts propounded by today's euthanasia advocates. They believed that there were three groups of people whose lives were so degraded and undignified that they constituted "life not worthy of life," and consequently these "useless eaters," as they later came to be known, could be killed ethically. Binding and Hoche deemed killable the terminally ill or mortally wounded, "incurable idiots," and the comatose.

1. TERMINALLY ILL OR MORTALLY WOUNDED INDIVIDUALS were those who "have been irretrievably lost as a result of illness or injury, who fully understand their situation, possess and have somehow expressed an urgent wish for release."[16] This view is virtually identical to euthanasia policies being urged upon us today.

2. "INCURABLE IDIOTS," WHOSE LIVES THE AUTHORS SAW AS "POINTLESS" AND "VALUELESS," were considered by them an economic and emotional "burden on society and their families." Hoche put it this way: "I have discovered that the average yearly (per head) cost for maintaining idiots has till now been thirteen hundred marks. . . . If we assume an average life expectancy of fifty years for individual cases, it is easy to estimate what *incredible capital* is withdrawn from the nation's wealth for food, clothing, and heating—for an unproductive purpose" (emphasis in original).[17] Today's advocates do not denigrate the mentally retarded as "idiots," nor do they go as far as Hoche and Binding in calling for their killing. However, the economic cost of caring for those labeled as having a low quality of life is frequently noted by euthanasia advocates.

3. THE "UNCONSCIOUS, if they ever again were roused from their comatose state, would waken to nameless suffering" and should be spared this.[18] The United States and other Western nations already ascribe to this criterion.

As euthanasia proponents always do, Binding and Hoche called for protective guidelines to govern the practice, including the need to make an application to an oversight board, the investigation by at least two physicians, a finding that the patients are "beyond help," with a report of the final act of killing to be given to the board.[19] Those who participated as killers, whether medical personnel, family members, or others, would, as in today's legislative proposals, be free from legal liability or culpability for their acts. These ideas later came to haunt Hoche; he would turn against the German euthanasia program—even though much of its rationale derived from his own writings—after one of his relatives became a victim.[20]

At the time Hoche and Binding were urging euthanasia upon Germany, another pernicious social revolution was catching on in Germany as well as in the United States and Britain: the eugenics movement. Eugenecists claimed the right to determine which human traits were better than other human traits, to determine a hierarchy of "hereditary worth." They intended to promote the desirable traits through selective "breeding" using the new science of genetics. Humans with traits considered worth keeping were encouraged to procreate. Those with undesirable characteristics were discouraged and even forcefully prevented from having children. Eugenics was a profound violation of the equality-of-human-life ethic and resulted in terrible oppression wherever it found official acceptance.

In Germany, eugenics theory created a growing obsession with purifying and strengthening the "Nordic race." Many Germans fervently believed that unless "inferior" Germans were kept from breeding, the *Volk* would weaken and eventually cease to exist. Moreover, Jost's idea that the state, rather than the individual, was the paramount decision maker also was widely accepted, popularizing the notion of forced sterilizations of those who, we might say, were deemed "useless breeders." Hitler was quite clear in *Mein Kampf* that he supported eugenics, seeing it as a method to "fight for one's own health." The alternative, according to Hitler, would be a national disaster, an end to what he called "the right to live in the world of struggle."[21]

When the Nazis took power in 1933, they quickly enacted laws authorizing involuntary sterilization. (Actually, they were years behind the United States, where some states had had eugenics laws in force since the 1920s.) To be kept from "breeding" were the mentally retarded, the blind and deaf, and "cripples" such as those with a clubfoot or even a cleft palate. Relatives of such people were even urged to voluntarily sterilize themselves to prevent the "defect" from being passed to the next generation. In the end, it is estimated that up to 350,000 Germans were sterilized in the years 1933–1945.[22]

In the years following the appearance of *Permitting the Destruction of Life Not Worthy of Life,* there was much debate about the so-called right to die that had been so forcefully propounded by Binding and Hoche. It soon became clear that the populace was in general agreement with the authors. For example, a 1925 survey among parents of children with mental disabilities disclosed that 74 percent of them would agree to the painless killing of their own children, revealing the extent to which euthanasia advocacy had already adversely impacted the population's moral values.[23] One can only imagine the attitude of nonparents.

Well aware that the German public supported euthanasia, the new Nazi government proposed to legalize the practice in 1933. A front-page *New York Times* article described the proposal as making it possible for physicians to end the tortures of incurable patients. Protective guidelines were to be included in the law, including the necessity that the patient "expressly and earnestly" request to die, or if unable to do so that relatives make the request, "acting from motives that do not contravene morals."[24]

This legislation never became law because of an outcry from the churches. But that did not stop the Nazi government from campaigning to increase public support for the killing of "useless eaters." Many propaganda films were produced depicting mentally retarded people as lower than beasts, a tactic also used against Jews. But it wasn't only the "idiots" who were at the receiving end of pro-euthanasia advocacy in Germany throughout the Nazi period. Various media also pushed the idea that physically disabled people had lives not worth living, and their deaths would be best for themselves, their families, and the state. One notable and very popular motion picture, *I Accuse,* sympathetically depicted a physician husband euthanizing his wife, who desperately wants to die because she has multiple sclerosis. The doctor and wife characters are lauded for their selflessness, wisdom, and courage in choosing her death. To assure that abuses will not occur with voluntary euthanasia, one character in the movie assures, "The most important precondition is always that the patient wants it."[25] (The values of *I Accuse* are virtually identical to those embraced by today's euthanasia movement. Witness the many suicides of disabled people, most with MS, facilitated by Jack Kevorkian. The reason many people state for countenancing these killings? It was what the patient wanted.)

All was now ready for the horror to follow, except for one thing. Just as Frankenstein's monster needed a bolt of lightning to come alive, for euthanasia to become a reality in Germany one last precondition was required: the mutation of traditional medical ethics.

For millennia, physicians have owed their sole allegiance to their patients. That changed dramatically in Germany. Many doctors and nurses came to accept the idea that they owed a professional duty to the state as well as to their patients—in their delivery of medical services. As a consequence, recalling the words spoken in 1806 by Dr. Christoph Wilhelm Hufeland, some doctors and nurses soon became among the most dangerous people in the state.

As the thirties came to a close, Germany had reached a dangerous point: Many physicians and most Germans believed that there was such a thing as a human life not worthy of life and that it was proper to terminate the lives of "useless eaters." Forced sterilizations were common and popularly accepted. Doctors believed they owed a professional duty to the state in their practice of medicine. All was now prepared for the euthanasia program to begin.

Euthanasia Comes to Germany

It is important to acknowledge that the consequences of the destruction of the equality-of-human-life ethic for Germany are not inevitably the same consequences that *will* ensue elsewhere. The United States is not a dictatorship as was Nazi Germany, and the late 1990s are not the early 1940s. Nevertheless, what happened in Germany demonstrates the dangers inherent in discarding the equality-of-human-life ethic.

For Hitler, the German euthanasia program, when it finally commenced, was the culmination of his long-held desire to legitimize medicalized killing in Germany. He had pulled back from the initial proposal to legalize euthanasia for fear of opposition from the churches at a time when he was consolidating his political power. According to Lifton, Hitler decided that "the best time to eliminate the incurably ill" would be to wait for the outbreak of war, a time when the general sense of the value of human life could be expected to be lessened.[26] But, as we have seen, many Germans were ahead of their Führer, already accepting the idea of life unworthy of life. By 1938, more than a year before the outbreak of actual hostilities, an outpouring of requests from the relatives of severely disabled infants and young children for permission to end the lives of their little useless eaters was flowing to the German government. Requests for euthanasia of the dying and disabled also were sent, some written by patients themselves and others from people who wanted euthanasia for relatives.

These requests were channeled directly to Hitler and his staff at the German Chancellery, who were looking for the right case with which to begin active euthanasia (killing by means of medical intervention) in Germany. That case came to their attention in late 1938. A baby had been born with birth defects: Baby Knauer was blind and had a leg and part of an arm missing. The parents were distraught and, accepting the general value system of their time, were deeply ashamed to have brought a useless eater into the world. They wrote requesting permission to have their child "put to sleep."

Hitler was quite interested in the case and sent one of his personal physicians, Karl Rudolph Brandt, to investigate. Brandt's instructions from the Führer were to verify the facts of the baby's condition and, if true, to assure the child's doctors and her parents that if she was killed, no one would face punishment or liability. Brandt was then to witness the euthanasia and report back to Hitler. The doctors in the case who met with Brandt agreed that there was "no justification for keeping the child alive," and Baby Knauer soon became one of the first victims of the Holocaust.[27]

By this time, Hitler, Brandt, and other Nazi social engineers had developed a detailed plan for the euthanasia program, and Hitler decided the moment had come for its implementation. Unlike the sterilization laws, a statute was not enacted legalizing euthanasia—it was never officially legalized in Germany. Rather, Hitler signed a decree permitting medicalized killing and named Brandt and a Nazi party member, Philip Bouhler, to head the program. Sympathetic physicians and nurses from around the country—many not even Nazi party members—cooperated in the horror that was to follow.

Disabled children were the first to suffer medicalized killing. Formal "protective guidelines" were created to prevent abuse, along the lines originally proposed by Binding and Hoche, including the creation of a panel of "expert referees," which judged who was eligible for killing and who was not. (The panel reviewed a questionnaire filled out by the child's doctor, not the child's actual medical records.) At first it took a unanimous verdict of all panel referees to allow a patient to be killed. Ironically, among the selected referees was Ernst Wentzler, the inventor of an incubator for prematurely born children, who unfortunately was also a devotee of Binding and Hoche. Wentzler was so committed to euthanasia that even in 1963 he remained unrepentant, recalling his work in sorting through the euthanasia requests as having been "a small contribution to human progress."[28]

In early 1939, children born with birth defects or with congenital diseases began to be killed under the euthanasia program. These unfortunate children were admitted to medical clinics by their doctors, where they would be euthanized. Most of these children were voluntarily turned over to medical authorities by their own parents; some (but certainly not all) knew, or at least suspected, that their disabled children were being sent to their deaths. New reporting rules made it mandatory for midwives and doctors to notify authorities when a baby was born with birth defects. Once the referees determined that the children were eligible for euthanasia, they were killed either by intentional starvation or an overdose of a drug, most typically a sedative called Luminal. The euphemism of choice for this butchery was "treatment."

It wasn't long before the list of those eligible to be killed expanded. The next group to be systematically euthanized, as authorized in an October 1939 decree from Hitler that was written on his private stationery, were severely mentally ill and retarded adults, a category that was expanded to include the criminally insane and people with conditions such as epilepsy, polio, schizophrenia, senile diseases, paralysis, and Huntington's disease. This was known as the T-4 program.* As with the children's euthanasia order, the matter was officially a secret.

Death for adult victims generally occurred at designated medical clinics and hospitals, which had been turned into killing centers. This was all a dress rehearsal for what was to come in the death camps. Like the later genocide, the T-4 program became highly bureaucratized, and government workers "coldly and calculatingly organized the murder of thousands of people" and kept meticulous records of what they were doing.[29] For example, secretaries "shared their offices with jars of foul-smelling gold-filled teeth, listening to dictation which enumerated 'bridge with three teeth,' 'a single tooth,' and so on."[30] The first Jews to be killed were exterminated as part of the T-4 program. Originally, Jews, as official undesirables, had not been eligible for euthanasia. But eventually they were included—only for them there were no protective guidelines, since, by definition, they were considered to embody "dangerous genes" in an individual medical sense and "racial poison" in a collective ethnic sense.[31] The killing of adults generally was accomplished with carbon monoxide, and eventually cyanide gas, with each center having its own crematorium. Within the framework of the T-4 program, experiments were performed to determine the most efficient way to kill masses of people, making more efficient the later slaughter at Auschwitz, Treblinka, Dachau, Buchenwald, and other genocide centers.

Modern euthanasia proponents, understandably wanting to distance their cause from these horrors, assert that German euthanasia is irrelevant to today's proposals because the German program was conducted in secret.[32] Officially, that was true, but not in actual practice. With so many people involved, it wasn't long before the German people began to com-

---

* T-4 was a code name based on the address of the German Chancellery, Tiergarten 4.

prehend what was happening. As Hitler's henchman Heinrich Himmler put it in 1941, "This is a secret that is no longer a secret."[33] "It's hard to keep a secret when whole wards are being emptied out," notes Hugh Gallagher, an expert on German euthanasia. "Sometimes buses of those to be killed would be chased after by children who would laugh, yell and taunt the patients about their pending appointments with crematoria ovens."[34]

To their credit, many Germans were appalled by what was happening. Some even found the courage to resist. According to Gallagher, "There were actually public demonstrations against the euthanasia program, which were anathema to the Nazis. Even some party members were appalled but they convinced themselves that the 'Führer must not know [about the program].' "[35] One of the most powerful voices in opposition to euthanasia was the Catholic archbishop Clemens August Graf von Galen, who courageously preached against the euthanasia program from the pulpit on August 3, 1941, stating in words still relevant today:

> If you establish and apply the principle that you can "kill" unproductive human beings, then woe betide us all when we become old and frail! If one is allowed to kill unproductive people, then woe betide the invalids who have used up, sacrificed and lost their health and strength in the productive process. . . . Poor people, sick people, unproductive people, so what? Have they somehow forfeited the right to live? Do you, do I have the right to live only as long as we are productive? . . . Nobody would be safe anymore. Who could trust his physician? It is inconceivable what depraved conduct, what suspicion would enter family life if this terrible doctrine is tolerated, adopted, carried out.[36]

To say the least, Hitler was not amused by the archbishop's brazen outspokenness. Yet he did nothing, not wishing to arouse domestic discontent by arresting the popular clergyman, especially when there were more pressing issues to worry about, such as the Eastern Front. Still, the Führer neither forgave nor forgot, vowing revenge at the end of the war, promising to "balance the accounts" with Archbishop Graf von Galen, so that "no 't' remains uncrossed, no 'i' left undotted."[37]

Because euthanasia was no longer secret and in response to the opposition the policy generated in some quarters, in August 1941 Hitler ordered Brandt to suspend the program. That was not the end of it, however. Participating doctors did not need an order from Hitler to kill their "patients." They were true believers, convinced they were performing a valuable medical service for their "patients" and their country. What little control had been exercised previously over the killing disappeared, the guidelines were cast aside, and from then until a few weeks *after* the end of the war, some doctors went on a killing rampage known today as "wild euthanasia," as they ended the lives of just about any patient they pleased, often without medical examination, usually by starvation or lethal injection.

It is important to reiterate that throughout the years in which euthanasia was performed in Germany, whether part of the officially sanctioned government program or otherwise, the government did not force one doctor to kill a patient nor were any doctors ever punished for refusing to euthanize a patient. It was the participating doctors themselves who had become the zealots.

Then, it was finally over. Brandt and a few other physicians were hanged by the Allies for crimes against humanity. But most doctors and nurses who had been involved in mass killing went unpunished, many continuing in their fields of practice. One physician who appears to have participated in the euthanasia Holocaust, Dr. Hans Joachim Sewerling, was even elected president of the World Medical Association in the 1980s. When the American Medical Association discovered his background and protested, Sewerling resigned, blaming a "Jewish conspiracy" for his troubles. However, he remains in good standing with the German Medical Association, which made him an honorary member of its board of trustees.[38]

Early Euthanasia Activism in the United States

The current efforts to legalize euthanasia are not the first in the United States, although they are the most sustained. During the 1920s and 1930s this country was not immune to the social forces and erosion of values that influenced Germany. Indeed, on the brink of World War II and even for a short time into the war, euthanasia was gaining respectability and acceptance among the people of the United States. Euthanasia advocacy in the pre–World War II United States had its roots in the infamous eugenics movement. As in Germany, this substantial deviation from the equality-of-human-life ethic led to widespread oppression and the profound injustice of involuntary sterilization, although not mass killing.

As difficult as it may be to believe, forced sterilization based on eugenic theories was specifically approved by the United States Supreme Court in 1927, with the case of *Buck v. Bell*.[39] Carrie Buck, the eighteen-year-old daughter of a prostitute, was pregnant out of wedlock, apparently after being raped by a relative of her foster father. Rather than rushing to her aid, the ashamed foster family had Carrie declared mentally and morally deficient and had her institutionalized in an asylum.

Asylum doctors, true believers in eugenics, decided to sterilize Carrie as a way to carry forward their eugenic theories. Carrie Buck sued, and the litigation eventually reached the United States Supreme Court. In a ruling that shows how judges' own prejudices can sometimes overcome facts and logic, Chief Justice Oliver Wendell Holmes issued the majority opinion permitting Carrie's sterilization, declaring, "Three generations of imbeciles is enough!" Holmes wrote:

> We have seen more than once that the public welfare may call upon the best citizens for their lives. It would be strange if it could not call upon those who already sap the strength of the State for these lesser sacrifices [sterilization], often not felt by those concerned, in order to prevent our being swamped by their incompetence. It is better for all the world . . . [if] society can prevent those who are manifestly unfit from continuing their kind.[40]

And so the real reason Carrie Buck was sterilized, along with tens of thousands of other Americans, was not because she was somehow genetically "defective" but because she was poor, powerless, and seen as an undesirable. Later in her life, she was released from the asylum, married twice, sang in a church choir, and took care of elderly people until her death in 1983.[41] Involuntary sterilization laws remained on the books in a few states into the 1960s.

Concurrent with the acceptance and practice of eugenics in the United States was a growing belief in euthanasia theory, and by the 1930s some euthanasia advocacy organizations had been formed in this country; one of these was the Euthanasia Society of America, now known as Choice in Dying. Like their German counterparts, these organizations urged the legalization of mercy killing, which they opined should be voluntary but which they hoped could be undertaken also on a nonvoluntary basis for those incapable of consent. For example, the president of the Euthanasia Society, a Cornell professor of neurology, Dr. Foster Kennedy, opined in a speech, "If the law sought to restrict euthanasia to those who could speak out for it, and thus overlooked those creatures who cannot speak, then I say as Dickens did, 'The law is an ass.' "[42] In a comment that echoes the views of some contemporary euthanasia advocates, especially Peter Singer, Kennedy later said that "defective children" up to the age of five should be permitted to be killed upon the request of parents or guardians, "if after careful board examination" it was determined that the child had no "future or hope."[43]

The American public responded favorably to arguments in favor of voluntary euthanasia, which then as now were couched in terms of the "right to die." Indeed, a 1939 public opinion poll of New York State doctors surveyed by the Euthanasia Society, published in *The New York Times,* found that 80 percent of respondents favored voluntary euthanasia for adults.[44]

Whatever chance euthanasia had to become accepted public policy in the United States at that time was obliterated with the country's shock and horror over the Holocaust. After the war, euthanasia theory fell into near total disrepute and the movement grew quiescent. It did not, however, die, as recent events clearly demonstrate. Indeed, many of today's euthanasia advocacy groups trace their roots back to euthanasia organizations formed in the 1930s.

Heeding the Warnings of History

It is tempting to demonize people and public-policy proposals with which we disagree by associating them with the Nazi period. Such comparisons are often facile exercises that discount and cheapen the horror of those awful days and the sacrifices of those who gave so much to bring them to an end. In that regard, the bioethicist Arthur Caplan has written, "Those who see analogies [to the Nazi period] must be specific about what they believe is similar between now and then. Blanket invocations such as . . . 'euthanasia, if legalized, will lead to Nazi Germany,' are to be avoided unless they can truly be supported in the scope of the claim being made."[45]

Caplan is right. Just because the Nazis said or believed something, or adopted certain public policies, doesn't mean, ipso facto, that the belief or policy is inherently evil or immoral. For example, Hitler also created the German autobahns. That does not mean that President Dwight Eisenhower was wrong when he facilitated the creation of the interstate highway system.

What relevance do the euthanasia horrors of Nazi Germany bear to euthanasia proposals in our own time? Some experts on that era see little relevance. Lifton, for one, has written, "One can speak of the Nazi state as a 'biocracy.' The model here is a theocracy, a system of rule by priests of a sacred order under the claim of divine prerogative."[46] There is no doubt that today's euthanasia advocates are not driven by the ideological madness that sees biology as destiny and the cleansing of the gene pool as a divine imperative.

Michael Burleigh, the author of *Death and Deliverance*, a study of the German euthanasia policies, specifically states that he has "no axes to grind regarding contemporary discussions about euthanasia," admitting to being "sympathetic to its voluntaristic implementation."[47] Still, Burleigh also acknowledges feeling "uneasy" about the "right to die [and] Dr. Death–style fanatics," as well as those he calls their extremist "counterparts" on the fringe of the anti-abortion movement.[48]

On the other hand, Hugh Gallagher sees a definite connection between the ideas that drive contemporary euthanasia advocacy and those of Germany's past, especially in current attitudes about choosing death for those who have a low "quality of life" and the emerging utilitarianism of the health-care cost-containment issue (discussed in Chapter 6), attitudes Gallagher sees as disturbingly reminiscent of some of those expressed by Binding and Hoche.

It is intriguing how closely many of the concepts advocated in *Permitting the Destruction of Life Not Worthy of Life* resemble in word and rationale many of the pro-euthanasia sentiments expressed in our current debate. Examples of this can be found by comparing Binding and Hoche's text with the text of the 1996 majority opinion of the U.S. Court of Appeals for the Ninth Circuit when it ruled, in *Compassion in Dying v. The State of Washington,* that Washington State's law banning assisted suicide is unconstitutional:

- Binding asserts that the "freedom to end [one's] own life . . . is the primary human right."[49]
  Judge Stephen Reinhardt, writing on behalf of seven other jurists, opined, "There is a Constitutionally protected liberty interest in determining the time and manner of one's own death."[50]

- *Binding:* "We are dealing with a legally permissible act of healing, which is most beneficial for patients in severe pain, and with the elimination of suffering. . . . This is not a matter of killing them."[51]
  Judge Reinhardt: "We have serious doubts that the terms 'suicide' and 'assisted suicide' are appropriate legal descriptions of the specific conduct at issue here."[52]

- *Binding:* "The permission of the suffering patient is not legally required."[53]
  Judge Reinhardt: "We should make it clear that a decision [to end a patient's life] of a duly appointed surrogate decision maker is for all legal purposes the decision of the patient himself."[54]

- *Binding:* "It is also completely unrestricted legally for a third party to help it along and encourage a decision to do it."[55]
  Judge Reinhardt: "We recognize that in some instances, the patient may be unable to self-administer the drugs and that administration by a physician, or a person acting under his direction or control, may be the only way the patient may receive them."[56]

- *Binding:* "The motto or rallying cry for this movement has been the expression 'the right to die.' "[57]
  Judge Reinhardt: "The terms 'right to die' . . . and 'hastening one's death' more accurately describe the liberty interest at issue here."[58]

- *Hoche:* "I consider it less important to work out all of the details than to admit that implementing this program obviously presupposes that all conceivable safeguards along these lines must be provided."[59]
  Judge Reinhardt: "While there is always room for error in any human endeavor, we believe that sufficient protections can and will be developed by the various states."[60]

- *Hoche:* "The idea of gaining relief from our national burden by permitting the destruction of life . . . will (from the start and for a very long time) encounter lively, strident, and passionately stated opposition."[61]
  Judge Reinhardt: "Those who believe strongly that death must come without physician assistance . . . are not free . . . to force their views, their religious convictions, or their philosophies on all other members of a democratic society."[62]

Many in the disability rights community are growing quite alarmed at the similarities between current euthanasia thought and the intellectual foundations of the German experience. Hugh Gallagher, who was himself disabled by polio as a child and who consequently would have been targeted for "treatment" by German physician-killers, worries about the analogy between "life not worthy of life" and "low quality of life," attitudes that he believes devalue the lives of disabled people in our day. Carol Gill, president of the Chicago Institute of Disability Research, also disabled by polio, agrees, noting that "disability has supplanted death in people's minds as the worst thing that can happen."[63]

These fears and prejudices about and against the disabled are shared by many physicians and sometimes affect their approaches to treatment. Gill notes that when "doctors don't believe the lives of disabled patients are tenable," they feel that ending the life of the patient by nontreatment (or, presumably, euthanasia) "is doing the patient and the family a favor."[64] In such medical attitudes there surely are disturbing echoes from Germany's past.

There can be little doubt, then, that there is a general, if not precise, analogy between the *attitudes* expressed during the pre-Nazi and Nazi periods in Germany and some of our own. That is not to say that we can thus anticipate the establishment in the United States of death camps for mass murder. However, the fact that death camps are extremely unlikely here—nay, virtually impossible—should not be the end of the analysis. There are, after all, other ways of falling off an ethical cliff.

Behavior is generally preceded by attitude. We tend to act out what we believe. That is why comprehending how the German euthanasia program could proceed—the widespread acceptance of apportioning relative worth to different categories of human lives, the lessening of the doctor's responsibility to the individual patient, etc.—is so important. These phenomena send messages that should resound through the decades: Making a virtue out of killing will have unpredictable consequences; deforming the traditional physician-patient relationship will be at the patient's peril; degrading the inherent perceived value of some humans leads directly to their oppression. The fact that we are flirting with some of the same ideas and value systems that led to horror in Germany is definite cause for concern.

Take the equality-of-human-life ethic. Here startling similarities between those awful times in Germany and contemporary attitudes can be found. To say, as modern euthanasia advocates do, that the lives of some people should be protected by the law while the lives of others should not be presumes that some human lives are inherently more valuable than others. This creates a subjective approach to the right to live, rather than the objective view inherent in the equality-of-human-life ethic.

Absent a strong adherence to the objective standard, decisions about life and death and access to appropriate medical care become power-based. That is what happened in Germany during the Holocaust. Another example of a subjective approach to the right to live, albeit on a much smaller scale, is Oregon's health-care rationing for Medicaid recipients. Under the Oregon rationing plan, a list of more than seven hundred treatments was created, and each treatment was given its own number. Every year, a cutoff number is determined, reflecting the amount of money available to fund Medicaid operations. Payment will be made for all appropriate treatments below the cutoff number. However, any treatment assigned a higher number will not be covered.

As first proposed, the Oregon plan placed healing treatment for end-stage AIDS patients very low on the list of treatment priorities, all but ensuring that Medicaid AIDS patients who wanted curative treatment at that stage in their disease would not receive it. AIDS activists were appropriately outraged, seeing this as a devaluation of the lives of people with AIDS. They were determined not to let Oregon abandon members of their community, no matter what the patients' prognosis. Through effective political advocacy, the activists successfully amended the plan so that AIDS patients who want healing treatment can obtain it, regardless of the stage of their disease.

If it is true that the politically powerful are better off in a quality-of-life-based system, the converse is true for people who are less organized and less powerful. In Oregon, although late-stage AIDS patients on Medicaid need not fear being cut off from treatment, categories of patients with little or no organized power—very low birth-weight babies and late-stage cancer patients, to name two—are on the nonpayment side of the cutoff.

Are the lives of late-stage AIDS patients any more or less precious than the lives of low-birth-weight infants or late-stage cancer patients? If the equality-of-human-life ethic is followed, the answer is no. But in Oregon, with its subjective Medicaid treatment standards and its policies of covered and uncovered treatment, the answer is yes. And woe betide the patient whose care is below the coverage cutoff.

We must not come to perceive killing as a virtue, as did the Germans of generations past. We have already decided that a whole class of patients, those assessed as P.V.S., can be killed by dehydration without consequence, and this has led directly to concerted efforts to expand the designation of those eligible for this "beneficence" to the conscious but cognitively disabled. Meanwhile, the growing public acceptance of allowing terminally ill people to be killed by doctors has already led to widespread calls for the same "right" to be accorded the nonterminal "hopelessly ill," before euthanasia is even legalized. That these policies mimic almost exactly many of the ideas and attitudes expressed by Binding and Hoche and the German medical biocracy that they helped inspire should start alarm bells ringing in our heads.

To be sure, differences between then and now should not be overlooked: German euthanasia attitudes were hate-filled, based to a great degree on bigotry, concepts of racial hygiene, and collectivist notions of the state as a living organism. Contemporary advocates, on the other hand, use much more passive language, intended to reflect sober deliberation and the balancing of competing interests, with attitudes most often based on concepts of personal autonomy. Yet when one cuts through the jargon, the *acts* that are being advocated are the same as those advocated by Binding and Hoche more than seventy-five years ago. That they are presented in warm tones of compassion or the bland prose of scholarly dispassion does not make them any less dangerous.

Those who sorted through the horror of the Holocaust in the years following the war earnestly wanted to learn how it could have happened and to ensure it never happened again. One man deeply involved in researching these issues with the Nuremberg Tribunal was Dr. Leo Alexander, who served with the U.S. Office of Chief Counsel for War Crimes. Dr. Alexander wrote a penetrating and important analysis about the foundation of the Holocaust in the July 14, 1949, issue of the *New England Journal of Medicine*, whose relevance is unblunted today:

> *Whatever proportions these crimes finally assumed, it became evident to all who investigated them that they had started from small beginnings. The beginnings at first were merely a subtle shift in emphasis in the basic attitudes of the physicians. It started with the acceptance of the attitude, basic to the euthanasia movement, that there is such a thing as a life not worthy to be lived. This attitude in its early stages concerned itself merely with the severely and chronically sick. Gradually the sphere of those to be included in this category was enlarged to encompass the socially unproductive, the ideologically unwanted, the racially unwanted and finally all non-Germans.*[65]

Looking at the state of the 1949 culture of American medicine, Dr. Alexander then warned:

> *In an increasingly utilitarian society these patients [with chronic diseases] are being looked down upon with increasing definiteness as unwanted ballast. A certain amount of rather open contempt for the*

people who cannot be rehabilitated with present knowledge has de-veloped. This is probably due to a good deal of unconscious hostility, because these people for whom there seem to be no effective remedies, have become a threat to newly acquired delusions of omnipo-tence. . . . At this point, Americans should remember that the enor-mity of the euthanasia movement is present in their own midst.[66]

CHAPTER 4

Dutch Treat

During World War II, the Germans occupied the Netherlands for nearly five years. To say the least, it was not a happy era for the Dutch. Yet it was also one of the most heroic times in that nation's notable history. The Dutch resisted the Nazis at every turn, some citizens risking their own lives to protect Jews and otherwise refusing to bend to the will of their cruel occupiers.

Dutch medical professionals were major participants in the resistance. The German commander of the occupation, Arthur Seyss-Inquart, now known derisively as "the Butcher of Holland," wanted to remake Dutch medical ethics in the German image. Toward that end he issued several orders, one of which required Dutch physicians to perform their professional services as "a public task," one that he defined as assisting as "helper . . . in the maintenance, improvement and re-establishment of [the patient's] vitality, physical efficiency and health."[1]

At first glance the order seems rather innocuous. But Dutch physicians knew better. They widely believed that the edict was a small first step designed to take them in an unethical direction, that of German medicine as then practiced. Accordingly, Dutch doctors unanimously rejected the order. Some went so far as to take down their shingles rather than violate their sacred duties to heal and protect their patients and to maintain a healthy separation between private obligation to each patient and public duty to the state.

Seyss-Inquart tried to coerce the doctors into compliance by stripping them of their licenses to practice. The doctors paid no heed; they stopped signing birth and death certificates but never stopped treating their patients. Seyss-Inquart then angrily upped the ante. One hundred doctors were arrested at random and shipped to concentration camps in the East, whence few returned. Dutch doctors still did not budge. They were willing to die before they would betray any of their patients.

Eventually it was the Germans, not the Dutch, who blinked. In one of history's great stories of successful peaceful civil disobedience, the Dutch doctors won. The Germans, unwilling to take more drastic action against the doctors of a hostile, occupied nation, eventually gave up trying to subvert Dutch medical ethics, and euthanasia never entered Dutch medical practice during World War II.

Of this episode Dr. Leo Alexander wrote:

> *Thus, it came about that not a single euthanasia or nontherapeutic sterilization was recommended or participated in by any Dutch physician. They had the foresight to resist before the first step was taken, and they acted unanimously and won out in the end. It is obvious that if the medical profession of a small nation under the conqueror's heel could resist so effectively the German medical profession could likewise have resisted had they not taken the fatal first step. It is the first seemingly innocent step away from principle that frequently decides a career of crime. Corrosion begins in microscopic proportions.*[2]

The Butcher of Holland was hanged after Nuremberg, in part because of his treatment of the Dutch medical community. Yet, in a painful irony, some of the very policies that Seyss-Inquart could not force upon heroic Dutch doctors during World War II have been willingly embraced by their modern counterparts—and not in microscopic proportions. Today, a majority of Dutch doctors openly accept euthanasia and assisted suicide as appropriate medical procedures.

Dr. I. van der Sluis, a Dutch opponent of his nation's euthanasia policies, told me exactly when and how such a radical change in values and ethics occurred in his country. "There was never propaganda in favor of euthanasia in my country before 1960," van der Sluis recalled. "Then came the cultural revolution of the late 1960s and early 1970s, which hit the Netherlands very hard. Traditional ethics collapsed in almost every area, including in the medical community. It got to the point that if you didn't accept the 'new ideas' you were a suspect person."[3]

A visit to Amsterdam reveals the truth of van der Sluis's observations about the depth of change that took place in the Netherlands. On the one hand, the city is the epitome of beautiful European charm, crisscrossed by canals, filled with magnificent architecture, giving all the appearance of Old World dignity and propriety. Amsterdam, like other Dutch cities, is a model of energy conservation. People walk everywhere and almost all are open and friendly. There are well-maintained bicycle paths. Indeed, it sometimes seems that more people in the streets are on bicycles than in cars. The trolley system is efficient and affordable.

On the other hand, for better or worse, a walk through the city streets of Amsterdam makes clear the new course that the Dutch have embarked upon, one radically different from that of their staid forebears. Amsterdam, once a community of proper merchants, is a city where decadence has become banal. In postcard racks in front of tourist-oriented stores are cards vividly depicting the Pope defecating, along with other equally taste-less offerings. In the main downtown shopping district, where families stroll in the evenings, restaurants are situated next to open-air slot-machine casinos, which are next to clothing stores, whose neighbors are pornography emporiums that have storefront window displays of sexual toys and explicit, full-color, gynecologically oriented photographs. Then there's the famous, or infamous, red-light district, where prostitutes sit in windows to be ogled and patronized by men like so much merchandise. "Coffee shops" abound, with names like the Grasshopper and Mellow Yel-low, where marijuana and hashish are legally sold and the pungent scent of the wares hangs in the breeze, even in the early morning, when patrons can be seen inside slumped in their chairs. Amsterdam's open hedonism has made the city a popular tourist attraction.

The Dutch pride themselves on their "nonjudgmentalism" about indi-vidual human behavior and they are strong advocates of finding consensus and compromise as a way of "managing" their social problems. Thus, in an attempt to reduce the use of hard drugs, marijuana and hashish are legal-ized if consumed in the coffee houses. To reduce out-of-wedlock births and abortion rates, the Dutch educational system and popular culture are very open about matters of sex, viewing it as a natural part of life, even for teenagers, while taking great pains to create a social milieu where the use of birth control and condoms is expected as part of the responsible man-agement of one's own sexuality. To reduce streetwalking, bordellos are free to operate, at least in Amsterdam, in the red-light district specifically zoned for that purpose.

The Dutch have adopted this same approach to the controversy sur-rounding the euthanasia issue. Because some doctors believed that euthanasia was appropriate, it was quasi-legalized in 1973 by a court decision. The idea was to create a compromise between proponents and opponents of legalization, whereby euthanasia would technically remain illegal but would be permitted in those few cases in which, supposedly, no other method could be found to alleviate a patient's suffering. As we shall see, however, it hasn't worked out that way. Instead of the medical establishment's managing and controlling death, the reverse seems to have occurred: The death imperative is controlling the practice and ethics of Dutch medicine. In only twenty-three years Dutch doctors have gone from being permitted to kill the terminally ill who ask for it, to killing the chronically ill who ask for it, to killing the depressed who have no physical illness who ask for it, to killing newborn babies in their cribs because they have birth defects, even though by definition they cannot ask for it. Dutch doctors also engage in involuntary euthanasia without significant legal consequence, even though such activity is officially prohibited.

These events are taking place within the context that despite euthanasia's being commonly practiced in the country, about 30 percent of the populace remains strongly opposed to it. As a consequence, the Dutch have never formally legalized euthanasia or physician-assisted suicide. Technically, both remain crimes punishable by long prison terms.[4] However, doctors who kill their patients or who help them kill themselves are not prosecuted if they follow the official protocols and guidelines that have been established, first by judicial rulings and more recently by statute.

To fully understand the context of the discussion, it is necessary to note the differences between the Dutch medical and legal systems and those here in the United States. America's health-care system is for the most part profit-driven, with financing primarily provided by private health insurance, although the poorest of the poor and the elderly receive government-financed health-care benefits. This leaves some of us out in the cold. At last count, 42 million Americans had no health insurance, which almost by definition means they receive inadequate health care.[5]

In contrast, virtually every Dutch citizen is legally entitled to quality medical care from birth until death. Money is not an issue for patients, since Dutch medicine is completely socialized; medical professionals are paid salaries by the government. The majority of physicians are general practitioners, family doctors who receive compensation on a per-patient basis, regardless of the level of care each individual patient requires. Dutch doctors are part of the broad middle class, and family doctors generally earn about $60,000 per year. Each citizen has a family doctor with whom he or she retains a long-lasting physician-patient relationship. Dutch doctors even make house calls!

The Dutch legal system has its roots in the Napoleonic Code, and generally one set of statutes governs the whole country. Eugene Sutorius, the lawyer primarily responsible for pushing the Dutch euthanasia movement in the nation's courts over the last several years, described the Dutch legal approach this way:

> We have professional judges and no jury system, which has a lot of consequences in the way controversial issues are dealt with. In Holland . . . the principle is that the judge is the . . . mouth of the law. Judges are to interpret law, not make it. . . . We are rather tied to the wording of the law. Thirdly, the system of criminal justice is centralized under the Ministry of Justice, [which] has broad discretion. . . . Prosecutions are not necessarily adversarial. Prosecutors may bring cases to establish legal precedents [rather than to punish wrongdoing].[6]

In contrast, the United States has a federal system of decentralized civil and criminal justice. Laws are made and enforced at all levels of government. Prosecutions are adversarial, based on attempts by prosecutors to punish wrongdoers, and nonprofessional juries generally decide outcomes. The United States Constitution is the supreme law of the land, superseding statutes and judicial rulings that violate its terms, but under that broad umbrella there are wide variations of law among federal, state, and local levels of government, and among the states themselves. Thus, what may be legal in one state may be illegal in another. This is not the case in Holland.

The Dutch System of Euthanasia

By the early seventies the Netherlands, deeply influenced by the cultural upheavals of the 1960s, was eschewing traditional values and ethical norms. In this milieu, as occurred to a somewhat lesser degree in the United States, the prevailing value system was turned on its head in areas such as drug use, sexual morality, and family issues.

Unlike in the United States, however, the euthanasia movement in the Netherlands quickly established a strong beachhead, finding respectability and acceptance, at least in theory. Euthanasia became a popular topic of discussion and analysis among the population and Dutch doctors, and many doctors and laypeople came to accept euthanasia as an appropriate response to the few cases at or near the end of life where suffering could not be alleviated.

These new attitudes on the issue profoundly affected Dutch law, beginning with a 1973 case in which Geetruida Postma, a Dutch physician, was charged with murder after she terminated the life of her seriously ill mother by giving her a lethal injection.[7] Postma appears to have intentionally used her mother's death to legitimize euthanasia among the populace and in law. Indeed, it is unlikely that the matter would have come to the attention of the authorities had she not insisted that her actions be made known.[8]

During the trial Postma was unrepentant. She testified that she acted out of compassion, stating that her mother was partly paralyzed, could hardly speak, had pneumonia, and was deaf. She further asserted that she killed her mother at the elder woman's request.

The highly visible case soon became a cause célèbre, much discussed and debated throughout the country. It became a rallying point for legalizing euthanasia and was the catalyst for the establishment of Holland's first voluntary euthanasia organization, the Voluntary Euthanasia Society. Postma's case generated such support that during the proceedings, doctors in her province signed an open letter to the Netherlands minister of justice stating that euthanasia was commonly practiced among physicians.[9]

The court found Dr. Postma guilty of murder. However, the court readily accepted the premise that most Dutch doctors supported euthanasia, at least in some cases. That being so, the court reasoned, the law should follow the medical consensus rather than the statute. Thus, in a departure from the Dutch legal requirement that changes in the law be enacted by the people through their representatives in Parliament, the court chose instead to create new law.

Dr. Postma received only a one-week suspended sentence and a year's probation.[10] To justify its action, the Dutch court relied heavily on expert testimony by the district's own medical inspector (illustrating the nonadversarial nature of the trial), who set forth certain conditions under which the average physician allegedly thought euthanasia should be considered acceptable. These conditions established the first boundaries for euthanasia practice in the Netherlands. Among these were the requirements that the patient be considered incurable, implying that the patient must suffer from a physical illness; that the patient's suffering be subjectively unbearable; that the request for termination of life be in writing; and that there should be adequate consultation with other physicians before euthanasia was carried out.[11] Inclusion of these conditions in the court's decision, which was not appealed and thus became a precedent, became the basis for subsequent acceptance of euthanasia in the Netherlands.

With the Postma decision, the Dutch stepped onto the slippery slope. Soon they were sliding down quickly as other court decisions followed, each widening the boundaries of acceptable medicalized killing and further liberalizing the conditions under which the practice of euthanasia would not be punished—although euthanasia technically remained illegal.

In 1993, the Dutch Parliament formalized the system that had been created by the courts: It enacted a statute that formalized the guidelines that doctors must follow to avoid punishment for euthanizing or assisting the suicides of patients.[12] These guidelines include the following:

- The request must be made entirely of the patient's own free will and not under pressure from others.

- The patient must have a lasting longing for death: The request must be made repeatedly over a period of time.

- The patient must be experiencing unbearable suffering.

- The patient must be given alternatives to euthanasia and time to consider these alternatives.

- There must be no reasonable alternatives to relieve suffering than euthanasia.

- Doctors must consult with at least one colleague who has faced the question of euthanasia before.

- The patient's death cannot inflict unnecessary suffering on others.

- Only a doctor can euthanize a patient.

- The euthanasia must be reported to the coroner, with a case history and a statement that the guidelines have been followed.[13]

In actual practice these guidelines offer precious little protection for the weak, vulnerable, and despairing, nor do they inhibit doctors from euthanizing patients who fall outside the guidelines' parameters.

It is important to recall that when euthanasia was first accepted in the Netherlands, it was supposed to be a rare event, to be resorted to only in the most unusual cases of "intolerable suffering." The guidelines were designed specifically to keep euthanasia occurrences few and far between by establishing demanding conditions that must be met. Over time, however, doctors began to interpret the conditions loosely and even ignore them.

This is the typical pattern of the euthanasia movement. Killing by doctors is always presented to the public as a "rare" occurrence, to be applied only when nothing else can be done. Proponents soothingly assure a doubtful public, as the New York euthanasia advocate Dr. Timothy Quill puts it, that euthanasia will be restricted to "the patient of last resort, [to be] taken only when hospice care stops providing comfort and dignity,"[14] when "all alternatives have been exhausted."[15] (Hospice medical care is designed to help terminally ill people. It does not seek to cure the terminal illness. Rather, it provides comfort, care, and alleviation of symptoms for dying people.) Unfortunately, the Dutch experience clearly demonstrates that once killing is accepted as a legitimate medical act, it quickly ceases to be rare or is resorted to only when all else fails. Instead, in the words of Dr. K. F. Gunning, perhaps the most notable Dutch opponent of euthanasia, "Once you accept killing as a solution for a single problem, you will find tomorrow hundreds of problems for which killing can be seen as a solution."[16]

In the twenty-plus years since euthanasia was redefined in the Netherlands as a legitimate tool of medical practice instead of a serious crime, cultural biases have changed, and many doctors now favor the practice. No longer constrained by conscience or culture, thanks to a redefinition of euthanasia as medical treatment instead of killing, Dutch doctors now terminate categories of people whose assisted deaths would have once provoked outrage, and do so in numbers that were not anticipated when the practice was first promoted. "Since my country came to accept euthanasia, there has been a steady increase in the categories of people who can be killed," says Dr. Gunning. "The numbers of cases in which doctors consciously cause their patients' death in my country is frightening."[17] Rather than being rare, statistics show that doctors intentionally kill almost 9 percent of all of the Dutch people who die each year.

The Remmelink Report

In 1990, responding to the heated debate about Dutch euthanasia and the many anecdotes being told about involuntary killings of patients by doctors, the Dutch government decided to determine how euthanasia was actually being carried out and appointed an investigative committee. Called the Committee to Investigate the Medical Practice Concerning Euthanasia, it was commonly known as the Remmelink Commission, after the committee's chairman, Professor J. Remmelink, then the attorney general of the Dutch Supreme Court.

Three studies were conducted by the Remmelink Commission. In the first, a retrospective study, more than four hundred physicians were interviewed about their opinions on the practice of euthanasia. Then for six months the same physicians were asked to record and report their actions in cases with a fatal outcome. Finally, a representative sampling of deaths was taken from the register at the Central Statistics Office, and the physicians who had been involved in the care of the deceased were asked to provide information about the cases. In all three instances, the doctors' anonymity was guaranteed.

The commission's two-volume report, known as the Remmelink Report, was issued in 1991.[18] The Remmelink Report was written so as to assure that euthanasia was rare and that the existing guidelines were effective in controlling the practice. This was done, in part, by severely restricting the definition of "euthanasia" to deliberate termination of another's life at his or her request, usually accomplished by a lethal injection of a sedative and a curarelike poison. Cases that did not explicitly fit that category were not called euthanasia. A doctor's lethally injecting a patient without request, a not uncommon occurrence in the Netherlands, was called not involuntary or nonvoluntary euthanasia but rather "termination of life without patient's explicit request." (Some Dutch doctors call involuntary euthanasia "life-terminating treatment," proving that the Dutch are not above resorting to euphemisms.) Other acts of intentional killing, such as purposefully overdosing a patient with pain-control medication for the purposes of killing him, also fell outside the Remmelink Report's working definition of euthanasia, because the drugs used in pain control, when properly applied, are palliative rather than lethal agents—unlike curare, always a lethal agent.

Although it dubiously narrowed the definition of euthanasia, the Remmelink Report did include the complete statistical data upon which it based its conclusions. Independent analysis of this rich source of information has had a profoundly negative impact on the world's view of Dutch euthanasia—so negative, in fact, that as these words are written the Dutch government has sponsored a new study.

According to the Remmelink Report, about 130,000 people die each year in the Netherlands.[19] Of these, approximately 43,300, or about one third, die suddenly—from catastrophic heart attacks, stroke, accidents, et cetera—thus precluding medical decision making about end-of-life care.[20]

That leaves approximately 90,000 people whose deaths involve end-of-life medical decision making each year. With that in mind, here are the figures about euthanasia-related deaths in 1990, derived from the Remmelink Report's published statistical data:

- 2,300 patients were euthanized (killed) by their doctors upon request, and 400 people died through physician-assisted suicide, for a total of 2,700 doctor-induced deaths.[21] That is approximately 3 percent of all deaths involving end-of-life medical care. The equivalent percentage in the United States would be 41,500 deaths.

- 1,040 died from involuntary euthanasia, lethal injections given without request or consent—three deaths every single day.[22] These deaths constitute slightly more than 1 percent of all cases involving end-of-life medical care. (The same percentage in the United States would be approximately 16,000 involuntary killings per year.) Of these involuntary euthanasia cases, 14 percent, or 145, were fully competent to make their own medical decisions but were killed without request or consent anyway.[23] (The same percentage in the United States would be more than 2,000 who would be killed.) Moreover, 72 percent of the people killed without their consent had never given any indication they would want their lives terminated.[24]

- 8,100 patients died from an intentional overdose of morphine or other pain-control medications, designed primarily to terminate life.[25] In other words, death was not a side effect of treatment to relieve pain, which can sometimes occur, but was the *intended result* of the overdose. Of these, 61 percent (4,941 patients) were intentionally overdosed without request or consent. The equivalent percentage in the United States would be approximately 78,000.

These figures are startling. Of the approximately 90,000 Dutch people whose deaths involved end-of-life medical decision making, 11,140 were intentionally killed (euthanized) or assisted in suicide—or 11.1 percent of all Dutch deaths involving medical decision making. This is approximately 8.5 percent of Dutch deaths from all causes. Of these killings, *more than half were involuntary* (1,040 involuntary lethal injections and 4,941 involuntary intentional overdoses). Applying those percentages to the U.S. death rate would mean more than 170,000 deaths each year caused by euthanasia or assisted suicide, and about 85,000 of these involuntary, more than the current number of U.S. suicides and homicides combined.[26]

It should also be kept in mind that the Remmelink statistics probably underestimate the actual number of deaths caused by euthanasia and assisted suicide. A study conducted by the Free University at Amsterdam revealed that two thirds of Dutch general practitioners have certified a patient's death as resulting from natural causes when in fact it was euthanasia or assisted suicide.[27] Another Dutch study arrived at a similar conclusion, finding that only 28 percent of doctors were honest about their euthanasia killings when filling out death certificates.[28] Moreover, a study conducted by the Medicolegal Group of Limburg University in Maastricht found that 41.1 percent of doctors who participated in the survey admitted to having engaged in involuntary euthanasia. A more recent Dutch study, written up in the *New England Journal of Medicine* in November 1996, found that only 41 percent of all euthanasia deaths were reported to the authorities. This same study revealed that 23 percent of physicians interviewed had killed patients without having received an explicit request. Also mentioned is a new wrinkle not touched upon in the Remmelink Report: At least half of Dutch physicians take the initiative by *suggesting* euthanasia to their patients.[29]

Guidelines That Do Not Protect

The Remmelink Report and other research into Dutch euthanasia practices suggest that guidelines do not protect and do not restrict. One reason is that guideline violations are rarely punished, and when they are, the sanctions are not meaningful. For example, a Dutch nurse was given a two-month suspended sentence for killing an AIDS patient in violation of the rule requiring that only doctors can perform euthanasia.[30]

But the issue goes much deeper than lack of proper enforcement. What is really involved is a profound change in Dutch society's definitions of right and wrong. With the widespread acceptance of a euthanasia consciousness in the Netherlands, the guideline limitations make little actual difference to doctors or, indeed, to much of the general public. The proverbial exception to the rule can always be rationalized, which in turn soon changes the exception into the rule. The official guidelines then expand to meet the actual practice.

These cases have real faces. Dr. Gunning tells of one such tragic circumstance:

> A friend of mine, an internist, was asked to see a lady with terminal lung cancer, who had a short time to live and was very short of breath. After the examination, he asked the patient to come to the hospital on

Saturday for a few days so that he could alleviate her distress. She re-
fused, being afraid of being euthanized there. My friend assured his
patient that he would be on duty and that no such thing would hap-
pen. So the lady came. On Sunday night she was breathing normally
and feeling much better. The doctor went home. When he came back
on Monday afternoon, the patient was dead. The doctor's colleague
told him, "What is the sense of having that woman here? It makes no
difference whether she dies today or after two weeks. We need the bed
for another case."[31]

In other words, the woman was euthanized against her explicit wishes to accommodate the killing doctor's priorities.

The psychiatrist Dr. Herbert Hendin, director of the American Foundation for Suicide Prevention, has done much in-depth research on Dutch euthanasia, including extensive discussions with Dutch doctors and review of cases. Dr. Hendin has concluded that many doctors in the Netherlands feel justified in performing involuntary euthanasia, because a system that permits them to kill "encourages some to feel entitled to make [euthanasia] decisions without consulting the patient."[32] As an example, Hendin recounts his interview with a pro-euthanasia doctor who justified killing a nun who had requested not to be killed on the basis of religious belief, because _he felt_ she was in too much pain.[33]

It is not only the involuntary cases that violate Dutch guidelines. Dr. Hendin describes his conversation with a Dutch doctor who has euthanized between fifty and a hundred patients. One of the cases in which he consulted was that of an elderly woman who wanted to die, not because she was ill but because she was haunted by memories of being a concentration camp survivor.[34] How could this case possibly meet the guidelines? The woman was not ill. The doctor in question was a family practitioner, not a psychiatrist, and there appears to have been no sustained attempt to alleviate the poor woman's anguish. Despite this, in an act that reeks of tragic irony, the doctor put her to death and is now afflicted himself by her memory.[35]

To prove the existence of cases that violate the official guidelines, it is not necessary to rely on anecdotal evidence. Such cases have even been documented in euthanasia-friendly documentaries originally produced in the Netherlands and later shown in the United States. One such documentary, broadcast over public television on the program *The Health Quarterly* in 1993, revealed how broadly the Dutch guidelines are interpreted—that is to say, how commonly they are ignored.[36]

One case documented in the film concerns a man named Henk Dykema, who at the time of filming was asymptomatic HIV-positive. Dykema feared the afflictions that he expected to befall him and had been asking his doctor to kill him for more than a year. The film shows the doctor telling Henk that he might live for years at his current stage of infection, but the patient wants none of it. The doctor, a general practitioner, then discussed Henk's case with a colleague, also a general practitioner. Significantly, no psychiatrist was consulted or involved. Finally, the doctor agreed to euthanize Dykema, even though he was not suffering any significant physical symptoms.

Dykema decided that he wanted to die on July 28, because the day had a symbolic importance for him. His doctor agreed to accommodate the request. The narrator tells us that Dykema died by drinking a poisonous brew supplied by his own doctor.[37]

Dykema's assisted suicide was clearly not a last resort, as required by the Dutch guidelines. He and his doctor did not explore all other possible options, such as psychiatric treatment, which could well have alleviated his anxiety. Nor was he told of the actions the doctor could have taken to relieve his suffering when he did become ill. The doctor didn't even wait until Henk had actual symptoms of AIDS. As Dr. Carlos Gomez, a specialist in hospice medicine at the University of Virginia and an expert on euthanasia issues, aptly put it, Dykema's physician was "responding to anticipation of suffering . . . which may or may not have been true. In a sense the physician was saying, 'You're absolutely right, your end is going to be a disaster.' "[38] There is a word for that kind of "care": abandonment.

Dr. Hendin has analyzed this case from a psychiatrist's perspective. He believes that "the patient was clearly depressed. The doctor kept establishing that the man was persistent in his request, but did not address the terror that underlay it."[39]

The documentary shows another patient who was euthanized, a psychiatrist named Jan Stricht, asking for euthanasia because he had blood clots on the brain. The malady was not terminal. Dr. Stricht, the viewer is told, might have lived "one year or twenty years."[40] Nor had the affliction caused significant physical pain. Rather, Dr. Stricht was emotionally upset at his greatly reduced physical capacities, caused primarily by significant difficulties in depth perception and other such motor deficiencies.

Dr. Stricht's own physician, a general practitioner, described the case as one of "mental suffering." The depressed man was feeling the effects of being dependent on others for the necessities of life:

I can depend on other people to do things, but the bad thing is they want to do it their way and not my way, so they don't help me. . . . I have to eat what they decide that I have to eat, which I don't want to eat at all. . . . Or, I want to drink, and they say, "You drink too much. It's wrong to do."[41]

The upset caused by growing dependent is seen by the doctor as legitimate grounds for euthanasia. No effort is taken to address and correct Dr. Stricht's legitimate complaints about his caregiving.

The documentary also shows Maria, a twenty-five-year-old woman with anorexia nervosa, asking for euthanasia. She is in remission but fears a recurrence of her malady, stating:

I've thought about dying day and night, and I know that if relief does not come, I will return to the old pattern, the pattern of self-punishment, hurting myself. I know it. I feel it, and therefore I hope the release will come soon and I die.[42]

Maria's doctor agreed to euthanize her, stating that "it is not possible to have a good quality of life for her." This case was even too much for the authorities, who brought charges against the doctor. However, the euthanasia consciousness had so permeated the justice system that the judge ruled that Maria's killing was justified because her suffering had made her life unbearable.

Similar tragedies can be found in many published investigations of Dutch euthanasia. For example, *The Oregonian* reported on a woman with skin cancer who was euthanized. She wasn't in pain, nor was she in a terminal stage of her illness. Rather, she was upset by the scars on her face and demanded euthanasia from her doctor, or else—the threat being that she would "jump from the balcony." Her doctor, to his later expressed regret, accommodated her wish to die.[43]

Studies indicate that families, rather than patients, generally decide when the time has come for euthanasia. According to Dr. Hendin, doctors called in such cases "usually advocate euthanasia," because they "support the relatives' desire to be free from the burden of caring for the patient."[44] One such case occurred when a wife told her husband to choose euthanasia or a nursing home. Not wanting to be cared for by strangers, he chose death. The doctor killed him, despite knowing of the coercion.[45]

Dr. Gunning tells of another such case related to him by a close physician friend of his who supports euthanasia: A man was hospitalized with terminal cancer and was in great pain. His son came to his father's doctor and said that the family wanted to bury the old man before they went on holiday. The doctor agreed and overdosed the man with pain-control medication. The next day, much to his shock, the old man was sitting up, feeling great. The intended overdose had not killed him but had killed the pain.[46]

If the guidelines don't protect a young, deeply emotionally disturbed woman such as Maria from being killed, if they allow a doctor to kill a woman on the basis of what the doctor himself called "a case of vanity," if they allow families to push the death agenda regardless of the desires of their ill relatives, whom can they protect?[47]

Death on Demand Comes to the Netherlands

The Dutch psychiatrist Boutdewijn Chabot has written, "If one accepts, as I do, that persistently suicidal patients are indeed terminal, then one must ask whether a persistently suicidal state can be diagnosed as an incurable disease. I believe in some cases, like that of my patient, it can."[48]

Hilly Bosscher was just such a deeply depressed and suicidal woman. She had lost her two sons, one to suicide in 1986 and the other to brain cancer in 1991. Her marriage, never very good and often abusive, took a turn for the worse after her first son's death and was dissolved in 1990. Bosscher had briefly received psychiatric treatment years earlier for the depression and suicidal thoughts she experienced after her son's suicide. On the day her second son died, she failed in an attempt to kill herself. She still wanted to die but hesitated at self-destruction for fear that she would be hospitalized if she tried and failed again. However, she moved the graves of her two sons to the same cemetery and purchased a burial plot for herself so that she could be buried between them.[49]

Bosscher began to attend meetings of the Dutch Euthanasia Society, where she met Dr. Chabot, who attended meetings to troll for patients. She told Dr. Chabot that she didn't want therapy, "because it would loosen the bonds with her deceased sons."[50] Dr. Chabot took her as a patient anyway and met with her on four occasions between August 2 and September 7, 1991. Dr. Chabot did not attempt to treat her. Rather, he interviewed her to determine her prognosis. After these interviews and his consultations, despite the complete absence of any physical illness, he agreed to help Bosscher kill herself, which he did on September 28, 1991.

Dr. Chabot was charged with the crime of assisted suicide. This is less dramatic than it sounds. As described earlier in the chapter, Dutch trials are not based strictly on the adversary system. Prosecutors sometimes file cases not to punish wrongdoers but rather to establish a legal precedent permitting a specific activity. This is the primary method by which euthanasia guidelines have been steadily loosened over the years in the Netherlands.

Dr. Chabot's lawyer was Eugene Sutorius, a charming man with a quick smile and a sharp legal mind any attorney would admire. Sutorius was no stranger to euthanasia cases, being a legal adviser to the Dutch Voluntary Euthanasia Society and the lawyer primarily responsible over many years for pushing the boundaries of euthanasia in the Dutch courts. Sutorius recalled for me his legal argument on behalf of Dr. Chabot:

> My . . . plea was [that] the doctor acted justifiably in [a situation of] a conflict of duties, one, the preponderant duty, which is preserving human life, and the second is fighting suffering or preventing it. . . . In this case, the duties could not be reconciled, one could not be fulfilled without violating the other. . . . So, I said, he could not escape the [patient's] request, and the request would be reasonable and understandable and it would be according to his prognosis, inevitable that the suffering would just continue. . . . So, I argued that a doctor may, under very strict circumstances, be justified in giving the priority to the other duty, the duty to relieve suffering. And that, they [the court] accepted.[51]

According to Sutorius the prosecutor vigorously presented the case, but even so there was never much question of Chabot's actually being meaningfully punished:

> The public prosecution, as a body, sees that this is not criminality in the normal sense. That he [the prosecutor] is not fighting real criminals here, he is fighting doctors that encounter a problem. . . . So, even the prosecutor, while bringing the case, he's more interested in making sure that we have strict definitions and order than he is in punishing the professional. He's trying to create a precedent. It's either yes or no, but he wants to make sure that there's order in society and that these things are done decently.[52]

Both the prosecutor and Sutorius got what they were looking for in the Chabot case. The lower court refused to punish the psychiatrist in any way, a decision blessed by the Dutch Supreme Court, with the minor caveat that Chabot erred by not having a colleague independently examine the patient. The basis of the ruling was that the law cannot distinguish between suffering caused by physical illness and suffering caused by mental anguish. Thus, Dutch guidelines now permit doctors in the Netherlands to kill their depressed patients on the basis of patient demand caused by depression, even if the patient refuses treatment that might overcome the suicidal fixation. In other words, in the Netherlands, people with a significant depression can obtain death virtually on demand.

Killing Children

In the Netherlands, infants are killed because they have birth defects, and doctors justify the practice. One Dutch pediatrician explained, "Some patients, if you withhold or withdraw treatment, the child will not die immediately. It might take hours or days or weeks. And then, I think it's better to support the child to die, and to help the child to die, and that's actually what we are doing, of course, in very rare occasions."[53]

Thanks to another "prosecution" of a doctor who euthanized an infant, euthanasia, already practiced on adults in the Netherlands, will soon openly enter the pediatric ward. Dr. Henk Prins killed a three-day-old girl who was born with spina bifida, hydrocephaly, and leg deformities. The doctor—a gynecologist, not a pediatrician or a medical expert in such cases, although experts were consulted—was defended by Sutorius. Prins testified in the trial court that he killed the child, with her parents' permission, because of the infant's poor prognosis and because the baby screamed in pain when touched. Yet the child was in agony because she was neglected medically. The open wound in her back, the primary characteristic of spina bifida, had not been closed, nor had the fluid been drained from her head, even though these medical treatments standard in spina bifida cases would have substantially reduced her pain. This shows the self-justifying, circular thinking involved in much medicalized killing.

The trial court refused to punish the doctor. Indeed, the judge praised Dr. Prins for "his integrity and courage and wished him well in any further legal proceedings he may face."[54] As of this writing, the prosecutor, wanting to create a precedent to govern euthanasia for people who cannot consent, is appealing to the Dutch Supreme Court to formally establish infanticide as a proper medical act.

It is noteworthy that the Remmelink Report did not include figures on the incidence of pediatric euthanasia, an accepted practice among most Dutch pediatricians. Nor did it include cases in which disabled children were allowed to die by medical neglect, the preferred Dutch method of killing newborns with birth defects. For example, children with Down syndrome are commonly born with a bowel obstruction that can easily be corrected with surgery. To refuse this treatment for a "normal" child would be considered an outrageous crime. But in the Netherlands, it is acceptable to leave the obstruction in place if the infant has Down syndrome, resulting in the baby's starving to death. One doctor has justified this form of killing by saying that the Down child would suffer if allowed to live because he or she "would always be dependent" and find it "very difficult to establish normal social relations, to create or bring up a family."[55] It is estimated that at least three hundred Dutch infants die from intentional medical neglect each year.[56] (Such deaths also occur in the United States.)

For several years now there has been consensus among Dutch pediatricians in support of infant euthanasia if neglect doesn't work. A 1990 report of the Royal Dutch Medical Association (K.N.M.G.), *Life-Terminating Actions with Incompetent Patients*, set forth "requirements for careful medical practice" when ending the lives of handicapped newborns. The standard for euthanasia is based on what Dutch doctors call an "unlivable life."[57] If this sounds familiar, it is: It differs little in its bigoted view of the value of disabled people from the attitudes expressed by Binding and Hoche in 1920 in *Permitting the Destruction of Life Not Worthy of Life*.

According to current Dutch medical ethics, the "livableness" of a life depends on a combination of factors, including the following:

1. THE EXPECTED MEASURE OF SUFFERING (NOT ONLY BODILY BUT ALSO EMOTIONAL—THE LEVEL OF HOPELESSNESS)
2. THE EXPECTED POTENTIAL FOR

    - communication and human relationships
    - independence (ability to move, to care for oneself, to live independently)
    - self-realization (being able to hear, read, write, labor)

3. THE CHILD'S LIFE EXPECTANCY[58]

If the infant's "prospects" don't measure up to what the doctor and parents believe is a life worth living, the child can be neglected to death or, if that doesn't work, killed.

These barbaric policies have been rationalized by Dutch doctors and ethicists on a number of grounds. A few resort to hard utilitarianism, asserting that the value of a life "depends on how valuable that life is for other people."[59] However, most rhetorical justifications of Dutch infanticide are couched in more compassionate tones, stressing that the killing is in the best interests of the child. Thus, the State Committee on Euthanasia of the K.N.M.G. declared support for killing newborns—as well as minors, mentally retarded persons, and the demented elderly—if "one can suppose that were the patients to express their will, they would opt for euthanasia."[60] It is doubtful that actual disabled people are often let into the decision making about whose lives are livable and whose lives are better off ended. They might have a contrary point of view.

This expansion of euthanasia guidelines has been several years in the making. In 1992, the Dutch Pediatric Association began drafting guidelines for the practice of physician-induced death for infants. The proposal recommended that the attending physician decide whether to end the child's life.[61] By 1993, three out of eight neonatal intensive-care units in the Netherlands had specific policies, endorsed by the Dutch Pediatric Society, that permitted infant euthanasia by fatal injection.[62] (In 1995, there were fifteen reported cases of infant euthanasia.)

Infants are not the only children who are eligible for euthanasia. Pediatric oncologists have provided a *hulp bij zelfoding* (self-help for ending life) program for adolescents since the 1980s, in which poisonous doses are prescribed for minors with terminal illness.[63] Moreover, children who want physician-assisted death may be able to receive it without consent of their parents. A 1986 report issued by the Central Committee of the Royal Dutch Medical Association explained its position on euthanasia of older minors:

> *The Central Committee is not in favour of including an exact limit in the law with respect to the "rights" of parents in the case of a minor making a request for euthanasia. Nor is the Central Committee in favour of giving a right of veto to one or both parents in such cases. The Central Committee does hold the view, however, that the physician should always consult the parents about their child's request for euthanasia. But with a view to the child's own good, this does not imply that parents have the power of decision. It goes without saying that where a young child is concerned, the state of affairs will be different from those where an older child is concerned.*

We would like to advocate not to include a separate age limit in the law, as it may be impossible as well as unjust in our opinion to lay down an exact age limit in this matter. Sometimes, a 15-year-old child can have a mature judgment. At all times, it will be a matter of acting carefully in medical respect [emphasis added].[64]

Where next for Dutch medical ethics? When I interviewed Eugene Sutorius, he was energetically preparing to defend yet another test case, that of a doctor who had euthanized a quadriplegic a year and a half after her injury because the woman did not want to live with her disability.

Drawing Conclusions

One of the pioneers of Dutch euthanasia, Dr. Pieter Admiraal, who has killed more than one hundred patients, told me, "Of our doctors, eighty-four percent will give euthanasia, while sixteen percent will not. Of these sixteen percent, most will send patients to another doctor for euthanasia. Only a few will not participate either directly or indirectly. . . . If you come to euthanasia like we did, you will come to the same result." I doubt that the Dutch physicians who died resisting Nazi pressure to begin killing their weakest and most vulnerable patients would admire Dr. Admiraal and his colleagues today. They would be horrified and appalled.

Unlike the Dutch, Americans do not come to the decision whether to accept legalized euthanasia blindly. We have the Dutch experience to guide us. On the basis of their experience with euthanasia, what can we learn about the death culture? First, the slippery slope is very real. As Dr. Gunning put it, the Dutch have proved that once killing is accepted as a solution for one problem, tomorrow it will be seen as the solution for hundreds of problems. Once we accept the killing of terminally ill patients, as did the Dutch, we will invariably accept the killing of chronically ill patients, depressed patients, and ultimately, even children.

Second, the substantive differences between the Dutch and U.S. health-care systems mean that the U.S. experience with the death culture would likely be far *worse* than that in the Netherlands. Recall that the Dutch have virtual universal health coverage. We, on the other hand, have over 42 million Americans without health insurance, which by definition means they receive inadequate health care. Moreover, for-profit health maintenance organizations are putting great financial pressure on the health-care system and are imposing a financial conflict of interest between patients and their own doctors by punishing physicians financially if they provide too much care (discussed in Chapter 6). Although cost containment is an issue in the Netherlands, financial pressures to hasten death are much more muted there than they would likely be here.

Third, the Netherlands is a much more tolerant society than we are, generally more accepting of differences among people, such as those of race, gender, and sexual orientation. Nevertheless, these attitudes filter into their medical practice; it is to be expected that our prevailing prejudices would filter more strongly into our medical practice. A recent editorial in the *New England Journal of Medicine* cited a plethora of studies that uncovered significant race-based inequality in the delivery of health care in the United States, and opined that the disparities in the delivery of health care apparently caused by racism need to be focused upon with the "rigor and attention given to other health concerns of similar magnitude."[65] These and other factors make it likely that legalizing and especially "routinizing" euthanasia in the United States would be especially dangerous for oppressed populations.

A legitimate question is: If euthanasia is so bad, why do a majority of the Dutch people support their country's policy? I put that very question to the Dutch ethicist W.C.M. Klijn, a retired professor of medical ethics who served as a member of a government-appointed committee that investigated whether euthanasia should be formally legalized and wrote the minority report recommending against legalization. (So far, the Dutch government still has not attempted to formally legalize euthanasia.) Professor Klijn told me:

> We Dutch pride ourselves on our history. We see ourselves as having been good in the past, therefore, we believe that we will always be good. It is an arrogance of goodness. Thus, even though there are striking resemblances to our euthanasia practices and those the Nazis sought to impose upon us, we assure ourselves: We resisted the Nazis. We are sophisticated, humane. We can't be doing wrong! To admit we are wrong on euthanasia would be to say that we are not the compassionate, sophisticated, enlightened people we think we are. It is very hard in the Dutch character to do that.[66]

Professor Klijn also believes that, much like the people of the United States, the Dutch have an almost reflexive response to arguments based on "personal autonomy." Because this concept is so deeply ingrained in the Dutch and U.S. value systems, upon hearing the magic word "choice," many people make up their minds and don't have the time or inclination to dig deeper. They don't see the whole picture: the abuses, the destruction of family cohesiveness, or the paternalism inherent in euthanasia, because the decision as to whether one lives or dies often depends more on the doctor's values than on the patient's.

Dr. van der Sluis, a secularist opponent of his country's euthanasia policies, raises another point germane to the ongoing debate in the United States. Many Dutch accept euthanasia so as not to be perceived as overly religious. "The proponents of euthanasia have falsely, but successfully, cast the argument as one of religion versus rationality," Dr. van der Sluis told me. "They assert that only fundamentalist Christians oppose euthanasia and since few Dutch are fundamentalist Christians, they tend to support euthanasia." Dr. Pieter Admiraal verified that point when he told me, "The only way to deny euthanasia is based on religion. Most Dutch are nonbelievers, and thus, they must support euthanasia."[67]

Dr. Herbert Hendin discovered another interesting reason why euthanasia may be accepted by the Dutch: The case studies, only some of which are recounted here, are not widely discussed in the Netherlands out of "loyalty to the system," and in order not to threaten the delicate consensus that has developed among the Dutch concerning the practice. Dr. Hendin writes that several Dutch euthanasia proponents admitted that they are not candid in their discussions about euthanasia "for political considerations." They don't want to "play into the hands of the Christian Democrats," the minority opposition party that opposes euthanasia.[68] Moreover, Dr. Hendin discovered that the Dutch are exquisitely sensitive to being criticized, and that "savage criticisms" of Dutch euthanasia policies by "physicians in the rest of Europe" have "forced the Dutch into a defensive position."[69] He also noted, "Virtually all of those who have played a role in advancing the cause of euthanasia [in the Netherlands] on humanitarian grounds were concerned about the problems in implementation yet seemed disinclined to express their doubts publicly."[70] Hendin confronted one such proponent who had published an article in favor of euthanasia that broadly contradicted his private conversations with Hendin. The doctor justified his hypocrisy on the basis of his not "wish[ing] to be critical of the system or perhaps to be viewed as being so in a culture in which uncritical support for Dutch euthanasia policies is politically correct."[71]

More than twenty years of legitimized euthanasia may also have desensitized the Dutch to activities that they once would have found abhorrent. One documentary televised on the Dutch television network showed the actual killing of a man with amyotrophic lateral sclerosis, generally known in this country as Lou Gehrig's disease, by his doctor. Even this documentary, intended to promote the legitimacy of euthanasia, showed how the Dutch euthanasia guidelines offer little actual protection. For example, the doctor who provides the required second opinion tells the patient bluntly, "You have an incurable disease which will soon end in death, and unless there is some intervention you will experience terrible suffering. You will probably suffocate."[72] In fact, according to Dame Cecily Saunders, the creator of the English hospice movement, if people with A.L.S. receive proper care, *they do not suffocate.* She has helped more than three hundred such patients die with dignity in hospice, so she should know. (I have confirmed this assessment with several U.S. neurologists and hospice doctors.) Yet neither the patient's doctor nor the rubber-stamp consultant bothered to tell the patient this news that might have caused him to change his mind about being killed. (An edited version of this documentary was shown in the United States on December 8, 1994, on ABC's magazine show *Prime Time.*)

Another example of the desensitization of a nation to indecency was a program aired on Dutch television that was partly financed by the Dutch Ministry of Health, called *A Matter of Life and Death.* The broadcast consisted of six segments; in each one, two seriously ill patients were pitted against each other. Both tell the audience about themselves and their respective illness and describe their current prognosis. The audience then votes on which of the two should receive life-prolonging treatment and which should not. The Dutch government defended the show as an effort to stimulate discussion about reducing health-care costs.[73]

Then there is the case of the little girl who fell into a lake and drowned. Normally, that would not be national news. But in this case, "Two hundred people stopped eating sandwiches, playing Frisbee, or walking the dog, and stood. Some moved to the bank and watched the girl drown. No one tried to help."[74] The little girl's death, captured on video, shook the Netherlands in much the same way the Rodney King video did in this country, as the Dutch, "in a rare moment of self-examination,"[75] wondered and worried about the decline of their culture.

Of course, these anecdotes don't prove anything one way or the other about whether euthanasia has adversely affected the Dutch national character. It is interesting to note, however, that some Dutch no longer trust their doctors. The Dutch Patients Association, a patients' rights group with sixty thousand members, distributes a wallet card to protect members from being involuntarily euthanized. The card specifically states that it is "intended to prevent involuntary euthanasia in case of admission of the signer to the hospital" and instructs that "no treatment be administered with the intention to terminate life."[76]

There are a few early indications that the Dutch may be having second thoughts about euthanasia. Eugene Sutorius conceded that the Chabot case had significantly raised the level and intensity of debate about its propriety. According to Dr. Gunning, recent opinion polls, while continuing to indicate popular support for euthanasia, show a pronounced increase in opposition since the early nineties. Even Dutch doctors seem to be disturbed about what euthanasia does to the human psyche. The K.N.M.G. has recommended that doctors have patients self-administer death rather than doing it themselves. Why? "Many doctors find euthanasia an extremely difficult and burdensome action."[77]

The purpose of this book is not to judge the Dutch or try to influence euthanasia practices in that country. It is to analyze what legalized euthanasia would mean to the United States. On that point, at least, Dutch proponents and opponents of euthanasia agree: Disaster lies ahead if the United States follows their country's lead. Dr. Pieter Admiraal told me:

> *I am totally against euthanasia in the U.S. as matters now stand. Before you have euthanasia, you have to have quality of care for terminally ill people, and the U.S. doesn't have that. Unless the U.S. can obtain it, it would be silly—ridiculous—for euthanasia to be legalized.*[78]

Eugene Sutorius, certainly no shirker when it comes to advancing the euthanasia agenda in his country, agrees. He believes that "in the States, euthanasia will become a substitute for care," and states further:

> *I think that a society that doesn't start with care cannot talk about euthanasia. I don't mean this as arrogance, but I think that care in Holland is in the center of what we feel that doctors should do and be there for. And I think doctors in a large degree mirror that. Because in Holland, the technological side didn't overthrow the care side. We didn't destroy the relationship between doctor and patient.*[79]

Sutorius chuckled as he told me that he now rarely receives invitations from U.S. proponents of euthanasia to come to the States and speak, largely because of his belief that policies he has worked so energetically to create in his country would be a terrible thing for America.

One pro-euthanasia book, which was underwritten by the Dutch government, put it thus:

> *Given the fact that euthanasia . . . can only be tolerated by society in [a] context where on the whole all human life is valued highly . . . in situations where the value of life becomes more uncertain due to violence, high suicide rates, disasters, economic uncertainties, etc., the basis of mutual trust on which this [euthanasia] decision-making should be founded cannot be sufficiently guaranteed.*[80]

In the United States, with its declining belief in the equality-of-human-life ethic, with its high rates of violence, significant suicide levels, pronounced economic uncertainties, divisions of race, gender, religion, sexual orientation, class, and the concomitant lack of mutual trust, euthanasia would be an ethical and moral catastrophe.

CHAPTER 5

Inventing the Right to Die

In 1992, Jack Kevorkian seriously proposed in the *American Journal of Forensic Psychiatry* that a pilot program of death clinics be established in Michigan. The clinics, which he calls "obitoria," would be staffed by physician-killers, known as "obitiatrists," who would be permitted legally to terminate patients who request it, in a procedure Kevorkian used to call "medicide" (which really means to kill a doctor, not to be killed by a doctor)* but now labels "patholysis."[1] Kevorkian foresaw that the first "patients" would be the terminally and chronically ill. However, he foresaw an eventual widening of obitiatry to people he calls "patients tortured by other than organic diseases."[2]

At the time such an idea seemed fantastical, almost laughable. It doesn't anymore. Euthanasia is no longer an abstract matter for intellectual debate in ethics classes or late-night musing among friends over drinks. Since 1994, serious political and legal actions taken by euthanasia advocates and their lawyers have brought assisted suicide to the brink of legal acceptance. Oregon has attempted to legalize physician-assisted suicide. Influential decisions in court cases in Washington and New York have bestowed a measure of moral and ethical respectability upon the death culture. It is important to analyze this trend in some detail if we are to understand the tactics and the

---

* When the Oakland County medical examiner Dr. Ljubisa J. Dragovic pointed out the actual meaning of "medicide" to local reporters, Kevorkian took some ribbing among the press. Later, after Kevorkian helped kill Ali Khalili, a physician, Dragovic told me he received an anonymous phone call on his voice mail, saying, "Ha, ha, ha. The first medicide has been accomplished."[3]

rhetoric that euthanasia's advocates are using to establish legalized killing as a routine medical practice.

Initiative 119 and Proposition 161

It is quite shocking to realize how fast and how far the death culture has advanced in recent years. As recently as 1988 the first attempt was made to qualify a euthanasia legalization initiative on California's ballot. That effort failed to get enough signatures to qualify for the ballot.

If death fundamentalists are anything, they are indomitable. Rather than being discouraged by their California failure, they redoubled their efforts: In 1991 they succeeded in qualifying a euthanasia legalization initiative in the state of Washington, known as Initiative 119, which would have permitted doctors to lethally inject patients under some circumstances. The early polls had the proposal far ahead, with some polls exceeding 70 percent approval. But that was before the anti-119 forces were able to present the reasons why legalizing euthanasia is a dangerous and unwise idea. In the end, support for euthanasia plummeted in Washington, and Initiative 119 lost decisively, 54 percent to 46 percent.

Undaunted by their loss, euthanasia advocates got right back to work. Again California was targeted, and Proposition 161, almost identical to Initiative 119, was successfully qualified for the November 1992 ballot. The campaign over Proposition 161 was a virtual replay of the earlier Washington battle. Once again, early polls showed public support in the 70 percentile range. But as usually is the case in debates over legalizing euthanasia, the more California voters learned about euthanasia and the more they considered the consequences that would flow from permitting doctors to kill, the less they liked Proposition 161. Following Washington's lead, California rejected legalized euthanasia 54–46 percent. Next, it was on to Oregon, where a different political strategy would lead to a dramatic victory for the death culture.

Oregon's Measure 16

After the passage of Oregon's Measure 16 in 1994, the first law in modern history explicitly legalizing physician-assisted suicide (P.A.S.), one would have expected suicide guru Derek Humphry to be ecstatic. He wasn't, warning in a letter to *The New York Times,* "The Oregon law, which forbids injections, could be disastrous. . . . Evidence I have accumulated shows that about 25 percent of assisted suicides fail. . . . The new Oregon way to die will work only if in every instance a doctor is standing by to administer the coup de grace, if necessary."[4]

Derek Humphry's newfound doubts about Measure 16 were not disclosed during the campaign for its passage. Not once did Humphry, an Oregon resident, warn his fellow citizens, as he would later in his letter to *The New York Times,* that "the only two 100 percent [effective] ways [of] accelerating dying are the lethal injection of barbiturates and curare or donning a plastic bag."[5] Rather, during the campaign Humphry professed great enthusiasm for the proposal, writing in a fund-raising letter on behalf of the initiative, "A break-through in Oregon will start a domino effect of law reform on assisted dying throughout America."

And so it came to pass. Euthanasia proponents received that break-through, albeit with a bare 51 percent of the Oregon vote, and nothing has been the same since.

The passage of Measure 16 illustrates the new step-by-step approach that euthanasia advocates have decided to take to promote their agenda: Take a half step back in order to propel the euthanasia cause two steps forward. Accordingly, Measure 16 was written in minimalist terms, the wording changed to make it appear less threatening and radical than had Initiative 119 and Proposition 161.

This was a pragmatic decision. Despite the death culture's recent successes, the prospect of doctors actively killing people remains a daunting idea. For example, in the same year that Oregonians would be voting on Measure 16, the Kevorkian gang in Michigan was unable to gather enough signatures to qualify an initiative to legalize euthanasia for that state's ballot—despite a very public and well-publicized petition drive seeking support. Even though what death fundamentalists really want is to legalize active euthanasia for the hopelessly ill, by restricting this proposal to assisted suicide for the terminally ill Measure 16's creators hoped they could finally obtain their longed-for foot-in-the-door breakthrough. Thus, for the same reason that Humphry didn't share with Oregon voters his belief that Measure 16 would be a disaster, backers also didn't tell Oregonians what a lawyer arguing on behalf of the newly enacted law later told U.S. District Court Judge Michael R. Hogan: that they viewed Measure 16 as merely a "first step."[6]

The Political Campaign

Both sides in the debate over legalizing euthanasia entered the Measure 16 campaign with reason for optimism. Opponents, buoyed by the victories in Washington and California, believed that an appropriately hard-hitting campaign would convince the people of Oregon to reject physician-induced death. Proponents, for their part, believed that the measure's minimizing text had sufficiently weakened the potent "abuse" issue, which had so damaged their cause in California and Washington. Besides, initial polls showed support for the initiative in the high 60 percent range.

The "Yes on 16" campaign led by Oregon Right to Die wasted no time getting out their emotion-driven appeal. Their poster woman was a nurse named Patty A. Rosen, head of the Bend, Oregon, chapter of the Hemlock Society. Rosen claimed in commercials to have helped her daughter, who she said was dying of bone cancer, kill herself some years before. In the ads she labeled herself a "criminal" because she had obtained the pills for her pain-racked daughter to take, and asserted that she had done so because her daughter "couldn't bear to be touched." Her voice cracking with emotion, Rosen recounted, "As she slipped peacefully away, I climbed into her bed and I took her in my arms for the first time in months. . . ." It was a poignant, touching bit of advocacy that left few viewers unmoved and fewer still thinking about the vital issues of the campaign, such as the potential for abuses; societal consequences; the availability and underutilization of compassionate caregiving opportunities like effective pain control (effective even for bone cancer when properly applied); and the issues of whether doctor-induced death would really reduce human suffering—not to mention where passage of the law might lead next.

Emotionalism and fear mongering about suffering and death were not the only tactics of Measure 16's proponents. There was also an unsubtle appeal to Oregon voter's reputed parochialism, mixed in with Catholic bashing. The Catholic church was very closely associated with the "No on 16" campaign, as it had been with the campaigns to defeat Initiative 119 and Proposition 161. Catholics provided significant funds to the "No on 16" campaign, and clerical collar–wearing church representatives were often selected by the media to express anti–Measure 16 sentiments. Soon, as had occurred in the Netherlands more than twenty years before, a false premise was created that Measure 16 was a battle between rigid religionists and compassionate rationalists.

In furtherance of this strategy, the "Yes on 16" campaign created ads that smelled of anti-Catholic bigotry. One ad asked, "Are we going to let one church make the rules for all of us?" A notable pro–Measure 16 radio commercial was more specific in its anti-Catholic appeal:

> *Who do you politicians and religious leaders think you are, trying to control my life? It's none of your business, so back off and back off now. I'm voting yes on 16 because what we have are some politicians and religious leaders who are playing politics all getting together to control my life. Listen, if I'm terminally ill, I don't want my family to be forced to drain their savings for unnecessary costly medical care while I suffer just because the politicians and religious leaders say that's the way it has to be. And don't buy the garbage the Catholic Church is putting out. The safeguards in 16 are as long as your arm. Multiple medical opinions, two oral requests and a written request that can be canceled at any time, a fifteen-day waiting period and another forty-eight-hour waiting period. You know, there are just some people who believe they have a divine right to control other people's lives, and they'd better back off because it's none of their business. Vote yes on 16.*[7]

Another ad complained that Catholic money was financing the opposition:

> *Their opposition is theological. They believe suffering is redemptive and that preserving physical life is always valued higher than relief of suffering, no matter how humiliating and intolerable that physical life is. And they apply that standard not only to themselves but to every Oregonian. They want to impose their unique theological perspective on the entire state.*[8]

It wasn't true, of course. Opponents of Measure 16 were not asserting that people have a duty to suffer. Nor were they seeking to impose some religious hegemony on the people of Oregon. But that didn't matter. If recent American political history proves anything, it is that negative ads work.

In contrast to the proponents' hardball, pull-out-all-the-stops advocacy, the opposition forces, under the umbrella of the Coalition for Compassionate Care (C.C.C.), took more of a Wiffle-ball approach to the campaign. The C.C.C. ran a fine commercial of a woman who had been misdiagnosed as being terminal within six months, warned of mistakes if Measure 16 passed, and financed rebuttals to the false assertion propounded by the "Yes on 16" crowd that only the Catholic church opposed the initiative. But the campaign did not go for the emotional jugular vein, as had opponents of Washington's Initiative 119 and California's Proposition 161. In California, for example, the political consultancy firm of Cavalier and Associates had created an award-winning television ad depicting a Kevorkian-esque doctor entering an elderly woman's room carrying a euthanasia syringe with which to kill her. That ad had resonated with voters, causing support for Proposition 161 to drop like a crowbar thrown off a bridge. But no similar advertisements were run in Oregon against Measure 16. Consequently, although support for Measure 16 dropped nearly 20 percent from original poll numbers, the C.C.C. was never able to drive support for the measure below the crucial 50 percent mark.

Critics contend this go-soft approach was a form of unilateral political disarmament leading directly to the measure's narrow passage. One experienced political strategist (who asked to remain anonymous) who has run many initiative campaigns and who watched the Measure 16 campaign closely is convinced that the initiative could have been defeated. "For whatever reasons, the opposition campaign decided to softball their campaign," this strategist says. "They simply chose not to use their most potent arguments, even though history proves that these arguments work."[9]

Perhaps the most vocal critic of the "No on 16" campaign is Rita Marker, executive director of the International Anti-Euthanasia Task Force, a nonprofit group dedicated to educating the public on issues related to the euthanasia debate. Marker, one of the world's preeminent experts on the subject, has spent nearly fifteen years researching and writing about euthanasia issues in the United States and internationally. She remains unhappy that the opposition to Measure 16 was so ineffective. "When someone takes on the responsibility of defeating a measure and says, 'I will lead and I will direct all that needs to be done,' they had better do it and do it well," she says. "Unfortunately, the opposition took on the responsibility and then engaged in political pacifism. [For] the leader of the campaign, that was irresponsible. For all appearances, it seemed they were more concerned with being nice to political opponents rather than protecting the lives of those who will be victimized by this law."[10]

This lack of aggressiveness is perhaps best illustrated by a crucial lapse during the critical last week of the campaign. Information surfaced that Patty Rosen had been, to put it kindly, less than candid about the death of her daughter in her commercials in support of Measure 16. In these ads, Rosen stated that her daughter had died from taking an overdose of pills. But a tape recording and transcript of a Rosen speech made in California two years previously on behalf of Proposition 161 revealed that she had actually given her daughter an injection because she feared the pills were not going to work.

Here was an opportunity rarely found in campaigns of this sort. Measure 16 proponents assured voters that passage of the measure would benefit the dying. Yet the poster woman for the campaign had stated earlier that she feared pills alone would not be sufficient to kill her dying daughter. If Patty Rosen's credibility could legitimately be questioned in the minds of voters (she admitted in a newspaper article that she had given her daughter an injection), then so could the veracity of all the arguments supporting Measure 16.

But no attempt was made to exploit Rosen's yawning credibility gap, even though the opposition campaign was well aware of her deception and still had money in the bank. As the opposition campaign limped to its conclusion, little mention was made of Rosen's lack of candor, which was discussed during the campaign only in a few low-key, inside-page newspaper stories.

In the end, it was a tragic matter of "so close, yet so far." Support for Measure 16 plummeted, as had support of Initiative 119 and Proposition 161—but not quite far enough. A bare 5 percent of Oregon's voters formally gave a state's formal imprimatur to physician-assisted suicide, for the first time in history.

The Nuts and Bolts of Measure 16

Measure 16, formally called the Oregon Death with Dignity Act, classifies a prescribed fatal overdose of drugs as a medical treatment. It authorizes patients who have been "determined by the attending physician and consulting physician to be suffering from a terminal disease" to make a written request for "medication for the purpose of ending his or her life."[11]

The following "safeguards" have been written into the act:

THE ATTENDING PHYSICIAN SHALL

1. MAKE THE INITIAL DETERMINATION OF WHETHER A PATIENT HAS A TERMINAL DISEASE, IS CAPABLE, AND HAS MADE THE REQUEST VOLUNTARILY

2. INFORM THE PATIENT OF

   a. His or her medical diagnosis
   b. His or her prognosis
   c. The potential risks associated with taking medication to be prescribed

    d. The probable result of taking the medication to be prescribed

    e. The feasible alternatives, including, but not limited to, comfort care, hospice care, and pain control

3. REFER THE PATIENT TO A CONSULTING PHYSICIAN FOR MEDICAL CONFIRMATION ... AND FOR A DETERMINATION THAT THE PATIENT IS CAPABLE AND ACTING VOLUNTARILY

4. REFER THE PATIENT FOR COUNSELING, IF APPROPRIATE [COUNSELING IS REQUIRED ONLY IF DEPRESSION OR ANOTHER MENTAL CONDITION CAUSES "IMPAIRED JUDGMENT"][12]

5. REQUEST THAT THE PATIENT NOTIFY NEXT OF KIN

6. INFORM THE PATIENT THAT HE OR SHE HAS THE OPPORTUNITY TO RESCIND THE REQUEST AT ANY TIME ... AND OFFER THE PATIENT AN OPPORTUNITY TO RESCIND AT THE END OF THE 15-DAY WAITING PERIOD ...

7. VERIFY, IMMEDIATELY PRIOR TO WRITING THE PRESCRIPTION ... THAT THE PATIENT IS MAKING AN INFORMED DECISION

8. FULFILL THE MEDICAL RECORD DOCUMENTATION REQUIREMENTS ...

9. ENSURE THAT ALL APPROPRIATE STEPS ARE CARRIED OUT IN ACCORDANCE WITH THIS ACT ...

The law also requires a waiting period of fifteen days between the initial request "and the writing of a prescription."[13]

Assuming the law goes into effect (it is currently tied up in the courts), the lives of people who have been diagnosed as dying, whether or not the diagnosis and prognosis is accurate, will have been removed from the parameter of state protection. This is a radical step fraught with danger or, as *The* (Portland) *Oregonian* put it, "sick—deadly sick."[14]

As for the so-called safeguards, such as they are, they consist mostly of smoke and mirrors. Measure 16 proponents insist that the only people eligible for doctor-hastened death are people at or near the brink of death. This is not true. The law defines terminal illness as "an incurable and irreversible disease that ... will, within reasonable medical judgment, produce death within six months."[15] The measure thus assumes that doctors who diagnose a terminal condition can be accurate in predicting the expected time of death. But that is just plain wrong. Many people who have been told they were going to die within months have lived for years. Indeed, some "terminally ill" people never die of the diagnosed disease at all. As an Oregon hospice doctor, Gary L. Lee, put it, "The 'six months to live' provision is bogus. Doctors usually can't predict the time of death in that fashion. I have had the experience where people were supposed to die, and didn't. I have seen cases where cancer suddenly cleared up for no apparent reason. You never know who is going to die. You just never know."[16]

Ira Byock, president of the American Academy of Hospice and Palliative Medicine, agrees, stating, "No one's life is over simply because a terminal prognosis has been given. There are people who don't die. Some people enter a hospice because of a terminal diagnosis, stabilize, and leave the hospice. Some live far longer than anyone ever anticipated. I had a patient who wanted to commit suicide because of the prognosis that he would soon die. Not only didn't he kill himself, he didn't die."[17]

Even Oregon doctors worry that they will be unable to accurately diagnose terminal illness in which death will occur within six months. A post–Measure 16 poll, conducted by the Oregon Medical Association, found that 50 percent of responding doctors "aren't confident they could predict that a patient had less than six months to live."[18]

In another telling lapse in the initiative's language, there is nothing in the definition of terminal illness requiring that the expected death will occur "despite appropriate medical treatment" or other such language, so as to weed out people who will be unlikely to die if they receive proper medical care. The clinical psychologist and disability rights activist Carol Gill, who specializes in issues of persons with disabilities, pain, and/or chronic illness, notes, "I am very concerned about the risks Measure 16 presents to people with disabilities or chronic progressive diseases. Countless such people would die without medical treatment that manages their conditions through medication, ventilation, nutritional support, or other medical treatment. Yet, with proper care, they can often live a full life expectancy. But, under Measure 16, these could be considered terminally ill."[19]

The journalist and poet Mark O'Brien, a quadriplegic who lives in an iron lung because of polio he contracted while very young, shares Gill's concerns. Writing about Measure 16's definition of terminal illness, O'Brien stated, "Without medical intervention in the form of my iron lung, I would die within six hours. Without medical intervention in the form of insulin, my sister, a diabetic, would die within six days."[20] O'Brien also sensed that the omission was not accidental but based on "the emotional needs of able-bodied people," which he sees as "often guiding policy decisions about disabled people." He writes, "I have long sensed the discomfort that people—including in the medical profession—feel at seeing me. I can almost hear them thinking, 'Get rid of these people, I don't care how, just get them out of my sight.' "[21]

There is little doubt that Gill's and O'Brien's fears are reasonable. The definition of terminal disease in Measure 16 takes the law almost all the way to the "hopelessly ill" category for authorizing hastened death. This is surely not an oversight. Remember, Measure 16 is a first step, designed as a bridge to all-out euthanasia. The law was coauthored by two lawyers, Cheryl K. Smith and Barbara Coombs Lee. The proposal was also gone over with a fine-tooth comb by pro-euthanasia types such as Derek Humphry, and "every element of the initiative was well debated" before being finalized. Reportedly there were nine different drafts.[22] It simply defies credulity to believe that such an obvious omission in the law's wording was an accident.

Worries about doctors killing patients are assuaged in Measure 16 with the blithe assurance that under the law doctors can't do the deed; that patients have to kill themselves. Yet nowhere in the initiative is there a stated requirement for self-administration of a lethal dose or, indeed, a prohibition against a physician's administering a lethal dose. The law merely says that such action is not specifically authorized by the law.

Proponents also assure that depressed people will not be helped to die under Measure 16 because doctors are supposed to refer those they believe to be depressed for "counseling." Yet the medical literature makes it clear that most doctors are not adept at identifying depression in their dying patients.[23] That means that many depressed people will slip through the Oregon suicide machinery without referral to a mental health professional.

But suppose a doctor believes a suicidal patient is depressed and refers him or her to counseling. Even that "safeguard" is more mirage than substance, given Measure 16's definition of counseling:

> Counseling means a consultation between a state licensed psychiatrist or psychologist and a patient for the purpose of determining whether the patient is suffering from a psychiatric or psychological disorder, or depression causing impaired judgment.[24]

Nowhere does the law mandate a formal psychiatric evaluation of the type required to accurately diagnose depression. Even if depression is diagnosed, there is no requirement that it be treated. Moreover, since depressed patients are not prevented from killing themselves, so long as they do not have "impaired judgment"—at best a vague and undefined legal term—assisted suicides of depressed people are very likely to take place should Measure 16 ever go into effect.

There's more. Incompetent patients might be allowed to receive a lethal dose of drugs under the act, since the doctor need only determine that the patient is "capable" before assisting in a suicide, not that a patient is "competent." This is a crucial distinction. Under the act, every person is capable who is not "incapable," defined as lacking "the ability to make and communicate health care decisions." Thus the ability to communicate decisions replaces the necessity of being competent to make decisions. Besides, depression is a mood disorder, not a thought disorder. Depressed people know they are not Napoleon or Cleopatra. They know that 2 plus 2 equals 4. But because they are depressed, they are likely to make self-destructive decisions—decisions that they can justify with apparent rationality but that they would not make were they free of depression.

Measure 16's consulting-physician protection is a joke. To be a consulting physician, a doctor need only be "qualified by specialty or experience in making a professional diagnosis and prognosis of the patient's disease."[25] That's no different from requiring that the consulting doctor be licensed, since the fact of licensure, by definition, means that the doctor is "qualified to make a professional diagnosis." (That is why it is legal for ob-gyns, for example, to perform plastic surgery, often with regrettable results.) Thus, a Kevorkian-type doctor who possesses few skills and little up-to-date training could make a specialty out of rubber-stamp death consultations. And as for being an attending physician, any doctor obtains that status as soon as a patient or surrogate decision maker asks him or her to become the patient's primary doctor. Thus, under Measure 16, a doctor with only a brief and superficial relationship with the patient could prescribe the deadly dose.

With so much missing from Measure 16's guidelines, they can hardly be called strict. Nor do they protect. What they do, as all euthanasia guidelines are intended to do, is falsely assure.

The Court Case

Shortly after Measure 16 passed, Dr. Gary Lee, among others, filed suit against the law. Dr. Lee participated in the lawsuit not out of a desire to control other people's "choices" but to protect the integrity of the patient-physician relationship. He explained why he was willing to put up with the inconvenience and anxiety of being part of a high-profile lawsuit:

> *I am convinced that this [Measure 16] is a bad bill, a dangerous bill, both for doctors and patients. It could affect the way I practice medi-*

cine and interfere with the way I interact with patients. Palliative care [hospice, pain control] requires nuance and a dedication to never giving up. Sometimes it can be very time-consuming. For example, if a palliative doctor gets stuck over a particularly intractable problem, we will solve it. It may take hours of research and calling around the country to see if a colleague has overcome the same problem before the solution is found, but we will solve it. I can see where legalized assisted suicide would push our value system away from such intense efforts and toward simple solutions to many of the patient problems we deal with. Then think about the docs who aren't experts in this area and only have one or two ideas about what to do about pain and suffering. . . . In that sense, I believe assisted suicide could eventually take the place of appropriate patient care.[26]

The lawsuit brought against Measure 16 by Dr. Lee and others, including a man dying of AIDS and a diabetic, was based on the belief that "Oregon's new assisted suicide law rests on a judgment that the lives of terminally ill and disabled patients are less deserving of protection than others."[27] The plaintiffs contended that the law "violates the constitutional guarantees to terminally ill and disabled individuals of equal protection of the law and due process with regard to the right of an individual to life."[28]

So far the lawsuit has been successful. United States District Court Judge Michael Hogan ruled that Measure 16 is unconstitutional, because the law creates a two-tiered system of justice. In his decision he wrote:

Measure 16 singles out terminally ill persons who want to commit suicide and excludes them from protection of Oregon laws that apply to others. Residents of Oregon are entitled to protection from committing suicide if found to be a danger to themselves, and after evaluation by a psychiatrist or other state certified mental health specialist. . . . Under Measure 16, the very lives of terminally ill persons depend on their own rational assessment of the value of their existence, and yet, there is no requirement that they be evaluated by a mental health specialist.[29]

Judge Hogan noted that doctors must treat their patients with medical competency but that Measure 16 established a lower standard of care for the terminally ill:

*Treating physicians may not be sufficiently qualified alone to eval-
uate mental impairments for the general public, but are given the significant role of deciding whether their patient may be suffering from a
"psychiatric or psychological disorder or depression causing impaired
judgment."... Contrary to the physicians "reasonable" standard of
care [the minimum level of competence required of physicians] for
other patients, under Measure 16 there is no bar to a physician acting
negligently [in assisting suicides].*[30]

Judge Hogan also believed that the law left the terminally ill open to coercion, exploitation, and victimization after the time the lethal prescription
is filled by the patient, ruling:

*Measure 16 abandons the terminally ill person at the time the
physician provides a lethal prescription. It fails to even acknowledge
the most critical time, that of death. It provides a means to commit
suicide to people who may be competent, incompetent, unduly influenced, and/or abused at the time of death. There is no distinction.*[31]

Judge Hogan ruled that Measure 16 violated the United States Constitution and issued an injunction against its enforcement, stating that Mea
sure 16's "safeguards are inadequate to bar incompetent, depressed but
treatable, judgment-impaired, or unduly influenced terminally ill patients from committing suicide."[32] In reaction, Derek Humphry, who
himself had labeled Measure 16 "disastrous" in a letter published in *The
New York Times* shortly after its passage, grumped that "the Oregon law
is as sound as any law in the world."[33] As this is written, Judge Hogan's
decision is being appealed in the U.S. Court of Appeals for the Ninth
Circuit.

Whether or not Measure 16 ever goes into effect is almost beside the
point. The initiative was designed as a way station on the road to general
acceptance of active euthanasia of the dying, the chronically ill, the elderly,
the disabled, and other vulnerable people. In this it has already succeeded,
causing shock waves and repercussions around the world. Anti-euthanasia
activists in Britain, Australia, and Canada have reported that Measure 16's
passage has reenergized euthanasia enthusiasts in those nations, leading to
the introduction of new legalization proposals in national parliaments
and/or regional governmental bodies. (Australia's Northern Territory
even passed an active euthanasia law, which as of this writing has been

used by three people to end their lives, but is now threatened in the national parliament and by lawsuits.)

Similarly, in this country the passage of Measure 16 spawned an energetic burst of death legislation throughout the country. From California to New Hampshire, advocates for euthanasia have sought to pass statutes legalizing physician-assisted suicide and/or euthanasia. Though few of these efforts even made it out of committee, as of this writing—and little noted in the media—three states have outlawed assisted suicide since Measure 16's passage: Louisiana, Rhode Island, and Iowa. Clearly it is not too late to reverse the trend.

Making Up Rights as They Go Along

State ballot initiatives and attempts to pass new legislation are only one part of a two-pronged strategy to legalize euthanasia. The second area of conflict is in America's courtrooms. Two major federal cases have been filed: *Compassion in Dying v. The State of Washington* and *Quill v. Dennis C. Vacco* in New York. (Dennis C. Vacco is the New York State attorney general.) While these initial cases deal primarily with the terminally ill, the attorney who filed both cases, Kathryn Tucker of the Seattle law firm Perkins Coie, readily admits that if she succeeds in making assisted suicide a legal right, she intends to represent litigants who test the limits of the law. Seen in this light, these early court cases, like Measure 16 in the political arena, are "first steps" down the slippery slope toward death on demand.

Compassion in Dying v. The State of Washington

The small group Compassion in Dying is an offshoot of the Hemlock Society, whose members "counsel" dying people who are contemplating suicide and help them carry it out. The group acts underground in order to avoid legal trouble, although it is not in the least shy about garnering sympathetic media publicity about its activities, such as Lisa Belkin's *New York Times Magazine* article "There's No Such Thing as a Simple Suicide," discussed in Chapter 1.

In 1994, Compassion in Dying joined with three dying patients and five physicians to challenge Washington's law banning assisted suicide. They won in the trial court but then lost in the U.S. Court of Appeals for the Ninth Circuit, where a three-judge panel ruled that Washington's law was constitutional. The matter was then reheard by an eleven-judge court (known as an en banc, or full-court, panel), which by an 8–3 decision over-ruled the three-judge panel and found that Washington's law against as-sisted suicide as it applied to the terminally ill was unconstitutional. The decision was written by Stephen Reinhardt, sometimes described as an "unreconstructed liberal," a "jurisprudential dinosaur" who is probably the most overturned judge on the most overturned federal court.[34] Judge Reinhardt's opinion quickly dismissed his court's obligation to apply the law as written and to depend on previous rulings:

> [W]e must strive to resist the natural judicial impulse to limit our vision to that which can plainly be observed on the face of the document before us, or even that which we have previously had the wisdom to recognize.[35]

Thus freeing themselves of the usual constraints that serve to limit the scope of judicial rulings, Judge Reinhardt and seven of his colleagues in ef-fect declared themselves licensed to create new constitutional rights from whole cloth.[36] The wording of the United States Constitution, the binding nature of judicial precedent, and even the vote of the people of Washing-ton only five years earlier that they did not want to legalize hastened death in their state carried little weight with Reinhardt and the judges who ruled with him.

The *Compassion in Dying* case relies on opinion polls for justification; it blurs sensitive and vital distinctions; and the opinion is rife with factual error. For example, the eleven-judge panel found:

> Unlike the depressed twenty-one-year-old, the romantically devas-tated twenty-eight-year-old, the alcoholic forty-year-old . . . who may be inclined to commit suicide, a terminally ill, competent adult can-not be cured.[37]

Yet, as noted earlier, "No clear definition of terminal illness is medically or legally possible, since only in hindsight is it known with certainty when someone is going to die."[38]

Judge Reinhardt also wrote:

> While some people who contemplate suicide can be restored to a state of physical and mental well-being, terminally ill adults who wish

to die can only be maintained in a debilitated and deteriorating state, unable to enjoy the presence of family or friends.[39]

There are many experts who disagree with this despairing view of the process of dying. Dr. Ira Byock, a hospice physician with extensive experience in these matters, says:

> *Every life-stage has value, including the time of dying. Obviously, it can be wrenching and require an abrupt adjustment, but over time, if treated with respect, compassion and expertise, dying people often achieve a sense of mastery. It is an arduous time but a very personal and extraordinary time. It should not be dismissed as unimportant or not worth living.*[40]

Perhaps the reason the appeals court was factually in error was that the original trial judge never held a fact-finding trial in the *Compassion in Dying* case, ruling instead on summary judgment that the law was unconstitutional as a matter of law. Judge Hogan, on the other hand, ruling on Measure 16 in Oregon, held a full trial before deciding against the measure. Since there was no trial in this case, little evidence was presented to serve as a factual basis for the decision making of the trial or the appeals court.

Factual inaccuracies are a minor problem compared to the rest of Judge Reinhardt's decision. Officially, the *Compassion in Dying* case stands on the proposition that there is a fundamental liberty interest in the United States Constitution in allowing citizens a "right to die." Unlike other constitutional rights, however, this "liberty interest" is not enjoyed by all people. Judge Reinhardt appears to create a sliding scale, in which he contends that while the state has a strong interest in protecting the life of the "young and healthy" and can prevent such a person's suicide, it does not have much interest at all in protecting the lives of people who are diagnosed as terminally ill.[41] So long as the dying are not coerced into choosing death and are mentally competent (extremely questionable propositions), they have an almost absolute right to choose to be assisted in their suicide by a doctor.

Judge Reinhardt has an unusual view of the state's obligation toward its citizens. The state isn't protecting lives by prohibiting assisted suicide, according to Judge Reinhardt. Rather, it is "forcing" people to stay alive. The state may engage in this totalitarianism against the young and healthy because "forcing a robust individual to continue living does not, at least absent extraordinary circumstances, subject him to 'pain . . . and suffering that is too intimate and personal for the state to insist on.' "[42] Note that if "extraordinary circumstances" exist, perhaps even young, healthy lives would not be protected. But if "suffering" is the primary issue, rather than the equal inherent worth of each individual, if it is somehow "wrong" for the state to "force" suffering people to stay alive, Reinhardt's decision could be interpreted to permit members of an oppressed minority to petition for suicide assistance because they could no longer stand to live as victims of perpetual injustice. To be logically consistent, the court would have to permit the killing if the minority member demonstrated sufficient anguish that was "too intimate and personal for the state to insist on."

Judge Reinhardt's decision also specifically opens the door for the hastened deaths of the disabled:

> *There are . . . subtle concerns . . . advanced by some representatives of the physically impaired, including the fear that certain physical disabilities will erroneously be deemed to make life "valueless." While we recognize the legitimacy of these concerns, however, we also recognize that seriously impaired individuals will, along with nonimpaired individuals, be the beneficiaries of the liberty interest asserted here—and that if they are not afforded the option to control their own fate, they like many others will be compelled against their will to endure protracted suffering.*[43]

Judge Reinhardt also legitimizes money worries as a reason for seeking medicalized suicide:

> *While state regulations can help ensure that patients do not make uninformed, or ill considered decisions, we are reluctant to say that, in a society in which the costs of protracted health care can be so exorbitant, it is improper for competent, terminally ill adults to take the economic welfare of their families and loved ones into consideration.*[44]

Judge Reinhardt's decision went even further, however, endorsing nonvoluntary killings of the incompetent—which by definition includes children, who generally are not allowed to make their own health-care decisions—people who want to die because they receive inadequate access to health care, and even outright euthanasia:

We should make it clear that a decision of a duly appointed surrogate decision maker, is for all legal purposes the decision of the patient himself.[45]

One of the prime arguments [in favor of laws prohibiting assisted suicide] is that the statute is necessary to protect the poor and minorities from exploitation. . . . In fact, . . . there is far more reason to raise the opposite concern: the concern that the poor and the minorities, who have historically received the least adequate health care, will not be afforded a fair opportunity to obtain the medical assistance [with suicide] to which they are entitled. . . .[46]

We agree that it may be difficult to make a principled distinction between physician-assisted suicide and the provision to terminally ill patients of other forms of life-ending medical assistance, such as the administration of drugs by a physician . . . or a person acting under his direction or control.[47]

Judge Reinhardt's opinion was so extreme that some of his colleagues took the extraordinary step of trying to have all twenty-four active judges of the U.S. Court of Appeals for the Ninth Circuit rehear the case. When that failed, several justices filed dissents, which, among other criticisms, complained that Judge Reinhardt and his cohorts nullified "the public will" of Washington's voters, who had voted not to allow assisted suicide in 1991. One judge, Diarmuid F. O'Scannlain, labeled the decision "embarrassing judicial excess" and a "shockingly broad act of judicial legislation."[48]

Quill v. Dennis C. Vacco

In the weeks following the Ninth Circuit's en banc decision in *Compassion in Dying,* the U.S. Court of Appeals for the Second Circuit, whose jurisdiction includes New York State, also ruled on the constitutionality of state laws that prohibit assisted suicide. The lawsuit had been filed by Dr. Timothy Quill, one of the nation's foremost euthanasia proponents, along with other physicians and terminally ill patients. The suit sought a ruling to declare unconstitutional New York's law, over a hundred years old, prohibiting assisted suicide. The trial court had dismissed Dr. Quill's suit as without merit. But the matter was appealed to a three-judge panel of the U.S. Court of Appeals for the Second Circuit.

The Second Circuit explicitly repudiated the Ninth Circuit's en banc decision by specifically ruling that assisted suicide is *not* a fundamental liberty interest founded in the United States Constitution. Rather, according to the court:

[T]he right [to assisted suicide,] considered here, cannot be consid-
ered so implicit in our understanding of ordered liberty that neither
justice nor liberty would exist if it were sacrificed. Nor can it be said
that the right to an assisted suicide claimed by plaintiffs is deeply
rooted in the nation's traditions and history. Indeed, the opposite is
true. Clearly, no "right" to assisted suicide ever has been recognized in
any state in the United States.[49]

Unfortunately, the judges found a different constitutional justification to permit legalized suicide: equal protection of the law.

The equal protection clause of the Fourteenth Amendment requires that similarly situated citizens must be treated alike under the law. Thus, requiring all six-year-old children to attend school treats similarly situated persons—six-year-old children—alike, whereas a law compelling six-year-old boys but not six-year-old girls to go to school would be to treat similarly situated persons differently, which would be an unconstitutional violation of the equal protection clause.

The Constitution does not require the law to treat matters that are not the same as if they were. Generally, the decision to decide what is a similar situation and what is not is up to lawmakers, requiring only that the distinctions made in law be "rationally related to a legitimate state interest."[50] In the example above, even though boys and girls are not exactly the same, the state would not be able to demonstrate a rational basis for allowing young girls and not young boys to stop attending school. But a law allowing seventeen-year-old minors to quit school would probably pass equal-protection muster, even though it treats some minors differently from others, the state having a rational basis for treating six-year-old minors and seventeen-year-old minors differently: Seventeen-year-olds can become emancipated, work legally, are close to adulthood, are more difficult to control, etc. In contrast, if a law restricts an activity deemed a fundamental liberty interest, such as freedom of speech (or in the Ninth Circuit's *Compassion in Dying* opinion, the right of an ill person to be killed by a doctor), the state can interfere with the activity only if it has a "compelling state interest," an extremely difficult legal standard to meet.

In the Quill case, the court decided:

- terminally ill patients who require life support and those who are dying but who do not require life support are similarly situated persons

- since it is legal for people to reject the medical treatment of life support, terminally ill people who are on life support and want to die can do so quickly by refusing such care

- terminally ill people who do not require life support are forced to stay alive, even if they want to die quickly, since rejecting treatment would not immediately accomplish that goal

- therefore, those who cannot die by refusing treatment should have the right to assisted suicide, to fulfill the requirement that the law treat them in a manner similar to their terminally ill counterparts who are on life support (in other words, by allowing patients to refuse life support, the state has created a right to die quickly that should apply to all terminally ill people)

- the state serves no rational interest in preventing the terminally ill from killing themselves, since their lives are all but over anyway

Thus, according to the court, since similarly situated people—i.e., the terminally ill—are being treated differently under the law, the assisted-suicide ban as applied to terminally ill people must fall before the equal protection clause.

Dying a natural death, which is what *may* happen if life support is terminated, is not the same thing as being killed. The former is by natural processes, while in the case of assisted suicide, the demise is intentionally induced by a death-causing agent. Moreover, when life-sustaining medical intervention is withheld or withdrawn from a patient, the result is uncertain. Death may or may not come. In an assisted suicide, however, the patient's death is inevitable. It will occur immediately following the injection or ingestion of the poisonous agent.

Here are just two illustrations:

A young woman named Karen Ann Quinlan overdosed on drugs and alcohol and became permanently unconscious. After several years, her parents sued Karen's hospital to compel her doctors to stop the unwanted medical treatment of machine-assisted breathing. Eventually, the New Jersey Supreme Court properly approved their request, and Karen was taken off the respirator.[51] But Karen didn't die. Indeed, she lived for ten years, finally succumbing to an infection.[52]

In the Ron Comeau case discussed in Chapter 2, when Comeau's respirator was cut off he too was expected to die. But he didn't—his condition began to improve. That was why the guardian decided to have him dehydrated!

The court of appeals decision in the Quill case also applies the wrong comparison. There is no analogy between a patient's right to refuse unwanted life-sustaining treatment and being killed by assisted suicide. It is freedom from *treatment,* not freedom from *life,* that has consistently served as the legal and ethical underpinning for the right to refuse medical treatment cases, from Karen Ann Quinlan to Nancy Cruzan to numerous others. This distinction is rational and vital. It protects people from unwanted physical intrusions. It does not, however, create a right to be killed with all of the dangers and potential for exploitation and abuse that such a right would entail.

Even if those dying who are on life support and those dying who are not on life support can be said to be similarly situated, there are abundant rational state interests served by the proscription against assisted suicide. Some of these were enunciated by Judge John T. Noonan, Jr., in the three-judge panel ruling in *Compassion in Dying* that upheld Washington's law prohibiting assisted suicide (subsequently overturned by the en banc ruling of the U.S. Court of Appeals for the Ninth Circuit).[53] Judge Noonan listed five rational state interests in Washington's law prohibiting assisted suicide:

- the interest in not having physicians in the role of killers of their patients

- the interest in not subjecting the elderly and even the not-elderly-but-infirm to psychological pressure to consent to their own deaths

- the interest in protecting the poor and minorities from exploitation (the poor would be especially open and vulnerable to manipulation in a regime of assisted suicide for two reasons: pain is a significant factor in creating a desire for assisted suicide, and the poor and minorities are notoriously less provided for in the alleviation of pain)

- the interest in protecting all of the handicapped from societal indifference and antipathy (an insidious bias against the handicapped— again coupled with a cost-saving mentality—makes them especially in need of Washington's statutory protection)

- an interest in preventing abuse similar to what has occurred in the Netherlands[54]

United States District Court Judge Thomas P. Griesa, in dismissing the Quill lawsuit at the trial court level, put it more succinctly:

> *It is hardly unreasonable or irrational for the state to recognize a difference between allowing nature to take its course . . . and inten-*

*tionally using an artificial death-producing device. The State has ob-
vious legitimate interests in preserving life, and in protecting vulnerable persons.*[55]

People of Michigan v. Jack Kevorkian

Although the media have paid more attention to the recent court rulings in
favor of assisted suicide, one major case has come down on the other side
of the issue. In 1991 the state of Michigan passed a law making it a crime
punishable by up to four years in prison to knowingly provide "the physical means" or participate "in a physical act" in the furtherance of another
person's suicide.[56] After Jack Kevorkian was arrested for breaking this law,
his lawyers sought to have the statute ruled unconstitutional. The case
wound its way through the lower courts, ending in the Michigan Supreme
Court, which ruled 5–2 that the law was constitutional.[57]

In reasoning directly contrary to that later adopted by U.S. circuit
courts of appeals rulings, the Michigan Supreme Court ruled that there is
a crucial difference between refusing life-sustaining medical treatment,
such as eschewing C.P.R. during cardiac arrest, and assisted suicide, "between choosing a natural death" and "deliberately seeking to terminate
one's life by resorting to death-inducing measures unrelated to the natural
process of dying."[58] In the former case, according to the court, "Nature [is
allowed] to proceed," whereas suicide "frustrates the natural course by introducing an outside agent to accelerate death."[59]

This commonsense distinction is easy to understand. If treatment is
stopped and the patient dies—which is not always the case—he or she dies
a natural death, from cancer, heart failure, pneumonia, etc. In assisted suicide or euthanasia, the patient is intentionally killed by means of an artificial cause of death, e.g., poison, a gunshot wound, carbon monoxide, etc.
Thus, in the court's words, "Persons who opt to discontinue life-sustaining
medical treatment [and who die as a result] are not, in effect, committing
suicide."[60]

The Michigan court cited the United States Supreme Court case
Planned Parenthood v. Casey,[61] which upheld a woman's right to abortion
first enunciated in *Roe v. Wade*[62] and which euthanasia advocates contend
opens the door for a "euthanasia *Roe.*" The Michigan Supreme Court
found that *Casey* did not dramatically "expand the liberty interests" identified by the reproductive cases (e.g., privacy, personal autonomy) into the
right to have death hastened. "In *Casey,*" the Michigan Supreme Court
ruled, "the [U.S. Supreme] Court was not directly concerned with the es-

tablishment of a new right, but rather with whether the Court should re-treat from the right previously recognized in *Roe v. Wade.*"[63] The Michigan court further noted that the primary point of *Casey* was to uphold the con-cept of *stare decisis* (precedent) and, moreover, that the U.S. Supreme Court emphasized in *Casey* that "abortion cases are unique."[64] The U.S. Court of Appeals for the Ninth Circuit subsequently ruled exactly the op-posite, but its decision would not have been binding on Michigan.

Rather than ruling that *Cruzan* created a right to die, the Michigan Supreme Court held that *Cruzan* actually affirmed the "sanctity of human life, and rejected the notion that there is a right of self-destruction in any . . . constitutional doctrine"[65] when it stated:

> As a general matter, the States—indeed, all civilized nations—
> demonstrate their commitment to life by treating homicide as a seri-
> ous crime. Moreover, the majority of States in this country have laws
> imposing criminal penalties on one who assists another to commit
> suicide.[66]

Thus, the Michigan Supreme Court concluded that "the right to commit suicide is neither implicit in the concept of ordered liberty nor deeply rooted in this nation's history or traditions," and that it would be "an im-permissible radical departure from existing tradition, and from the princi-ples that underlie that tradition, to declare that there is such a fundamental right protected by the due process clause.[67] (In contrast, the U.S. Court of Appeals for the Ninth Circuit claimed that *Cruzan* did create a "right to die.")

The Michigan Supreme Court not only found that there was no consti-tutional right to an assisted suicide, but also ruled that the Michigan statute prohibiting the crime met constitutional muster, and further, that Michigan common law (law based in judicial rulings rather than statutes) criminalized assisted suicide even in the absence of a statute.

After this rebuke by his state's highest court, Kevorkian petitioned the United States Supreme Court to hear the matter. The Court refused to take his appeal. Thus, in Michigan at least, laws against assisted suicide are deemed constitutional. Indeed, the Michigan Supreme Court ruled that the act is a common-law crime (the original statute has lapsed).

Three high courts—the Michigan Supreme Court, the U.S. Court of Appeals for the Ninth Circuit, and the U.S. Court of Appeals for the Second Circuit—

have all considered whether there is a constitutional right to assisted suicide, and all have come to different conclusions. The final answer to this controversial legal question will be decided by the United States Supreme Court. On October 1, 1996, the Court, which had refused Jack Kevorkian's request that it review the Michigan Supreme Court's ruling, agreed to review the decisions of both the Ninth and Second Circuit appeals courts. On January 8, 1997, oral arguments were heard in the Supreme Court; most of the justices appeared skeptical that there is a constitutional right to die. As this is written, the Court has not issued its decision.

Upcoming Euthanasia Legalization Proposals

As the courts wrangle over the constitutionality of existing laws prohibiting assisted suicide, pro-euthanasia advocates are working to create "model statutes" that they hope will be utilized by state legislatures in legalizing euthanasia or regulating it, should existing prohibitions ultimately be ruled unconstitutional. These proposals do not reflect the ultimate scope of the practice that will come into being. In a sense, like Measure 16, they are merely way stations, steps on a path leading us to death on demand. As proponents of one of the most discussed euthanasia proposals said about their efforts to draft a model law, "Anyone . . . [would be] eligible [for assisted suicide] whose illness is incurable and who subjectively feels that the accompanying suffering is worse than death."[68]

Most of these active proposals discard the terminal-illness limitation, embracing less restrictive categories of people who would be eligible for killing by physicians. Moreover, judging by the experience of the Netherlands, and considering the attitudes expressed by Judge Reinhardt in the *Compassion in Dying* case, were these proposals to become law, it would be no time at all before killing became accepted for the depressed and the incompetent, justified by poor quality of life (as is already happening in the food and fluids cases), in addition to the physically afflicted.

One such model statute recently created is "the Massachusetts Model," published in the *Harvard Journal on Legislation*. The proposal was written by committee and its terms were arrived at through a process of consensus. The proposed law would legalize physician-assisted suicide along the lines of Measure 16 for hopelessly ill people (but not the depressed) and for people who are dying. The following groups would be eligible for physician participation in their killing:

- patients eighteen or older

- patients who have a "terminal illness," defined as an illness that is likely to cause death within six months, or an "intractable and unbearable illness," which the model act defines as one which "cannot be cured or successfully palliated," and which "causes such severe suffering that a patient prefers death" (no proof of suffering would be required if the patient was diagnosed as terminal within six months)

- patients whose decision is not the result of a "distortion of the patient's judgment due to clinical depression or any other mental illness," and in whom the decision is a "reasoned choice," made "free of undue influence by any person" (that such determinations would take months or longer to truly ferret out is not addressed)[69]

The doctor who participates in the killing need not be the patient's primary physician. Indeed, the doctor who has assumed only "partial responsibility" for the patient can still help with the suicide. This leaves wide open the possibility of doctors developing practices based solely on providing death, doctors who may have no significant history with the patient or expertise in the particular malady of the patient. In other words, physicians such as Jack Kevorkian would be able to find a new lease on professional life.

Similar proposals have been made by Dr. Timothy E. Quill, the Rochester, New York, internist who was the plaintiff in *Quill v. Vacco.* Sometimes called "the respectable Kevorkian," Dr. Quill came to national attention when he wrote a piece for the *New England Journal of Medicine* in which he admitted to having assisted the suicide of a patient whom he calls Diane. According to Dr. Quill, Diane had a history of family and personal problems with alcoholism and depression. She had been cured of vaginal cancer years before. Immediately upon hearing a leukemia diagnosis, not wanting to face another serious illness, Diane refused treatment, despite having a 25 percent chance of long-term survival from the disease. Fearing suffering and anguish, Diane told Dr. Quill that she did not want to linger in relative comfort either.[70]

Dr. Quill readily accepted Diane's decision. Indeed, he reinforced it by referring her to the Hemlock Society for advice and support. Later, when Diane decided the time had come to die, Dr. Quill wrote a prescription for a lethal dose of pills because "she was sad and frightened to be leaving, but . . . even more terrified to stay and suffer."[71] After her suicide, Dr. Quill falsified her death certificate by claiming her death was caused by leukemia.

This sad tale rocketed Dr. Quill to star status among death fundamentalists and in the media. He has since written and lectured extensively concerning laws he hopes will legalize physician-assisted suicide. In some of these proposals Dr. Quill eliminates any requirement that the patient have a terminal illness, writing that those eligible for hastened deaths need only have "incurable" and "debilitating" conditions associated with "severe, unrelenting suffering," in other words, hopeless illness.[72] (Dr. Quill sometimes speaks out of both sides of his mouth on the issue of terminal illness. In more public forums, he has stated that assisted suicide should be restricted to the terminally ill. But he has written so extensively to the contrary that this assertion lacks credibility and appears to be a tactical decision designed to make assisted suicide more palatable to a doubting nation.[73] It is also important to realize that as used by Dr. Quill, the term *suffering* does not appear to be synonymous with *pain*. Suffering can include such difficulties as the fear of future suffering, loss of dignity, and other such completely subjective criteria.)

As to safeguards, Dr. Quill proposes that the patient's death request not be the "result of inadequate comfort care" and opines further that "all reasonable comfort measures must at least have been considered, and preferably tried" before assisted suicide is carried out.[74] He also suggests that the patient be required to request death repeatedly. The same requirement exists in the Netherlands, and we have seen that the repeated requests rather than the underlying condition can become the primary consideration. Dr. Quill also believes the physician must ensure that the patient's "judgment is not distorted," meaning only that the patient must "be capable of understanding the decision and its implications."[75] Since, as stated earlier, depression alters mood but does not inhibit thought processes, depressed people could easily qualify for killing, since they would be capable of understanding that their decision would result in death. Thus, this "safeguard" is essentially meaningless. Dr. Quill believes that physician-assisted suicide, which he also calls "controlled death," should be "carried out only in the context of a meaningful doctor-patient relationship."[76] Finally, there should be a consultation with another doctor to "ensure the patient's request is voluntary and rational."[77]

Note the false assumptions made by these euthanasia proponents. In their idealized death ideology, killing would take place only amid meaningfully deep relationships between noble and courageous patients who have tried everything else first, and doctors who are supercareful Marcus Welby clones, all based on mutual exploration and respect of the patient's values and a deeply held desire to alleviate suffering. Indeed, Dr. Quill has unequivocally declared, "In my opinion, physician assisted death only becomes a legitimate option in those infrequent circumstances when patients are suffering intolerably in spite of excellent hospice care."[78]

But this is a country in which 42 million citizens have no health insurance. It is a country where hospice care is underfunded and underpublicized. It is a country whose doctors are woefully undertrained and unskilled in treating pain and diagnosing depression. It is a country in which the health-care system itself is undergoing wrenching transformation, with for-profit H.M.O.s changing the face of medicine and driving a wedge between patients and doctors. Unfortunately, it is also a country known to discriminate against minorities, the disabled, and, increasingly, those with health problems. It is difficult to imagine that Dr. Quill and other euthanasia advocates believe that the conditions they say they require can easily be found in America's health-care system, still less that their proposals will contribute toward bringing such a system into being.

CHAPTER 6

Euthanasia's Betrayal of Medicine

Imagine a world where everyone receives optimum health care, regardless of financial means. Imagine a world where all seriously ill or disabled persons are surrounded by a loving and supportive community of family, friends, and professionals dedicated solely to their welfare. Imagine a world where family members are ever supportive and never pressure, intimidate, manipulate, or abandon their loved ones. Imagine a world where everyone has altruistic motives. Imagine a world where depression is immediately recognized and treated. Imagine a world where disabled people are universally valued and are provided the services they require for full participation in the community. Imagine a world where choices are made with due deliberation and rational analysis, where people do not act in haste and are free of duress, menace, coercion, or fraud.

Anyone who believes that such a world actually exists has gone to one too many Grateful Dead concerts. But don't tell that to death fundamentalists, because this is the environment in which they claim euthanasia would be practiced.

Read the words of Dr. Timothy Quill:

> *Assisting death either by direct or indirect methods, is not something to undertake without careful assessment of mental status and exploration of all alternatives. It is the path of last resort, taken only when hospice care stops providing comfort and dignity, and when there are no good options for regaining quality of life.*[12]

Read the words of Jack Kevorkian:

> *The medical profession must display the moral virility expected of that once noble calling by taking absolute control of its ethical prerogatives. The ideal doctor, armed with a good medical education and practical training . . . with strong character . . . with honesty and common sense . . . and with a completely free mind . . . can handle any medical challenge. . . . This can be true only if . . . the highest respect is given for the personal autonomy . . . of every patient. . . . Under those conditions of patients' autonomy coupled with medical competence and honesty, how could any overwhelming or insuperable bioethical problem arise?*[3]

The "death counselor" and pro–assisted suicide author Stephen Jamison, Ph.D., has written:

> *I believe it [hastened death] will be reserved for extraordinary cases that fail to respond to efforts at palliative care. Moreover, it should be provided in such a way that promotes an ideal of medical intervention that carefully looks at each case and balances a patient's suffering with the principles of beneficence, nonmaleficence, autonomy, and justice. . . . [A] team approach to implementation [would] ensure that a patient has received the best quality of pain management and comfort care available.*[4]

Lonny Shavelson, a photojournalist and emergency-room physician whose book, *A Chosen Death,* was discussed in Chapter 1, states:

> *Assisted suicide, active euthanasia, and even passive euthanasia should be available only to patients who have first had the fullest chance to control the suffering of dying by every possible means other than by bringing on their own death.*[5]

A Dysfunctional Health-Care Delivery System

What these and other euthanasia advocates ignore, or perhaps choose not to see, is that these fundamental conditions do not exist in our money-driven health-care system. They don't take into account the difficulties and stresses of family life, the vulnerability of people who are depressed or in pain to pressure and coercion, or, indeed, the reality of human nature as it too often relates to money issues such as inheritance or life insurance. Nor do they acknowledge that it is likely that some physicians, perhaps those with a bias in favor of assisted suicide, may become death doctors whose primary "practice" is to kill patients.

Death doctors would be very unlikely to have the kind of long-term patient-physician relationships that Dr. Timothy Quill and Stephen Jamison envision. Rather, they would more likely resemble Jack Kevorkian, not treating patients or seeking to relieve their suffering but just helping to kill them. If Kevorkian is any indication, the last thing a death doctor would want is a close relationship with the patient—after all, the "relationship" would be rather short-lived. When questions arose about his assisted killing of Judith Curren, a nonterminally ill Massachusetts woman alleged to have been depressed, addicted to drugs, and perhaps abused by her husband, Kevorkian was asked by an NBC reporter whether he should have had a more intimate relationship with his "patient" before helping her die. Kevorkian responded angrily, "Who says I have to have an intimate relationship with the patient [to assist in her suicide]? I'm a medical doctor. I can review records and see patients, and can examine them. Who says I have to learn what their family history is and who their children are and what they did fifty years ago? Who says that?"[6]

Ironically, legal assisted suicide and euthanasia are not only unlikely to be intimate but in fact are likely to cause more misery and suffering than they would alleviate. This was the conclusion of the twenty-five-member New York State Task Force on Life and the Law, a permanent commission created by Governor Mario Cuomo in 1985, which spent more than a year intensely investigating whether assisted suicide should be legalized. Despite having some members who supported assisted suicide and euthanasia in theory before beginning their investigation, the task force's recommendation was unanimous that killing should not be legalized.

The task force's report, *When Death Is Sought: Assisted Suicide and Euthanasia in the Medical Context,* is must-reading for anyone interested in the euthanasia debate.[7] A striking feature of the report is that it does not rely on abstract notions of religion, morality, or philosophy but rather on a pragmatic and practical realization:

> *In light of the pervasive failure of our health care system to treat pain and diagnose and treat depression, legalizing assisted suicide*

and euthanasia would be profoundly dangerous for r
als who are ill and vulnerable. The risks would be
those who are elderly, poor, socially disadvantaged, o
to good medical care.[8]

When Death Is Sought effectively punctures the idyllic picture of assisted suicide put forth by euthanasia advocates. According to the task force, the "good case," i.e., in which all "safeguards would be satisfied . . . bears little relation to prevalent social and medical practices."[9] In other words, despite their advocacy of high ideals, the world envisioned by euthanasia advocates simply doesn't exist—and will not exist in the foreseeable future.

Many social risks inherent in euthanasia were also cited by the task force as a reason not to legalize euthanasia, among them the following:

- Euthanasia would be practiced through the "prism of social inequality and bias that characterizes the delivery of services in all segments of our society, including health care."[10] In other words, racism, ageism, sexism, bigotry against disabled people, and issues of class and socioeconomic status would all materially affect killing decisions. The level of care, time, caution, personal attention, and gentility that would be accorded a Jackie Kennedy who requested hastened death versus a dishwasher without health insurance who requested hastened death would be as different as every other comparison that could be made between two such lives.

- "Most doctors do not have a long-standing relationship with their patients or information about the complex personal factors" that go into a request to be killed. Moreover, "neither treatment for pain nor diagnosis of and treatment for depression is widely available in clinical practice."[11] Yet untreated pain and depression are the primary reasons dying patients request physician-assisted suicide.

- "As long as the [killing] policies hinge on notions of pain and suffering, they are uncontainable,"[12] because "neither pain nor suffering can be gauged objectively, nor are they subject to the kind of judgments needed to fashion coherent public policy."[13] Legalized killing based on "unbearable suffering" cannot logically be limited to the dying and, if legalized, would soon be available to anyone who claimed to be in agony. As we saw in Chapter 4, this inexorable widening of killing categories has already occurred in the Netherlands.

Perhaps most important, the task force found that euthanasia and assisted suicide are unnecessary to relieve suffering. "Contrary to what many
believe," the task force noted, "the vast majority of individuals who are terminally ill or facing severe pain or disability are not suicidal. Moreover, terminally ill patients who do desire suicide or euthanasia often suffer from a
treatable mental disorder, most commonly depression. When these patients receive appropriate treatment for depression, they usually abandon
the wish to commit suicide."[14]

Indeed, the task force noted that techniques to control pain, treat depression, and provide support for patients and families already exist. The
problem isn't with whether these truly beneficent care opportunities
work; if properly applied, they do in nearly every case. Rather, society still
must overcome the "numerous barriers" that exist to their proper application, "including a lack of professional knowledge and training, unjusti-
fied fears about physical and psychological dependence, poor pain
assessment . . . and reluctance of patients and their families to seek pain
relief."[15] That will require dedicated effort and sustained energy, which
too often are diverted from these important tasks to the struggle over legalizing euthanasia.

The New York State Task Force is not alone in making these points.
When Dr. Timothy Quill began his assisted suicide crusade, his colleagues
at the University of Rochester Medical Center conducted a study of the
issue. After more than a year's investigation, which included significant
input by Dr. Quill, the University of Rochester Task Force unanimously
recommended against legalization, for reasons similar to those detailed by
the New York State Task Force, including the existence of "practical treatments and management techniques available at the present time which
should prove adequate for palliation of suffering in virtually all clinical situations."[16] The Rochester report also noted that doctors have done an insufficient job of treating dying and suffering patients and recommended
greater attention be paid to these vital care issues.

The conclusions of these studies are echoed by internal discussion
within the medical profession, which has finally come to realize its partial responsibility for the fear and anxiety over suffering at the end of life
felt by many of their patients, and the scandalous undertreatment of
pain and depression, major sources of the energy driving the euthanasia
movement.

For example, the *Journal of the American Medical Association* has
stated that "inadequate treatment of pain continues to be a problem de-

spite more knowledge about its causes and control and despite widespread efforts of governments and multiple medical and voluntary organizations to disseminate this knowledge. . . . All types of pain in all parts of the world are inadequately treated."[17] *American Medical News* editorialized, "Evidence suggests that there is a significant gap between the most effective pain treatment and what most patients actually get."[18] And the authors of a special report on pain control in the *New England Journal of Medicine* wrote, "Undertreatment of cancer pain is common because of clinicians' inadequate knowledge of effective assessment and management practices, negative attitudes of patients and clinicians toward the use of drugs for the relief of pain, and a variety of problems related to reimbursement for effective pain management."[19]

Likewise, the state of California has determined that the paucity of effective pain-control treatment is such a pervasive problem that it convened an official Summit on Effective Pain Management, in which more than 120 health-care practitioners, professional and public educators, representatives of professional schools, and health-care consumers met to identify problems and recommend solutions. The official report of the summit acknowledged that pain is significantly undertreated. Especially relevant to the question of class-based factors in euthanasia advocacy was the finding that pain is "more likely to be undertreated if the patient is minority, female, elderly, or a child."[20]

If doctors currently do such a poor job, generally, of relieving the pain and depression of suffering people when doctor-induced death is illegal, what kind of a job would they do if killing a patient were considered just another "treatment option," and a less expensive and time-consuming option at that? To put it another way, why would we trust doctors to kill us, when too often they don't do an adequate job of caring for us? With so many Americans uninsured, the "last resort" scenario is a virtual impossibility.

Financial Incentives in American Medicine

Money drives the American health-care system. Doctors' fees generally amount to hundreds of dollars an hour. One day in the hospital alone can cost well over a thousand dollars, and that doesn't include the "extras" for which hospitals also charge, such as intensive care, oxygen, bandages, and aspirin. Come down with a condition or injury that requires a few weeks of hospitalization followed by extended follow-up care and the tab will easily rise into six figures.

This money imperative, which has increased substantially in the vacuum following in the wake of President Bill Clinton's health-care reform fiasco, makes euthanasia even more dangerous here than it is in the Netherlands.

At last count, 42 million Americans had no health insurance, and this figure doesn't include tens of millions of other Americans who are temporarily uninsured at any given time.[21] As of 1994 approximately 14.2 percent of all American children—nearly 10 million—had no health insurance, whether private or public, up from 12.4 percent in 1992.[22]

Almost by definition, being uninsured means that one lacks sustained access to quality health-care services. Most doctors refuse to accept new patients who do not have health insurance, and most private hospitals will only help uninsured ill people when required to do so by law in a life-threatening emergency. Being uninsured means that health care, when it is received, is generally delivered in a public hospital emergency room, where, after hours of waiting, a harried doctor (often in training) will be assigned to deal as quickly and cheaply as possible with the problem. Those with chronic conditions often face similar barriers to effective care, relying on free clinics or emergency rooms where the lack of consistent treatment can cause complications requiring an expensive emergency response later.

With the near geometric growth of for-profit hospitals and health-care financing systems, even this meager measure of care for the uninsured poor is now actively threatened. With a health-care delivery system increasingly dominated by for-profit corporations, the delivery of charity health care traditionally made available by nonprofit religious or community hospitals may be endangered. According to Bruce Hilton, director of the National Center for Bioethics, a study in Florida indicated that for-profit hospitals, which make up more than half of that state's health-care institutions, only supply 8 percent of the state's charity care.[23]

In this context, euthanasia would be a potential form of oppression against the uninsured, the working poor, divorced persons, minorities, the unemployed, the mentally ill, and those lacking education who may not even speak English. For these people, the presumption that assisted suicide would be considered only after every other conceivable method of care has been tried is unlikely to apply. If euthanasia advocates really believed that doctor-hastened death should be performed only if there is no other way to alleviate suffering, they would put their issue on the shelf until the structural flaws in American medicine are solved. To do otherwise is putting the cart before the horse. Hospice, extended pain control, psychiatric treatment of depression—services essential to the "last resort" scenario—are usually inaccessible to the uninsured. Many who would want to live were they to receive proper care might out of desperation express a desire to die when they have difficulty obtaining it. Doctors might be tempted to follow the line of least resistance by going along with such desires or even recommending the "final treatment."

Such a scenario is not purely imaginary. In July 1996, Rebecca Badger, age thirty-nine, traveled from California to Michigan to become Jack Kevorkian's thirty-third known assisted-suicide victim. In a KEYT-TV (Santa Barbara) television interview taped only days before her death, Badger, who believed she had multiple sclerosis and who lost her private health insurance after a divorce forced her onto MediCal (California's Medicaid program), complained bitterly about five-hour hospital waits to see a doctor and explained that the reason she was going to Kevorkian was her constant, unrelieved pain. Badger also said that if her pain were only relieved, she would want to live.[24]

According to press reports, at least one doctor who cared for Rebecca, when contacted by a self-identified Kevorkian associate, did nothing to try to protect his patient but rather "presumed they [Kevorkian and associates] would talk her out of it."[25] The Kevorkian people either did not thoroughly investigate Badger's reasons for wanting to commit suicide or, if they did, didn't provide the pain relief she specifically said would change her desire to die into a will to live.

According to Badger's autopsy report, she did not have M.S. at all. Dr. Ljubisa J. Dragovic, a neuropathologist with specialized training as a pathologist in detecting neurological conditions and thus an expert in detecting M.S., performed Badger's autopsy. He told me, "Rebecca Badger had no sign of the disease. The findings are completely negative. The problem with M.S. is that a lot of conditions can simulate M.S. and M.S. can simulate a lot of conditions."[26]

What Badger did suffer from was diagnosed depression and abandonment by the health-care system. According to her daughter, Badger, a recovering alcoholic who was addicted to prescription medications, had lost faith in the medicine and believed that her maladies would never be taken seriously, leading to her fatal trip to Michigan.[27]

H.M.O.s and Euthanasia: A Deadly Combination

The uninsured aren't the only ones who are threatened by the commercialization of health care and the approach of legalized euthanasia. We all are.

It is no secret that health-care costs are skyrocketing. In 1996 alone it is expected that the total spent on health care, including research, will top $1 trillion, or approximately 14 percent of the nation's entire gross domestic product.[28] Controlling unnecessary medical costs and improving the efficiency of health-care delivery is both desirable and necessary. But cost cutting in the context of a medical system in which assisted suicide and euthanasia were legal would be a lethal threat to us all. Health-care financing is in the midst of a transition from traditional "fee-for-service" medicine, in which the health-care provider is paid a fee for each service performed, to a "managed-care" system, in which money is made by not providing services and by controlling costs in other ways. This turns the traditional presumptions about health-care financing and the delivery of medical services inside out.

The hottest trend in managed care is the for-profit health-maintenance organization. H.M.O.s have become so ubiquitous that by the turn of the century, approximately 50 percent of all health-insured Americans will be H.M.O. members.[29] So, too, will most public-health-care recipients, both Medicaid (the federal/state funded and state-administered health insurance for the poorest of the poor) and Medicare (the health insurance plan for the elderly and some disabled) recipients, who are increasingly pushed toward accepting care in H.M.O. settings. Thus, it is safe to assume that within the next ten years, almost all health-insured Americans, whether through private or publicly financed plans, will be members of an H.M.O. An H.M.O. receives a fixed monthly premium from the insured person or, more commonly, from his or her employer, union, or government financing authority. In return for premiums, plan members (in H.M.O. parlance) are entitled to have all of their medical services provided (subject to the terms of the plan), generally including primary care, specialty care, hospitalization, prescriptions, and a broad range of other health-care services.

There is a trade-off for this depth of coverage. Unlike in fee-for-service medicine, where the patient can pick any doctor he or she chooses, H.M.O. members can only use the services of plan-approved doctors, hospitals, labs, etc., except in a bona fide life-threatening emergency. Failing to comply with this strict rule relieves the H.M.O. of the responsibility to pay for the unauthorized medical services. This exclusivity clause permits the H.M.O. to contract with physicians, hospitals, labs, and other health-care providers to provide the services at a lower price, and in return the providers have a guaranteed patient base.

H.M.O.s also place great emphasis on preventive care and early diagnosis of health problems. Many offer wellness education classes and free clinics to help people quit smoking. This all saves money because people stay healthier and require less medical care. When they do become ill, treatment is generally less expensive because the malady will have been caught earlier, thereby increasing the likeliness of a quicker cure.

The theory behind H.M.O.s, then, is win-win: People give up freedom of choice over doctors and hospitals but significantly limit their out-of-pocket expenses, since H.M.O. premiums and patients' copayments (payments made by the patient to the health-care provider) are lower than with fee-for-service insurance. At the same time, members are encouraged to accept preventive care and obtain regular health-care screenings, such as mammograms. If all works as designed, patients are healthier and illnesses are caught sooner when they are easier and less expensive to treat. Doctors and other health-care providers reduce the prices they charge to the H.M.O. for their services and in return have better access to patients. The H.M.O. can lower its charges for health insurance, allowing greater access to coverage by more people.

Originally, most H.M.O.s were nonprofit organizations that allowed doctors significant participation in health-care delivery policy guidelines. Unfortunately, in recent years big business has seen a huge profit potential in H.M.O.s, and many nonprofit companies have been converted into for-profit business enterprises. With the entry of big business into the H.M.O. marketplace, the influence of doctors over care guidelines has waned, while the influence of the bean counters and executives has waxed. In fact, some for-profit health-care company executives hope to drive nonprofit hospitals completely out of existence. Richard Scott, the CEO of Columbia/HCA, one of the nation's largest owners of for-profit hospitals (it earned $1 billion in profits in 1995[30]), has said, "Non-taxpaying [i.e., non-profit] hospitals shouldn't be in business."[31]

There is nothing wrong with making money in health care, so long as profits don't come at the expense of the health and well-being of patients. But with the advent of for-profit H.M.O.s, business success may be coming at the expense of patient care. The jury is still out, but there are disturbing signs. The national media have frequently reported that plan members with chronic conditions or serious diseases—just the people who might opt for euthanasia if not properly cared for—too often receive inadequate care.[32] Physicians, consumer advocates, and even some H.M.O. executives complain that the big-business drive to make high profits has created such intense competitive pressures to cut costs that critics have labeled it a "race to the bottom."

Critics point to horror stories of new mothers forced to leave the hospital within a day of giving birth, and of decimated nursing staff levels at some hospitals, where personnel have been laid off under intense financial pressures from H.M.O.s. There are even a few reported cases of patients *in hospitals* calling 911 for a response to their medical emergencies because they could not get help from the hospital's stretched-too-thin nursing staffs![33] Doctors have had their "face time" with patients reduced and have had gag rules imposed upon them, by contract in some cases, to prevent them from discussing all medical options with patients and from criticizing their contract H.M.O.s.[34] Physicians have been warned to restrict the number of referrals to specialists or face losing a part or all of their livelihood. *The Washington Post* reported that Washington, D.C.'s, largest managed health-care plan, Mid-Atlantic Medical Services, Inc., informed physicians that their referrals to specialists could include only one visit and that their contracts would be terminated if they failed to meet referral patterns for their specialty.[35] A San Diego–based H.M.O., Sharp HealthCare, had a clause in its employee handbook that said, "All employees have the responsibility to place the interests of Sharp HealthCare above their own and others." The definition of the term *others* included "patients."[36]

The H.M.O.s claim that these cuts and rigid rules simply improve efficiency and reduce waste. But in some markets, the cuts are becoming so deep that observers are highly skeptical of the claim. For example, Kaiser Permanente of Southern California planned a 25–27 percent cut in costs in its 1995–97 business plan.[37] The plan, which was leaked to consumer advocates, foresaw reductions of 30 percent in the number of days plan members spend in the hospital, proposed cuts in outpatient costs of 22–27 percent, and advocated that managers get doctors to prescribe less expensive drugs to patients, which could result in patients' receiving older drugs that are less effective. In order to achieve these cuts, Kaiser physicians would receive bonuses tied to achieving these targets.[38] These bonuses could place a financial conflict of interest between patients and their doctors.

In the stampede to cut costs, some H.M.O.s have even threatened their members' ability to access community emergency response systems. The

Tampa cardiologist Peter Alagona, Jr., whose patients' lives sometimes depend on quick, unequivocal responses to emergencies, was very disturbed when some Florida H.M.O.s attempted to remodel the 911 emergency response system into an H.M.O. image by requiring plan members to call a number to get permission to call 911 in a medical emergency! Had the plan gone through, plan members who in the anxiety of the moment called 911 might not have had their emergency care covered by their H.M.O. Moreover, with time often of the essence in emergencies, the delay in accessing emergency response might have cost lives. Fortunately, the plan was never adopted.

The quality of care in H.M.O.s affects publicly financed health care as well as privately insured plan members. Many states are moving to an H.M.O. model to care for their Medicaid patients. Some of these programs have worked well, particularly since Medicaid recipients in H.M.O.s generally obtain a personal physician, often for the first time.[39] But other Medicaid H.M.O. recipients have not been as fortunate. It often takes tenacity, time, and strength of personality to fully access all care to which a plan member is entitled in an H.M.O. Many on Medicaid don't have the education or the sense of personal power to do that. That may be why *American Medical News* has reported that several states have run into significant problems with quality of care in Medicaid-funded H.M.O.s, including " 'poor' or 'very poor' . . . care of children and pregnant women" and "hundreds of confirmed cases of poor and life-threatening care" for recipients. Simultaneously, these H.M.O.s had excessive administrative costs, including "executive salaries in excess of $1 million."[40]

Now, consider the intense pressure to cut costs in connection with legalized euthanasia. If killing patients because they are seriously ill or disabled becomes a legitimate method of "treatment," patients who require depth of care will be endangered. Remember, for H.M.O.s, profits come not through providing services but from limiting costs, meaning reducing services in some cases. Imagine the money that could be saved—and thus profits earned—by H.M.O.s by *not* treating cancer patients because they "choose" instead to be killed; in *not* treating AIDS patients because they "choose" instead to be killed; in *not* treating M.S. patients because they "choose" instead to be killed; in *not* treating quadriplegic patients because they "choose" instead to be killed.

This disturbing paradigm is one reason why managed care is now called "managed death" by those who worry about legalized euthanasia in a health-care system dominated by H.M.O.s. As Dr. Daniel P. Salmasy, of the Center for Clinical Bioethics at the Georgetown University Medical Center, has written in *Archives of Internal Medicine,* we may be heading toward a health-care system where cost control and the killing of patients go hand in hand:

> *As providers of managed death, many physicians will be sincerely motivated by respect for patient autonomy, but the cost factor will always lurk silently in the background. This will be especially true if they are providing managed death in a setting of managed care. A perilous line of argument might then emerge: . . . 1) Too much money is spent on health care; 2) certain patients are expensive to take care of (i.e., those with physical disabilities and the elderly); 3) these patients appear to suffer a great deal, lead lives of diminished dignity, and are a burden to others; . . . 4) recognizing the diminished dignity, suffering and burdens borne by these persons and those around them, their right to euthanasia or assisted suicide should be legally recognized; and 5) the happy side effect will be health care cost savings.*[41]

Lending credence to Dr. Salmasy's warning is the intense pressure already placed on doctors at the clinical level to cut costs. One of the hallmarks of H.M.O. care is the dual role of the plan member's primary-care physician (P.C.P.). First, the P.C.P., usually an internist, family-care specialist, or, for children, a pediatrician, is the plan member's personal doctor, in charge of preventive care, managing chronic conditions, providing inoculations, and the like. The P.C.P. also serves a function on behalf of the H.M.O. as cost-cutting "gatekeeper," the person in charge of controlling the cost of each patient's care.

It is the gatekeeper function that has so many physicians and consumer advocates worried about financial conflicts of interest between doctors and their patients. Doctors in many H.M.O.s are paid individually (or as part of a small group) on a capitation basis. That means that the P.C.P. (or the group) receives a flat monthly fee for each patient, regardless of the frequency of care the patient requires. Some capitation payments are extremely low, as little as $8 per month per patient.[42] If a patient required four visits per month, the doctor would be paid $2 per consultation, a figure so low that it could discourage depth of care. (H.M.O. defenders point out that some patients rarely see the doctor and so the capitation system evens out, with the doctor compensated for care he or she is never called upon to provide.)

That a doctor receives no extra compensation for additional effort isn't the primary worry about capitation. The real concern is that some companies impose a capitation system in which the P.C.P. is held *personally financially responsible* by the H.M.O. for any referrals made outside his or her group, to specialists or for tests. In such contracts, the P.C.P. receives a higher-than-usual capitation payment, perhaps $40 per month per patient, but in return must personally pay for each patient's lab tests, consultations with specialists, and emergency care, up to a maximum per patient that may be as high as $5,000, after which the H.M.O. pays.[43] In a system where doctors lose money every time they refer a patient out of house, they may be reluctant to allow their patients to consult specialists, including pain-control experts or psychiatrists, physicians who are crucial to the proper care of many dying or chronically ill patients. Without such treatment, these patients might turn in despair to a death doctor—or ask their P.C.P. to become one—in search of relief.

These and other financial pressures placed on doctors in clinical practice by H.M.O.s may already be having life-and-death repercussions. Take the case of the Christie family of Woodside, California. In 1993, Katherine and Harry Christie joined an H.M.O. known as TakeCare Health Plan. They chose the Palo Alto Medical Clinic as their primary medical group (a group of doctors of varying specialties who would be responsible for the family's medical care). At the time, Carley, the Christies' nine-year-old daughter, was having significant kidney problems. According to a Petition to Assess Civil Penalties filed by the California Department of Corporations, the agency in charge of regulating H.M.O.s in the state, Carley's P.C.P., Dr. Susan Smith, referred her to Dr. James Bassett, a Palo Alto Medical Clinic colleague, for consultation, despite the fact that Dr. Bassett had little experience in pediatric urology.[44]

Dr. Bassett diagnosed Carley with a rare and life-threatening cancer known as Wilms' tumor. Having no experience in treating Wilms' tumor, and knowing that he was not the doctor to adequately care for Carley, Dr. Bassett suggested that the Christies take Carley to Dr. Michael Link, a pediatric urologist with extensive experience in treating Wilms' tumor, which often requires surgery, chemotherapy, and radiation. Dr. Link and other members of his specialized multidisciplinary team were not part of the Palo Alto Medical Clinic group practice.

Under the H.M.O. contract with the Christies, any out-of-group referral needed the go-ahead of Carley's P.C.P., Dr. Smith. Refusing to abide by what the Department of Corporations called "good professional practice,"[45] Dr. Smith refused to authorize a referral to Dr. Link and instead insisted that her colleague Dr. Bassett, with no experience in Wilms' tumor surgery or treatment, perform the surgery. Adding to the outrageousness of this decision was the worry that Dr. Bassett may have worsened Carley's condition previously during a biopsy by "causing spillage of the tumor [into other parts of her body]. This spillage triggered an additional nine months of painful chemotherapy. . . ."[46]

The Christies were in a dreadful bind: Their daughter needed immediate surgery to save her life, yet they faced paying for it themselves unless they permitted an unqualified doctor to provide the care. As the clock was ticking toward the time surgery would have to be performed, Dr. Smith's position softened: Dr. Bassett would have to assist at the surgery if the referral were to be made. The Christies agreed, but he declined to participate.[47] Their daughter's life being paramount, the Christies transferred Carley's care to the experienced medical team. The surgery was successful. Carley's life was saved.

TakeCare soon informed the Christies that it would not pay for Carley's treatment, "in retaliation," according to the Department of Corporations, "for the Christies' choosing a qualified pediatrician surgeon to remove Carley's tumor."[48] The H.M.O. also refused to pay for the cost of hospitalization, which represented $47,000 of the $55,000 total cost of Carley's care, despite the fact that the same hospital would have been used regardless of which doctors treated Carley. Thus, in addition to worrying about their daughter's recuperation, the Christies were now facing pronounced financial difficulty.

The Christies entered the contractual grievance process of the H.M.O. (Owing to a binding arbitration clause, they were unable to sue.) They obtained an arbitration award recovering their medical expenses and arbitration fees, but not their legal fees. They then filed a complaint with the Department of Corporations, alleging that the H.M.O. had violated the California Health and Safety Code. The Christies were not after a monetary settlement for themselves, but rather, hoped the D.O.C. would fine the company to set an example for all of the state's H.M.O.s. An administrative fine of $500,000 was levied against TakeCare, which was upheld on appeal. As of early 1997, TakeCare has not decided whether to pursue further appeals.

The California Department of Corporations contends that a primary reason Carley was refused referral to a qualified specialist was the H.M.O.'s capitation agreement with Palo Alto Medical Clinic, which required the physicians group to pay for Carley's surgery out of its own funds if it were performed by nongroup physicians, money that would have been saved by keeping her care in-house.[49] The H.M.O. denies the charge.

The Christie family story was not a tale of euthanasia, of course. But if a capitation-based financial conflict may have put at significant risk a nine-year-old girl with a good chance of recovery, imagine what these financial conundrums would mean to elderly cancer patients, disabled persons requiring long-term specialized care, or dying people who require intensive and perhaps costly pain control. In order to save their own money, unscrupulous P.C.P.s might deny expensive specialized care to their most needful and vulnerable patients, leading to unrelieved suffering and resulting despair. This in turn could propel patients toward wanting euthanasia. Indeed, the doctor could legally recommend the killing as a "treatment option." This is an especially worrying scenario considering the depth of trust and hope seriously ill patients place in their physicians and the ease with which physicians could maneuver suffering patients toward requesting euthanasia.

Physicians organizations, consumer advocates, and legislators have attempted to curtail the financial conflict of interest some H.M.O.s place between patients and their doctors. As of this writing, these efforts have mostly failed, although a federal law was passed in October 1996 that prohibits forced discharge of new mothers until at least forty-eight hours after they have given birth. In March 1996, regulatory rules proposed by the United States Department of Health and Human Services were quashed under a well-financed and organized blitzkrieg of negative political pressure by the H.M.O. industry.[50] The H.M.O. comments revealed that capitation bonuses and penalties in some plans constitute up to 25 percent of their physicians' compensation.[51] Efforts at reform at the state level are also finding tough sledding. As of this writing, 350 bills have been introduced in forty state legislatures seeking to protect patients from H.M.O. abuse. So far, only 34 of these bills have passed.[52]

Not coincidentally, Wall Street investors and for-profit H.M.O. executives are getting rich from the money made off of draconian compensation controls that can be dangerous to their members' health. When Pacificare Health Systems, Inc., purchased FHP International, it paid $2.07 billion[53] for a company that had been valued at only $32 million when it converted to for-profit in 1985.[54] When U.S. Healthcare merged with Aetna Life & Casualty Company in 1996 to form a huge H.M.O. conglomerate, U.S. Healthcare's founder and chief executive officer, Leonard

Abramson, gained a *$1 billion* bonus! Of course, $1 billion doesn't go as far as it used to. Apparently, Mr. Abramson also needed some pin money and will also "earn" $10 million over five years from a part-time consulting contract when the merger is completed.[55] The average health-care industry CEO earned $2.9 million per year in 1995. Several earned between $8.8 million and $15.5 million per year,[56] and that doesn't take into account dividends paid to CEOs who were investors.

What would it be like to know that the doctor who is licensed to kill you also benefits financially from the act? Or to know that a doctor who recommends suicide for your spouse could be financially punished for providing him or her with "too much" care? What would happen to the trust between you and your doctor? How would potential financial gain affect your doctor's attitude toward your care if you develop a problem that requires specialized treatment? Would you have ready access to pain control, psychiatric treatment, hospice, and other care opportunities that would be more expensive than euthanasia? Moreover, if killing the weak and sick becomes a major area of cost cutting—and thus a profit center in the immensely powerful health-care industry—what would happen to medical ethics overall? And would legalized killing change society's attitudes toward the value of the lives of people deemed eligible for hastened death: the dying, the ill, the elderly, and the disabled? With H.M.O.s becoming the norm, these questions must be answered before we embrace euthanasia or take seriously the "last resort" scenarios spun by death fundamentalists.

The Silent Epidemic: Medical Malpractice

Another disturbing truth about our health-care delivery system routinely overlooked in euthanasia advocacy is the "silent epidemic" of medical malpractice.[57] According to Charles Inlander, president of the People's Medical Society, one of the nation's largest patient advocacy groups with more than 100,000 dues-paying members, "Between 136,000 and 310,000 people a year are injured or killed due to medical mistakes by their doctors," a figure Inlander calls "conservative."[58] An authoritative study published in 1991 by the Harvard Medical Practice Study Group, conducted at Harvard's School of Public Health and one of the most comprehensive and objective investigations of medical malpractice ever performed, found that more than 98,000 patients in hospitals located in New York State suffered "adverse events," injuries from medical care rather than disease, in one year, 1984. Twenty-seven percent of these adverse events were the result of medical negligence, causing 6,895 patient deaths in the state's hospitals that year.[59] Projecting these figures nationwide, the study's authors project that at least 80,000 people are killed in hospitals each year by medical malpractice, more than deaths caused by suicide, homicide, and AIDS combined.[60] These figures only represent deaths in hospitals. They don't measure misdiagnoses, failure to properly alleviate pain or depression, or other failings in the clinical setting. Moreover, it must be kept in mind that these disturbing projections have been derived from data that predate the ascendancy of managed care, when the financial incentives of fee-for-service health care lay in providing too much care, rather than too little as they do today.

Between 5 and 15 percent of the physician population are believed to be "incompetent or dangerous," and these doctors would be as entitled to kill patients as any other physician.[61] Indeed, some might be attracted to a euthanasia "practice," as legalization proposals provide civil and criminal legal immunity to doctors who kill their patients. Legalizing killing by doctors could even become a way for a few very unscrupulous doctors to cover up their malpractice or limit damages from lawsuits, by killing the victims they have injured in the name of "death with dignity" and the "right to die."

A recent euthanasia case in San Francisco illustrates how easy it would be for a doctor to kill a patient in order to cover up malpractice. In March 1995 a nine-year-old girl with a neurological condition that affected her physical development was admitted into the University of California Medical Center for elective surgery to realign her jaw. The surgery, which required that her jaws be wired shut, went well, but afterward, an apparent case of medical malpractice led to the girl's jaws not being unwired when she became nauseated. The girl aspirated on her own vomit and was left with severe brain damage.[62]

The girl had been unconscious for a few weeks when a pediatrician specialist, an employee of the hospital who was not the cause of the girl's aspiration-caused injury, undertook her care for a couple of hours while on duty. A different doctor had previously convinced the girl's mother to suspend life support, but the girl hadn't died. After being removed from a respirator she began to breathe spontaneously, after which, apparently, the hospital refused to support the girl nutritionally. A few hours after the decision to cut off food and fluids, the employee-doctor injected the child with potassium chloride, which paralyzed the girl's heart and killed her. (A legal dispute later arose over whether the girl's distraught mother had asked the doctor to administer the lethal injection.)

This intentional killing of a child did not result in criminal prosecution. Nor, as far as is publicly known, was the doctor disciplined by the California Medical Board, although one source told me the case is still being investigated. However, three nurses who blew the whistle on the doctor were initially suspended without pay, allegedly owing to their supposed delay in reporting the incident. (The nurses' suspension was overturned on administrative appeal. However, one of the lawyers in the case told me that they were all reassigned to other duties, prompting at least one nurse to quit her job and move to another city.) The employee-doctor, however, only had her hospital staff privileges suspended but did not lose pay.

An astonishing level of secrecy and obfuscation was imposed on the case from the beginning, depriving the public of very important information about the quality of care being rendered in an important local public hospital, about the professional competency of the doctors involved, and about the intentional killing of a nine-year-old child. The hospital's press release on the killing referred to it as "an atypical" case of "withdrawing life support."[63] The doctor's name was not publicly disclosed, nor were the names of the killed child or her mother. Even the nurses' names remain a secret, and two of them weren't even on duty when the girl was killed!

The killing doctor has claimed, in anonymous interviews, that her decision to inject the girl was motivated solely by a "compassionate" desire to end the girl's suffering at the request of the mother.[64] Perhaps. But what if her motive had actually been venal, to reduce the malpractice legal exposure to her hospital or, say, to protect a friend who had actually injured the girl? What if she had been the original malpracticing doctor (which she wasn't) and her motive was self-protection? Who would know? She could claim she was acting as an angel of mercy to provide "death with dignity" when her actual motive was to reduce the monetary damages to be paid out of the malpractice case, since the "value" of a case involving a dead child is usually less, perhaps far less, than a malpractice case involving a child who will require a lifetime of assisted care. (In the former, the damages generally are limited to the emotional anguish of the parents and the loss of love and companionship, certainly no small matter, and to awards to compensate pain and suffering, which in many states are capped by law. In the latter case, the expenses associated with providing a lifetime of medical care for the injured child are added to the distress damages, meaning that such cases are usually worth many millions of dollars.)

The malpractice civil suit brought by her mother involving the girl's postsurgery injury and subsequent killing was settled quickly for an undisclosed amount. If the terms of the settlement were those usually utilized in legal settlements of this kind, the hospital and doctors involved did not admit liability or wrongdoing. (My request to the University of California Medical Center for an interview with the killing doctor was refused, nor would it release the name of anyone involved.)

Euthanasia advocates often use cases such as this to support their contention that euthanasia is common and, as Dr. Quill put it, must be "brought out of the darkness into the light." In fact, there is no reliable information on the frequency or infrequency of euthanasia in the clinical setting. No one knows whether, or how often, doctors actually kill their patients.

Surveys taken of doctors about this issue tend to rebut the claim that euthanasia and assisted suicide are common occurrences. For example, in the wake of the passage of Measure 16, Oregon doctors were surveyed by the *New England Journal of Medicine* to determine their attitudes and experiences with assisted suicide. Only 7 percent of the responding doctors had ever written a lethal prescription for use in a patient's suicide, 187 out of 2,761 doctors surveyed.[65] A similar study published in the same journal in 1994 found that only 9.4 percent of physicians had taken action to "directly" cause a patient to die (not necessarily euthanasia or assisted suicide), and only 3.7 percent had provided information that would cause a patient's death.[66]

The polling also suggests that physicians, while reflecting society's deep divisions about legalizing assisted suicide, are generally quite worried about its application in the real world. The Oregon poll found that more than half of Oregon physicians would be unwilling because of moral objections to prescribe an overdose. Adding to their unease was the fear felt by more than 90 percent of the doctors that their patients would seek hastened death so as not to be a burden on others. This fear was born out in the October 1996 Gallup Poll cited earlier in which "being a burden to family and friends" was cited as the respondents' primary fear associated with death and dying.[67] Eighty-three percent of Oregon doctors thought that their patients might decide to self-destruct because of financial pressures. Moreover, fully half were not confident they could diagnose whether a patient has six months or less to live, the time frame required in the statute to permit assisted suicide. Twenty-eight percent weren't confident they could recognize depression in a patient asking for a lethal dose.[68] When a 1994 survey of Washington doctors asked respondents whether they would actively euthanize a patient, a more hands-on endeavor than assisted suicide, only 33 percent said they would.[69] (The Oregon poll dealt only with prescribing an overdose and not with participating in the actual killing of the patient. The Washington poll considered actual euthanasia.)

Virtually all professional health-care organizations oppose legalization of euthanasia and assisted suicide. The American Medical Association, the National Hospice Organization, and the American Nurses Association are all staunchly opposed to both practices and have issued public statements of their position. The A.M.A.'s opinion is worth citing:

> *The medical profession will not tolerate being put in a position to judge the value of human lives. . . . To allow or force physicians to participate in actively ending the lives of patients would so dramatically and fundamentally change the entire patient/physician relationship that it would undermine the principles we, as a society, hold most dear. We must never lose sight of the caveat that physicians are healers, and where we cannot heal, our role is to comfort.[70]*

These opinions are almost universally shared by the medical profession around the world. The British Medical Association (B.M.A.), like its American counterpart, has consistently maintained firm opposition to assisted suicide and euthanasia. In the early 1980s, the B.M.A. responded to calls for a policy change by undertaking a study of euthanasia in the Netherlands. The study resulted in a 1988 report, reiterated in 1993, which concluded:

> *The law should not be changed and the deliberate taking of a human life should remain a crime. This rejection of a change in the law to permit doctors to intervene to end a person's life is not just a subordination of individual well-being to social policy. It is, instead, an affirmation of the supreme value of the individual, no matter how worthless and hopeless that individual may feel.[71]*

Similarly, the World Medical Association, whose members are physicians from forty-one countries, has also adopted a position opposing physician-induced death. It states:

> *Physician-assisted suicide, like euthanasia, is unethical and must be condemned by the medical profession. Where the assistance of the*

physician is intentionally and deliberately directed at enabling an individual to end his or her own life, the physician acts unethically.[72]

Despite the intense public campaign to legitimize and legalize assisted suicide and euthanasia, despite the unremitting "educational" efforts by bioethics institutes (often funded by health-care foundations affiliated with profit-making corporations), which regularly present the pro-euthanasia point of view in professional symposia and seminars, doctors cannot be said to have come close to endorsing the death culture.

"Doctor Knows Best"

So far, we have seen that euthanasia advocacy is based in large measure on respecting patient autonomy: the right to choose the place, manner, and time of one's own death. So too is the killing of cognitively disabled people by dehydration, justified as a matter of ceasing treatment out of respect for the personal values and decision making of the patient and/or surrogates.

But what if the "choice" of the patient and/or surrogates is to continue treatment? What if the patient's personal value system holds that it is right and proper to fight for life until death can no longer be held at bay? As a matter of consistency, one would expect that such decisions to resist dying would be as respected in a society that values personal autonomy as the decision to seek death or refuse life-sustaining medical treatment. To a growing extent, however, one would be wrong.

Denying Wanted Care

While society and the media have been focusing on respecting patient autonomy as an exercise in a "right to die," little attention is being paid to concurrent efforts to disregard patient autonomy when the patient wants care, and thereby create a medical system in which there is no right to live. This is the emerging ethical debate over "futile care," in which many bioethicists, academics, members of the medical intelligentsia, and social engineers argue that treatment requests can be disregarded ethically by physicians if the request is deemed to be futile, regardless of the desires of the patient. "The decision about futile therapy cannot and should not be abdicated by the physician to the patient, family, surrogate, court, or society in general," says Allen J. Bennett, M.D., vice chairman of the Committee on Bioethical Issues of the Medical Society of the State of New York. "To abdicate a decision about the futility of a procedure or medical treatment is to abdicate professional responsibility for the patient. . . . Futility decisions should be left to physicians."[73]

Futilitarianism, as it is sometimes called, is social Darwinism. It proposes that the old, the dying, those on the margins, and the profoundly disabled must be pushed out of the lifeboat in order to allow others in or, indeed, to keep the boat afloat. Thus, it can be described as a first cousin to euthanasia in that it rejects the equality-of-human-life ethic in favor of a subjective value system that determines whose lives are worth protecting and whose lives are not.

The theory of futilitarianism goes something like this: When a patient reaches a certain stage of age, illness, or injury, any further treatment other than comfort care is futile and should be withheld or stopped. That the patient may want the treatment anyway, because of deeply held values or a desire to improve medical condition, is not decisive; the doctors involved have the right to refuse treatment, period.

At this point, let me make it clear that I am not talking about "futile" care as an objective concept. No one expects doctors to perform services that have no possibility of providing a medical benefit to patients. Thus, someone afflicted with a simple ear infection does not have the "right" to demand an appendectomy. A doctor could and should refuse to perform such a procedure. But futilitarians are bending this traditional objective concept of futile care in order to promote a radical view of health-care decision making. This would allow health-care professionals, health insurance company executives, or even community "consensus" to take precedence over patients' wishes for their care.

Futilitarianism has quietly been gaining momentum for the last several years. Mandatory treatment guidelines have already been drafted by bioethics think tanks and are nearing implementation. These are not rules intended to define minimum allowable standards (which are desperately needed in this age of the development of H.M.O.s), but rather to serve as guidelines for the *maximum care* that a physician must provide for patients or for which health insurance companies and H.M.O.s must pay. If desired medical care falls outside the guidelines, the treatment is deemed "futile" or "inappropriate." If patients want an inappropriate treatment, it will not be rendered unless they are willing to pay out of their own pockets.

Dr. Marcia Angell, executive editor of the *New England Journal of Medicine,* editorialized that current presumptions in favor of life as they apply to the permanently unconscious must be changed so that "demoralized" caregivers won't have to provide care *they* believe is futile—or wastes "valuable resources."[74] Dr. Angell offered three proposals. The first would be to broaden the definition of death to include diagnosis of permanent unconsciousness. There are currently two primary and appropriate definitions of death in use: brain death, the total cessation of all measurable electrical activity in the brain, and complete cessation of heartbeat and respiration.[75] Dr. Angell's radical suggestion would be to take living people with functioning bodies, including brain systems, and pretend that they were deceased. Dr. Angell notes that these "patients do not 'look dead.' " Thus, she observes that "it would, paradoxically, be necessary to withdraw life-sustaining treatment, including artificial feeding, to stop the cardiopulmonary function."

Dr. Angell's second proposal is to pass laws that prohibit medical care for the unconscious after the passage of a specified period of time. Under this approach the decision to make a person die by withholding nutrition would be made in advance by society without regard to any individual case. Thus, according to Dr. Angell, the family who wanted care to continue would be comforted by the knowledge that the decision to terminate their loved one's life was not personal. This is an example of futilitarianism.

The third and "less sweeping" proposal, favored personally by Dr. Angell, would create a legal presumption that persons who are unconscious would not want treatment after a specified time. In that way, a family that held the "idiosyncratic" view that their loved one should not be dehydrated to death would have to prove that the patient had expressed a specific desire to be treated under these specific circumstances.[76] In other words, the current (weak) presumption in favor of life for the profoundly cognitively disabled would change to an explicit presumption in favor of death.

Dr. Angell and many others who agree with her believe, on the basis of *their* personal value systems, that unconscious patients do not have lives worth living. They believe that, by definition, medical treatment for such patients should be deemed futile. Ironically, their reason for stopping "treatment" with food and fluids is not because the treatment fails but because it succeeds in keeping patients alive—to futilitarians, an unacceptable outcome.

This is rank hypocrisy. Recall from Chapter 2 that if patients or their families want to be dehydrated to death when the patient is in a cognitively disabled condition, the killing will be done supposedly out of a deep and abiding respect for patient autonomy. But if a family should rebel against the prevailing medical value system and want to keep their unconscious loved one alive, apparently the right to autonomy is no longer important—even though unconscious patients sometimes wake up years after being diagnosed as permanently unconscious. (Robert Wendland regained consciousness sixteen months after his accident. There's also the famous case of the unconscious policeman who unexpectedly awoke and began to talk seven and a half years after being shot in the head.)

Note, too, the values expressed in Dr. Angell's editorial. As Thomas Marzen of the National Center for the Medically Dependent and Disabled, a legal advocacy group for the profoundly disabled, says, it seems that we "have lost the virtue of caring for people simply because they are people."[77] Indeed, nowhere in her editorial does Dr. Angell speak of unconscious patients as people. Rather, they are viewed as problems, patients who "demoralize" caregivers and waste resources.

There is another flaw in Dr. Angell's thesis. She gives short shrift to the fact that people diagnosed by doctors as permanently unconscious often aren't. According to a growing body of medical literature, misdiagnosis of the persistent vegetative state is common. For example, a study published in the June 1991 *Archives of Neurology* found that of eighty-four patients with a firm diagnosis of P.V.S., 58 percent recovered consciousness within a three-year period. Studies also show that researchers have been unable to identify objective "predictors of recovery," to differentiate between those who may awaken and those who most likely will not. Moreover, some "unconscious" patients who later awaken report that they were not unaware as is supposed, but rather had "visions" or "out-of-body experiences" or were aware and emotionally responsive to everything going on around them but were unable to communicate.[78] A recent study in Great Britain reveals that perhaps 40 percent of patients diagnosed with P.V.S. actually are conscious.[79] If these and other similar studies are accurate, Dr. Angell's proposed ethic, if accepted, would likely cause the deaths of some people who would have recovered consciousness given sufficient time. It also means that those dehydrated to death on the assumption that they were completely unaware and hence unable to suffer could die in a most agonizing manner, whether or not they or their families wanted that outcome.

The elderly are also targets of the medical futilitarian movement, with some proposing age-based health-care rationing. Professor Margaret P. Battin, an influential pro-euthanasia philosopher and academic, while not favoring age-based rationing at this time, has written, "It is not at all difficult to imagine the development of social expectations around the notion that there is a time to die, or, indeed, that it is a matter of virtue or obligation to choose to die." Such a policy, she wrote, need not be "viewed as a violation of rights. In an age-rationing society there is no *right* [Battin's emphasis] to live maximally on, nor to receive the necessary medical care." The young and middle-aged would have the right to "medical prolongation of life," but "each person will be equally subject to the expectation that his life shall come to an end before the sustained terminal morbidity sets in." Elderly people would "continue to enjoy the rights of persons in society, but the right to extensive medical continuation of their lives [would not be] among them."[80] As of this writing, Professor Battin has not urged the actual adoption of these policies. She prefers "termination procedures which are dignified and humane"[81]—euthanasia—to mandatory rationing if some future resource scarcity "requires" that the length of human lives be limited. Battin believes that there is a "cogent argument for . . . voluntary but socially encouraged killing or self-killing of the elderly as their infirmities overcome them."[82] Derek Humphry, meanwhile, has predicted that after it is legal for the terminally ill to have suicide assistance, "Aid to the elderly in dying [will] by sheer force of public opinion [be] addressed ethically and legally."[83]

While philosophers like Professor Battin muse about future age-based health-care rationing for and/or voluntary euthanasia of the elderly, a growing number of bioethicists already hold the nihilistic view that the needs and wants of the aged must be pitted against the needs and wants of other groups in society, leading to limitations of elder-health care through categorical rules, in order to ensure that "older persons, as an age group, do not take a disproportionate share of resources needed by other age groups for their welfare."[84]

That older people may have contributed a disproportionate share of resources by the time they need significant medical services seems to have escaped age-futilitarians' notice, as does the fact that everything can't be measured in terms of money and resources. For example, many (this author included) believe that the current generation of elderly people contributed more to the welfare of our country than any generation since the Civil War: weathering the Great Depression; defeating the Axis powers in World War II; creating a just and lasting peace; containing communism; building unheard-of national prosperity; financing the growth of a nationwide service infrastructure, including the amazing advances in health care of recent decades; and educating the Baby Boomers at an unprecedented level. That's quite a record of accomplishment that should count for something.

The futilitarian movement to withhold wanted medical care from those deemed unworthy to receive it is expanding its list of targets as it gains momentum. Daniel Callahan, until recently the head of the bioethics think tank the Hastings Center and a supporter of age-based health-care rationing, now believes that futilitarianism should expand beyond elderly and unconscious patients into the entire health-care system. Callahan, like most futilitarians, defines "futile care" vaguely. It exists when "there is a likely, though not necessarily certain, downward course of an illness, making death a strong probability," or when "successful treatment is more likely to bring extended unconsciousness or advanced dementia than cure or significant amelioration," or when "the available treatments for a potentially fatal condition entail a significant likelihood of extended pain or suffering," or when available treatments "significantly increase to probability of a bad death."[85] These are extremely loose categories. For example, if a treatment has a 51 percent chance to cause unconsciousness and a 49 percent chance of not having that result, then technically unconsciousness is "more likely" to occur. Even though Callahan acknowledges that "great precision in making treatment decisions of this kind will not be possible,"[86] he asserts that patients who want "futile" treatment as he defines it should have to pay for it themselves.

Callahan's embrace of health-care rationing based on futilitarianism is helping drive medical ethics toward extremely dangerous and rocky shores, namely, that individual medical treatment decisions can be based ethically on determinations of "social consensus and political will"[87] rather than on private determinations between patient and physician. This radical proposal is being further fostered and prepared for use in the clinical setting by an organization known as the Colorado Collective for Medical Decisions (C.C.M.D.) (formerly known as GUIDe), which has already drafted preliminary guidelines to define "inappropriate" care. C.C.M.D.'s director, Dr. Donald J. Murphy, hopes the work of his group will empower doctors, hospitals, nursing homes, and health-care financing entities all over the country, including for-profit H.M.O.s, to refuse "futile" medical treatment, even when the care is desired by the patient. What kind of treatment will be denied if C.C.M.D. has its way? According to its published preliminary guidelines, "futile care" will include food and fluids and other forms of life support for people in P.V.S. And it will include denying C.P.R.—even when wanted by, for example, family members—to the "frail, institutionalized elderly"; people with a "terminal illness" where there is "less than a 5% chance of surviving to discharge after C.P.R."; if the patient is "receiving hospice care"; and if more than "7 minutes pass from the cardiac arrest before C.P.R. can be initiated"—to name a few.[88] C.C.M.D. is also creating guidelines permitting refusal of other forms of intensive medical care that take into account a comparison of "resources used for acute illnesses" and "chronic illnesses"; "expected mental status" of the patient if his or her life is saved; "the role of substance abuse or high-risk behaviors in the current illness"; in the case of low-birth-weight infants, "the role of substance abuse or high-risk behavior by the mother"; and an analysis of "the benefits and burdens on caregivers"[89]—again, among other planned restrictions.[90] This means that the elderly in nursing homes, children with birth defects, and people whose lives are threatened because of "lifestyle" choices could be denied medical treatment, whether they or their surrogate decision makers want it or not.

If C.C.M.D. gets its way, it will mutate traditional Western values and the ethics of health care. In a C.C.M.D.-crafted world—as in Germany earlier in this century—doctors will not owe their sole loyalty to their patients. Rather, they will also be responsible to serve the needs of the community in their practices, as determined by the political process. The advocates of such changes maintain they will better promote "health," a concept that Dr. Murphy expands from current usage, which focuses on the individual, to a definition including broad community issues of "education, transportation, and recreation, as much as medical care."[91]

The stated purpose behind C.C.M.D. futilitarianism is to save resources for those whom "society" deems more worthy of its dollars. If that means sacrificing the ill, the elderly, even people who would have a "5, 10, or even 20 percent chance of surviving," that difficult decision will have to be made.[92] But not by the patients. Rather, doctors, health insurance executives, and those with political power will choose. And you can lay odds that those deemed "inappropriate for treatment" won't be members of the elite or those who are organized into effective political constituencies. Those forced to walk the futilitarian plank will be the comparatively powerless, the uneducated, and people on the margins of society.

This dynamic already has been at work in Oregon, which instituted health-care rationing for Medicaid recipients in 1987 (see Chapter 3). The purported aim of Oregon's rationing plan was to bring more recipients into the Medicaid program. In order to accommodate that desire, rationing was created, based on limiting treatments.

To accomplish this, a list of medical treatments was created, currently 1 through 745. Every two years, a decision is made as to the highest treatment number that will be covered; the highest number covered for the years 1993 and 1994 was number 606.[93] The treatments at or below 606 are paid for by Medicaid. Treatments above 606 are not paid for by Medicaid, which generally means the care will not be sought.

The relative value of each treatment listed in the Oregon plan was established in part on the basis of "community input"—in other words, politics. The consequences of playing politics with people's health care were obvious. Those with political clout generally did well. Those without clout often found their treatment needs on the wrong side of the line. For example, as initially envisioned, late-stage AIDS patients were to be excluded from payment for treatment other than for comfort care, based on a presumption that aggressive treatment for such dying patients is generally ineffective. However, when the AIDS community learned of the plan, they organized, protested, agitated, and debated to prevent AIDS patients from being written off. As a consequence of their political acumen, treatment of late-stage AIDS patients continues to be covered by Oregon Medicaid. Yet some advanced-stage cancers remain outside the line because cancer patients did not have equivalent political power, or at least did not exercise it. The same proved true of very-low-birth-weight infants, whose treatment is not paid for.

Legalized euthanasia and assisted suicide would have the potential to save financially strapped government programs, such as Oregon's Medicaid plan, millions by eradicating people whose care is expensive. Perhaps that is why, when Measure 16 passed, the director of Oregon's Medicaid plan announced that assisted suicide would be considered "comfort care" and thus paid for by the state's Medicaid plan.

The belief that the health-care system will be destroyed unless we cease spending so much money on dying people is fundamentally misguided. End-of-life care takes up only 10–12 percent of the entire health-care budget, so unless we kill every patient as soon as the terminal diagnosis is given, reductions from eliminating end-of-life medical care will not produce significant savings.[94]

Dr. Joanne Lynn, professor of medicine and of community and family medicine at the Center for the Evaluation of Clinical Sciences, Dartmouth Medical School, testifying before the Senate Finance Committee in 1994, said:

> *There is a widespread myth that enormous resources are wasted on the dying. The evidence for this is actually quite frail. About one-*

quarter of payments under Medicare are directed at the care of those who die during that year. This seems to be a reasonable proportion— after all, persons are commonly quite sick in the year before they die. . . . Very few dying persons now have resuscitation efforts or extended stays in intensive care.[95]

"The Economics of Dying," an article published in the *New England Journal of Medicine* in 1994, is even more to the point. Its authors, Drs. Ezekiel Emanuel and Linda Emanuel, reviewed studies of the cost savings that could be achieved by Medicare if more people signed advance directives (such as durable powers of attorney for health care; see pages 240–42), if there were broader use of D.N.R.s ("do not resuscitate" orders), if futile care guidelines advocated by C.C.M.D. were enacted, and the like. Although the studies were not definitive, the Emanuels concluded:

> *The amount that might be saved by reducing the use of aggressive life-sustaining interventions for dying patients is at most 3.3 percent of total national health care expenditures. In 1993, with $900 billion going to health care, this savings would amount to $29.7 billion. . . . We must stop deluding ourselves that advance directives and less aggressive care at the end of life will solve the financial problems of the health care system.*[96]

Even rationing advocates admit that there is little money to be saved by forcing people out of desired end-of-life treatment opportunities. Dr. Murphy himself admits it will not save the health-care system a lot of money.

The health-care funding problem in this country stems, at least in part, from our other spending priorities. For example, the United States accounts for almost 40 percent of all the military spending on earth.[97] While nonprofit H.M.O.s generally allocate more than 90 percent of their revenue to medical care, many for-profit H.M.O.s allocate only between 50 and 80 percent to medical care.[98] According to a study published by the California Medical Association, Wellpoint Health Networks, Inc., a for-profit, spent 70.2 percent of its revenues on medical care, the balance going to administrative costs and profits. Foundation Health, another for-profit, took more than 25 percent of the health-care dollar for administrative expenses and profits, while TakeCare of California, the for-profit H.M.O. that insured the Christies, spent 76.7 percent of its revenues on medical care.[99] But the first prize for diverting funds from patients has to go to Cigna Health Care of Illinois, which, according to the Illinois State Medical Society, used only 47.15 percent of its income on medical care in 1995.[100] A billion-dollar profit was extracted from a merger between two for-profit H.M.O.s,[101] and Columbia/HCA, a corporation that controls approximately 7 percent of all U.S. hospital beds, earned a profit of almost $1 billion in 1995.[102]

Eliminating "futile" care is only the first step in the proverbial thousand-mile journey. In the end, Dr. Murphy and C.C.M.D. hope to arrive at a health-care system where "community consensus" determines the parameters of medical care. Dr. Murphy says, "If we can't get a compromise on [futile care], we will never be able to restrict marginally beneficial care," where greater resource savings are to be found.[103] According to Dr. Murphy, marginal medical procedures include "mammograms for women over 80" or medical treatment that the community finds inappropriate for some people because of, say, age or state of health, but which the community considers acceptable for those it deems more deserving of care.[104] It may be worthwhile to reduce overutilization of marginally beneficial treatment, perhaps through public education and better communication between physicians and patients. But achieving mandatory restrictions by pitting different populations against each other in the political process hardly seems an appropriate way to establish an ethical health-care delivery system.

Readers might not be surprised to learn that former Colorado Governor Richard Lamm, a one-time Reform Party presidential hopeful who gained notoriety for opining that old people "have a duty to die and get out of the way," was one of the incorporators of C.C.M.D. and is one of its directors. Lamm is also notorious for expressing an anti–disabled person prejudice, as when he claimed that money spent on educating the mentally retarded is wasted, because "we must ask ourselves, in a world of limited resources, does it make sense to spend ten thousand dollars a year to educate a child to roll over?"[105]

Dr. Murphy expects to have the C.C.M.D. guidelines completed and a community "consensus" obtained through public forums that C.C.M.D. will sponsor by spring 1999. Then, hoping to bypass the legal system, C.C.M.D. intends to "go to the institutions, the nursing homes, the hospitals, the H.M.O.s, and tell them, 'Here. This is where the community is right now.' " From that point onward, Dr. Murphy hopes patients will be denied wanted care that "the community" disapproves of, if necessary by means of unilateral decisions by health-care providers and/or financers.[106]

Patient autonomy is not a consideration for C.C.M.D. Dr. Murphy believes that the time has come to "put some boundaries on patient autonomy" for the "good of the community."[107] This isn't surprising. I believe that for many activists and advocates involved in these end-of-life issues, patient autonomy in end-of-life decision making isn't the goal—the death of the patient is. Stopping "inappropriate life-saving treatment" isn't the goal—the death of the patient is. Certain people are seen as better off deceased—for their own benefit, for that of their families, as a service to society. If patient autonomy obtains that end, well and good. If families can be convinced that their loved ones' deaths are for the best and agree to shut off life nutritional support, fine. But if patients or families want to "rage, rage, against the dying of the light," then the theory of futile treatment will be applied. Whichever method gets the job done, the result is the same: death.

Futilitarianism isn't just a future danger; it is already here. One early victim was Catherine Gilgunn. Gilgunn, a woman in her early seventies, was in poor health. She had undergone a mastectomy for breast cancer a few years prior to the incident described here, she had diabetes, heart disease, and chronic urinary tract infections, and she had not fully recovered from a stroke. Then, in June of 1989, she fell and broke her hip for the third time.

Despite her many maladies, Mrs. Gilgunn had a burning desire to live. Indeed, she was unequivocal: In the event of a health-care emergency, she instructed her doctors and her family, everything that could be done to save her was to be done. She named her daughter, Joan, as her health-care proxy to make decisions for her in the event of incapacity. There was no doubt in anybody's mind what Mrs. Gilgunn wanted: medical treatment to prolong her life.

Several days after being hospitalized for her broken hip, Mrs. Gilgunn had several seizures, which ultimately left her in a coma. Joan Gilgunn complied with her mother's stated desires and instructed the doctors to treat her mother to the end. But the doctors paid no heed. Over Joan's and the family's objections, on July 5, Mrs. Gilgunn's attending physician placed a D.N.R. (do not resuscitate) order on her chart. That meant that if Mrs. Gilgunn had a cardiac arrest, the medical team would not attempt C.P.R.

The hospital's Optimum Care Committee (perhaps with the bottom line in mind) had encouraged the attending physician to place the D.N.R.

on Mrs. Gilgunn's chart; the head of the committee, Father Edwin Cassem, M.D., had decided that C.P.R. was not a "genuine therapeutic option." A social worker also approved, concluding that the wishes of the family and patient did not justify "mistreating the patient,"[108] even though the treatment was exactly what the patient wanted.

The D.N.R. order was, however, soon rescinded by the attending physician, who felt duty-bound to comply with the family's strong desires. Perhaps that is why, in August, the hospital had a new attending physician take over Mrs. Gilgunn's care. The Optimum Care Committee again urged that a D.N.R. order be placed on her chart because *its members believed* that C.P.R. would be "inhumane and unethical."[109]

Not only did the new doctor comply with the committee's wishes, but without asking the family's consent the doctor ordered that Mrs. Gilgunn be weaned from her respirator—not to see whether she could survive without this medical intervention but, as the doctor later testified, so that she "would go out with some dignity and to not have her on a respirator at the time she died." Three days later, Mrs. Gilgunn expired.

The case ended in a courtroom with the hospital and doctors sued for medical malpractice. But if the family thought that the jury would sympathize with Mrs. Gilgunn's right to patient autonomy, they were sadly mistaken. Instead, the jury decided that the doctors were justified in making unilateral decisions over the objections of the family and the patient's stated desires. (Perhaps they were influenced by the judge's bizarre instructions that futile care is treatment that does not bring about a cure.)

In the end, it was not Mrs. Gilgunn's or her daughter's opinions, values, or autonomy that counted. Only the opinions of the doctors and hospital administrators mattered. In kowtowing to the physicians' values the jury may have opened a very dangerous door. As bioethicist Alexander Morgan Capron, codirector of the Pacific Center for Health Policy and Ethics, wrote about the case, "To allow Mrs. Gilgunn's physicians to impose this view [that treatment of Mrs. Gilgunn would not promote her meaningful existence] on their patient is the equivalent of allowing them to abandon the patient."[110]

Mrs. Gilgunn's case, like Nancy Cruzan's, was an early indicator of a growing trend whereby many doctors now feel justified in personally determining which patients are to be denied C.P.R., regardless of patient desires. This has caused some controversy, although not nearly enough. One dissenter, the bioethicist Arthur Caplan, has written, "When it comes to life and death, there's not much room for unilateral decisions by physicians. . . . It [C.P.R.] is a personal, value question. Patients who want to base their care on hope or take long shots ought to have that right."[111]

Increasingly, social workers, doctors, and courts believe that doctors, not families, have the ultimate right to decide when to "pull the plug" on sick patients, including children. In several cases, state bureaucrats have even gone so far as to strip parental rights because mothers and fathers insisted that their catastrophically ill children be continued on "futile" life support.

One such child was known as Baby Terry. On May 22, 1993, Terry Achtabowski, Jr., was born prematurely, at twenty-three weeks' gestation. (The normal gestation period for a human infant is thirty-eight to forty weeks. Babies born as low as twenty weeks have been known to survive.) Baby Terry, who weighed 1 pound, 7 ounces, at birth, was desperately ill. Deprived of oxygen, his brain had been damaged and he required a respirator to stay alive.

Doctors at Hurley Medical Center in Flint, Michigan, advised the infant's parents, Rosetta Christle, twenty-one, and Terry Achtabowski, twenty-two, that Baby Terry's life support should be discontinued as futile care that did not benefit their son. But Christle and Achtabowski disagreed. They weren't ready to give up. Baby Terry had gained a pound since birth and had successfully fought off a bacterial infection, and they wanted to protect his human right to fight for his own life. Accordingly, they refused to consent to discontinued care.

This was unacceptable to Baby Terry's doctors and the hospital administration. The Michigan Department of Social Services quickly brought court action to strip the young parents of their right to make decisions about Baby Terry's medical care. (Ordinarily such action is taken only when parents refuse needed medical treatment for a child.) A hearing was convened and court testimony elicited. The physicians were unanimous in their desire to terminate care, testifying that the child was in pain, although relieved by morphine, that his bodily systems were slowly breaking down, and that he had no chance of long-term survival. The Hurley bioethics committee weighed in on August 9, 1993, opining that removing the ventilator would be ethical and "the insistence of continued, useless, painful and harmful treatment of infant Terry [Achtabowski] would be contrary to medical judgment and to *moral and ethical beliefs of physicians* caring for the patient"[112] (my emphasis). In other words, when it came to choosing between the values of Baby Terry's parents, based in large part on their religious faith, and the values of the doctors, the hospital, and the state, only the latter opinions mattered. The parents were seen as emotionally unfit to make the hard choices.

Solely on the basis of their disagreement with the physicians' prognosis, Judge Thomas L. Gadola of the Genesee County Probate Court found Christle and Achtabowski unfit to make proper health-care decisions for their baby and stripped them of their rights as parents. He then awarded temporary guardianship of Baby Terry to his maternal great-aunt, who had previously stated her willingness to obey the doctors and cut off life support.[113]

Legal wrangling continued. Before the case concluded, Baby Terry died in his mother's arms, aged two and a half months, on August 12, 1993. Lawyers for Christle and Achtabowski still wanted a court decision overruling the trial court. But the court of appeals dismissed the case as moot.

Some readers may be wondering what difference these stories really make, as in both cases the doctors were probably right about the medical prognosis. But life and medical decision making isn't that simple. Doctors are not gods, and prognoses aren't cast in stone. It isn't always easy, even for medical professionals, to know who is going to live and who is going to die.

On October 27, 1994, Ryan Nguyen was born eight weeks prematurely by emergency cesarean section at Sacred Heart Medical Center in Spokane, Washington. Ryan was soon diagnosed with acute and chronic loss of kidney function, a bowel obstruction, severe brain damage, and other maladies. He was placed in the neonatal intensive-care unit, where he was put on kidney dialysis, and because of the bowel obstruction, was fed intravenously. A few days later he was refused as a candidate for a kidney transplant, nor was he considered by doctors at several facilities as a candidate for long-term dialysis.

Just ten days after Ryan's birth, doctors at Sacred Heart Medical Center told his parents, Nghia and Darla Nguyen, that their son's continuing kidney dialysis was futile and therefore they wanted to terminate his life support. Nghia and Darla objected, but their opinion didn't matter to the doctors. Without his parents' consent, Ryan was taken off dialysis on November 13, 1994.

On November 16, Nghia Nguyen called a conference with Ryan's doctors, where, according to legal briefs, he was informed that "Ryan had no future and they were giving him no options, and that for the good of his son, he should sign no-code [no C.P.R., etc.] orders because there was no chance for his son to survive."[114] Nghia refused to sign the orders and instructed the doctors to put his son back on dialysis. They did not do so.

In desperation, Nguyen retained Spokane attorney Russell Van Camp. Van Camp obtained a temporary court order on November 22 that required Sacred Heart and Ryan's doctors to restore dialysis and other life support, including C.P.R. if necessary, a judicial act that saved the infant's life when, soon thereafter, he experienced a profound medical emergency.

Sacred Heart administrators and Ryan's doctors were not happy that their will had been thwarted. The day after the temporary injunction was issued, Sacred Heart's vice president filed a complaint with the state's Child Protective Services in which they accused the Nguyens of "physical abuse" and "physical neglect" of Ryan. According to the intake summary report of the complaint, Child Protective Services was told that the "parents contacted W. Russell Van Camp, attorney at law. He has obtained a restraining order . . . that enjoins the hospital from stopping dialysis. . . . Hospital feels like it's cruel and inhumane to continue treatment as child is suffering because of it."[115] The complaint was investigated by Child Support Services and eventually dropped.

Meanwhile, the November 22 court order being temporary, Ryan's future hinged on a December court hearing in which a judge would decide whether to permanently enjoin Sacred Heart from taking Ryan off of life support. The hospital's lawyers vigorously fought against continuing the court's protection of Ryan, asserting in one court brief:

> *Ryan's condition is universally fatal, with or without court-ordered dialysis. Sacred Heart and the physicians plead that the Court remove the order and allow them to once again provide Ryan with the best possible care—care that is appropriate under his circumstances, and consistent with* their ethics *[my emphasis], the acceptable medical standard of care, their training, and within Sacred Heart's capabilities. . . . Ryan's physicians are unanimous in their opinion that there is* no chance *[my emphasis] that dialysis will cure or serve any therapeutic benefit to Ryan; nor will it serve as a bridge to future care. . . . Although medical technology has advanced, medical ethics remain constant. The fundamental principle remains—to do no harm. There will always come a time when medicine can do no more. It is inevitable that it must eventually fail and, sadly, it has now failed Ryan.*[116]

The only thing that had failed Ryan were his doctors and their insistence that their values and those of hospital administration about Ryan's care and his future should supersede the desires of his parents. For despite their absolute insistence that "recovery was not possible" and that continued dialysis would impose "pain and suffering without possible benefit," Ryan didn't die.[117] In fact, once another doctor agreed to treat Ryan and his care was transferred to Emanuel Children's Hospital in Portland, Oregon, he was soon weaned off dialysis and it was determined that he did not have profound brain damage. Ryan continues to receive treatment for the bowel obstruction, and once this is finally cleared up, he is expected to be fine and probably will not need a kidney transplant until late puberty, if at all. (It is too early to tell whether he will have a learning disability.) Indeed, as of September 1996 Ryan was a responsive, happy eighteen-month-old who weighed over thirty-five pounds, who could stand but not yet walk, and who happily gave friends "high fives"—no thanks to his former doctors and hospital.

As this is written, the Nguyens have filed a lawsuit against Sacred Heart Medical Center and some of the physicians and other professionals who tried to terminate his care and thereby cause his death. They claimed that the medical professionals and hospital administrators were acting out of desire to cover up a botched delivery and to save money for the hospital, since Ryan was a Washington Medicaid patient.[118] The lawsuit seeks damages for medical malpractice and the violation of federal and state law, including the Americans with Disabilities Act.[119] The defendants deny the charges. The case is pending.

The cost of the acceptance of futilitarianism will be the death of future Baby Ryans, admits the C.C.M.D.'s Dr. Murphy. "There is no question that there are risks," he told me. "And there's no question that those with less power will be at greater risk. There are going to be the Baby Ryans. There are going to be nursing home patients who would have survived and who wanted to accept their quality of life. But by shifting our priorities, we will be able to do a better job for more people."[120]

In a futilitarian world, as the German physician Christoph Wilhelm Hufeland said so long ago, in 1806, the physician could become the "most dangerous person in the state."

When it comes to euthanasia, it is increasingly difficult to believe that killing by doctors will only be a "last resort," when it is already becoming more difficult to obtain desired treatment that doctors or health insurance companies don't want delivered. Moreover, in America's evolving ethical milieu where some doctors have come to believe they have the professional right to refuse treatment over the objections of patients, if euthanasia were "just another medical treatment," what would prevent doctors from coming to believe they were entitled to actively kill patients whose continued care they deemed futile? It is a very short stride from refusing wanted life-saving care to actively killing patients without request, as Dutch doctors already do. Both death decisions give top priority to physician morale and values over patient desires and choices. Both serve the financial bottom line of H.M.O.s, publicly funded health-care entities, hospitals, and perhaps physicians themselves. Both substantially devalue the inherent worth of vulnerable human lives.

CHAPTER 7

Euthanasia as a Form of Oppression

The idea that legalized euthanasia would be a form of oppression will undoubtedly offend believers in "rational suicide" who strongly hold to the idea that legal recognition of assisted suicide and euthanasia is a matter of maximizing individual liberty. While it is not my intention to give offense, I believe that the contrary is true, that what proponents actually are doing—even if they don't mean to—is creating a new form of oppression based on state of health.

Let's explore this premise for a moment. At its core, all oppression is based on a division of human beings into different categories, some of whom receive special rights and privileges or greater protection than others do, because of a false belief that some humans are somehow better/different/more valuable than other humans. Oppression has been based on differences of race, gender, sexual orientation, national origin, religion, tribe, age, and other categories that have served the purposes of oppressors. Now perhaps we can include state of health or happiness as bases for oppression.

As the history of this country demonstrates, oppression is especially insidious when formalized into law. The Jim Crow statutes in the Old South, which legalized discrimination based on race, are illustrative. They not only gave African-Americans short legal shrift but actively promoted a racist and oppressive culture by giving the states' imprimatur to bigotry, thereby encouraging and legitimizing the overt, extralegal racism that was then common in Southern society. Thus, the laws that required segregated schools were essential ingredients in creating the oppressive climate that permitted and even encouraged lynching, even though such vigilante murders were technically against the law.

So too would it be if the state created a doctor's legal right to help kill his patients. The law's wording would be couched in words of compassion and liberty, but language—e.g., "separate but equal"—does not always mean what it says. By making assisted suicide a legally recognized and enforceable right, the underlying message would be for the state to proclaim that all human lives are not of equal inherent worth, that some of us (the healthy, able-bodied, and relatively happy) are worth protecting, even from self-destruction, while others of us (the "hopelessly ill") are people whose lives are of such little use that their deaths are best for all concerned. The impact of this would be no different from the consequences that flowed from institutionalizing racism in the law: It would create a new category for culling humans into privileged and oppressed classes, thereby influencing cultural outlook as well as impacting upon the state's legal obligations toward its citizens. In other words, "rational suicides" would be not only permitted but actively encouraged, just as the societal message behind Jim Crow laws promoted overt and covert racism.

Prejudice Against the Disabled

Increasingly, disabled people are the focus of the euthanasia movement, which views them as potential "beneficiaries" (in the words of Ninth Circuit Court of Appeals Judge Stephen Reinhardt) of the right to be killed by a doctor. Many in the disability rights community have a dramatically different view. Rather than seeing euthanasia as a guarantee of "liberty," they view legalization as a dire threat and a form of bigotry against disabled people that sends the loud message that disabled people's lives are worthless.

Paul Longmore, a nationally respected disability rights activist, writer, and associate professor of history at California State University at San Francisco, says, "Current euthanasia activists talk a lot about personal autonomy and choice. Well, for people with disabilities who have opted for assisted suicide, it was a spurious choice. These are people who have been denied the ability to choose about virtually every other option in their lives: They have been segregated out of society; they have been denied the right to work; they have been discriminated against in getting an education; they have been blocked from expressing themselves romantically and sexually; they have been penalized for marrying by having public benefits shut off, including desperately needed health insurance; they have been shunned by loved ones and friends. In virtually every case in which a person with a disability has sought legal assistance in ending their lives, they have been discriminated against in most if not all of these ways."[1]

Evan Kemp, the chairman of the Equal Employment Opportunities Commission under former President Bush, an entrepreneur and a conservative with very different political affiliations from Longmore's, agrees. About hastened death, he states simply: "Euthanasia is nothing more than human beings—often doctors—killing disabled, ill, or elderly people."[2]

Those of us who are able-bodied may think that the worst form of discrimination that disabled people generally face is having their "handicapped" parking spaces taken by those who have no right to use them. Actually, hate crimes against disabled people are a pervasive problem (so bad, in fact, that the law now requires the F.B.I. to gather statistics on the issue). Disabled people not only face the danger of physical assault but face hurtful insults and thoughtless comments by friends, neighbors, and even total strangers. "Every day I run into people who will say, 'If I were you, I'd give up,' " says Kathi Wolfe, a writer who is legally blind. "A taxi driver recently refused to pick me up, telling me he won't allow handicapped people in his cab. A few months ago, when I was heading for the subway, someone took my cane and threw it down the escalator, hissing at me, 'You people belong in a concentration camp.' I've even had a *doctor* tell me that if he were blind like me, he would kill himself."[3]

Paul Longmore, who can't use his arms because of polio and who has curvature of the spine requiring the frequent use of a respirator, tells a similar story. "Strangers have come up to me on the streets telling me that they would rather be dead than in my position, that before they would be disabled, they would kill themselves. A lot of people would rather not see us and be reminded that life is fragile and not totally within our control. They wish we would just go away."[4]

"Disability has supplanted death in people's minds as the worst thing that can happen," says the psychologist Carol Gill, a disability rights activist and head of the Chicago Institute on Disability Research. "These prejudices are sometimes shared by physicians, ethicists, and others in the health care hierarchy. That can be frightening. If a doctor doesn't think that a life with disability is tenable, they think they are doing a [disabled] patient a favor by advocating an end to treatment [so death will occur]."[5] One assumes that if euthanasia were legalized, the same could be said about it.

"Kevorkian and other 'death with dignity' proponents are broadening the definition of 'extreme human suffering' to encompass mental and physical disabilities that leave individuals unable to live life unassisted," a disability rights journal has recently noted. "Activists fear that such thinking will reinforce society's acceptance of health care rationing and the denial of adequate funding for assistive technology and personal assistance services. One activist attending a recent meeting on disability and euthanasia scoffed, 'Dignity my eye; all that concern about dignity boils down to society's contempt for people who need help to go to the bathroom!' "[6]

These prejudices seep into the delivery of health care that those of us who are able-bodied take for granted. Examples of such biases are routinely reported in disability rights literature. The following excerpt from an article in the disability health and wellness journal, *One Step Ahead's Second Opinion,* is typical of the impediments placed in the paths of disabled people:

> *Robert Powell has lived with partial paralysis since childhood and learned two years ago he has a heart condition. . . . [The] hospital staff repeatedly asked him how much he wanted done to save his life should his condition fail to respond to routine treatment. Having barely reached middle age, he assured them he wanted aggressive measures to save his life. Staff continued to question him about his decision. They finally requested a psychiatric consult because they felt he was "having trouble accepting death."*[7]

Facing and overcoming this type of prejudice is difficult enough in a health-care system whose official ethics still value all lives equally. But now, with the equality-of-human-life ideal under attack from the euthanasia movement, and in the context of society's prejudice against people with disabilities, many in the disability rights movement are very concerned that they will be victimized by legalized euthanasia. One prominent disabled disability rights activist, extremely alarmed by society's apparent acceptance of euthanasia, told me, "I don't expect to die a natural death."

William G. Strothers, the editor of *Mainstream* magazine, a monthly serving the disabled community, recently issued a clarion call to anti-euthanasia activists after two women with multiple sclerosis were assisted in suicides, one by Jack Kevorkian and one by a man named George Delury, who participated in his wife's death. (The Delury case is discussed in the next section.) Strothers wrote:

> *What's troubling is that medical professionals and others are eager to pursue assisted suicide as a viable option when they and society at*

large have a fairly limited understanding of life. For example, nega-
tive stereotypes of disability as a fate worse than death persist, even
among people with disabilities. . . . As active participants in society,
people with disabilities have the opportunity to counter Kevorkian
and be evangelists for life. We had better get to it quickly.[8]

Some disability activists are doing just that. Diane Coleman and others
in the disability rights movement have formed an organization called Not
Dead Yet. "Not Dead Yet is declaring war on the ultimate form of discrimination, euthanasia," Coleman asserts angrily. "We've watched over the
last decade as our brothers and sisters have been denied suicide prevention that nondisabled people take for granted. We've watched as families
have been allowed to withhold food and water from their disabled children. Now, the courts [Ninth and Second Circuit courts of appeals] have
ruled that assisted suicide is a constitutional right, not for everyone, mind
you, but for us. We can't trust the courts and we can't trust the medical
profession. It's time to act before it is too late."[9]

Not Dead Yet has begun a series of demonstrations and other educational efforts around the country to alert the general public to the threat
euthanasia poses to disabled people. Fittingly, the first demonstration, in
June 1996, was in front of the house of Jack Kevorkian, whom Not Dead
Yet believes is a bigot on the basis of his disdainful statements about the
value of the lives of disabled people and because he has helped so many
depressed disabled people kill themselves.

Not Dead Yet next targeted a medical ethics conference where a
keynote presenter advocated limiting medical treatments for certain disabled people as futile "exoticare." Rather than endure the adverse publicity of people in wheelchairs demonstrating against discrimination, the
ethicists invited representatives of Not Dead Yet to address the convention. What could have been a confrontation became, instead, an educational opportunity. "We asked the ethicists how many of the hospital
ethics committees had disabled people as members," Diane Coleman recalls. "Only two out of forty or fifty of the people raised their hands. When
we asked if the disabled people who were represented had knowledge and
experience in independent living, no one raised their hands. Yet, these
committees continually make decisions about life and death based on the
perceived quality of disabled people's lives."[10] Not Dead Yet also was
present to support the American Medical Association's decision to maintain its strong stand against legalizing physician-assisted suicide at its 1996
national convention.

Few events illustrate the antidisability attitudes of society better than the reaction of much of Canada to the murder of twelve-year-old Tracy Latimer, who had a severe case of cerebral palsy. Tracy was killed by her father, Robert, one Sunday, when the rest of the Latimer family was at church. After the family had left, Latimer carried Tracy to the garage, put her inside the cab of the family pickup truck, turned on the ignition, closed the garage door, and walked away, leaving his daughter to die alone, choking on carbon monoxide fumes.

Robert Latimer was arrested, convicted of second-degree murder, and given a sentence of life in prison, of which he would have to serve a minimum of ten years. The Latimer case caused a national uproar, but not against the father. Rather, his conviction and jail sentence outraged many Canadians. The case turned into a cause célèbre for legalizing euthanasia. One columnist asked, "Where were the doctors when Robert Latimer needed them?" and advocated, in the guise of sharing a correspondent's opinion, that "a committee to make life and death decisions" be formed when "life becomes intolerable and death may be the most compassionate thing."[11] Tens of thousands of dollars were donated by supporters to the Latimer legal defense fund and the pro-Latimer uproar was crucial in obtaining Robert Latimer's release from prison, pending appeal. One judge, dissenting from an early court of appeals decision affirming Latimer's sentence, even included in the text of his dissent letters from outraged citizens demanding that Latimer be freed rather than punished for his "act of love."[12]

Within months of Tracy's death, an American parent, Susan Smith, killed her two sons by pushing her car into a lake with the boys firmly buckled into their car safety seats. Like Tracy, the Smith children died alone as their murderous parent watched from only a short distance away. But unlike in Tracy's case, the entire country leapt to the posthumous defense of the Smith boys. Susan Smith was branded a monster and had to be protected from an angry crowd, while Robert Latimer was widely hailed as a loving father.

Why the difference? There is only one explanation: Smith's children were able-bodied and pleasant to look at, and therefore they had a right to their lives. Tracy Latimer was disabled and unphotogenic, and therefore she was seen by many as better off dead.

That was certainly the message received by another Canadian youngster who took Tracy's killing and Robert Latimer's popular support quite personally. His name was Teague Johnson. Teague and Tracy had a lot in common. They were about the same age. Both had severe cases of cerebral palsy. Both were quadriplegic. Both were often in pain and required various treatments to alleviate their discomfort. Both had severe communication difficulties. Unlike Tracy, Teague had learned facilitated communication techniques that allowed him to express himself to his close relatives and friends.

"I remember Teague was very distressed by the idea that a father could take it upon himself to choose death for his disabled daughter," Teague's father, Larry Johnson, recalls. "And he was distressed that so many Canadians reacted with sympathy for the man who killed a daughter who differed from Teague only in the fact that five or six people in Teague's life had been able to help him say his own words and clarify his own wishes."[13]

Teague was so anguished by Tracy's murder and the widespread approval of it by his fellow Canadians that he wrote an opinion column, which was published in *The Vancouver Sun* on December 9, 1994:*

> *My name is Teague. I am 11 years old and have really severe cerebral palsy. The Latimer case . . . has caused me a great deal of unhappiness and worry. . . . I feel strongly that all children are valuable and deserve to live full and complete lives. No one should make the decision for another person about whether their life is worth living or not. . . .*
>
> *I have to fight pain all the time. When I was little life* was *pain. My foster Mom Cara helped me to learn to manage and control my pain. Now my life is so full of joy. There isn't time enough in the day for me to learn and experience all I wish to do. I have a family and many friends who love me. I have a world of knowledge to discover. I have so much to give.*
>
> *I can't walk or feed myself. But I am not "suffering from cerebral palsy." I use a wheelchair but I am not "confined to a wheelchair." I have pain but I do not need to be "put out of my misery."*
>
> *My body is not my enemy. It is that which allows me to enjoy Mozart, experience Shakespeare, savor a bouillabaisse feast, and cuddle my Mom. Life is a precious gift. It belongs to the person to whom it was given. Not to her parents, nor to the state. Tracy's life was hers "to make of it what she could" [quoting the Latimer trial judge]. My life is going to be astounding.*[14]

* This and other writings of Teague Johnson quoted herein are copyrighted by Larry Johnson and are reprinted with his permission.

Teague's loved ones helped him communicate his values of love, mutual connectedness, and universal equality to people all over the world on the Internet. In a letter to a friend dated April 4, 1994, facilitated by Teague's foster mother, "Ca.," Teague wrote:

> *I am really working hard these days to be strong and healthy. I really want to live a long, long time because I have so much to do. There is so much I want to learn and many people who need me. My Ca. loves me and really needs me to be her foster boy. That's right, I used to think that I needed my Ca. but she really needs me. I thought really I was a burden to my Ca. But really, I discovered that the best place for my Ca. to be is living with me. My Ca. needs me to be really happy. My L. [Larry, Teague's father] needs me to really help him with his master's thesis. Really, without me these grownups would actually stop learning new things. And I have lots to teach the world. I am going to be an important teacher.* [15]

Another note from Teague:

> *I am working on helping the world understand that children with disabilities are really the same as other children and need love and a good education. Really people shouldn't make assumptions on what someone is like based on what they look like. I hope [to show] people that those assumptions about people based on religion and race and sexual orientation are really wrong too. I am doing this by talking to people, and making speeches, and writing articles for newspapers. This is really my mission. And really if one segment of the population, like . . . people with disabilities, are considered second class citizens, then that makes it easier for people to start treating other segments of the population too.* [16]

Facilitated communication is a matter of some controversy. Some experts contend that the disabled person isn't doing the actual communicating, but rather, that well-meaning facilitators are unconsciously supplying words and thoughts that are not really there. Other experts accept facilitated communication as genuine.

Be that as it may, the sentiments expressed by Teague are important and meaningful, whether or not they were actually his. For, as Paul Longmore says of the Tracy Latimer case, "One of the serious dangers to all disabled people is that there is an ideal, a standard, a norm, against which people with disabilities are measured. The further you depart from the ideal, the less human you are deemed, until you get to people who are nonverbal and quadriplegic, where many see the disabled person as literally nonhuman. That appears to be driving the public attitudes in the Tracy Latimer case."[17]

Teague Johnson died in his father's arms from natural causes at age twelve. "Teague never doubted that his own life was worth living," Larry Johnson says. "He was excited about the future, and he continually made plans to advance his education and to engage in new and exciting projects. He lived to communicate his thoughts to the people and to help them understand that peace, love, and joy were possible for every human being."[18]

As for Robert Latimer, who had a different view about the value of his daughter's life, he remains free on bail while his case is on appeal. He has been granted a new trial because the prosecution asked jury members about their feelings toward assisted suicide before the trial, which is not permitted under Canadian law.

Few cases enrage disability rights activists nor prove to them as convincingly the bigotry faced by disabled people as does that of Elizabeth Bouvia. In the early 1980s, Bouvia was suicidal after undergoing one devastating emotional crisis after another within two years: Her brother died, she was in deep financial distress, she left graduate school because of discrimination, she had a miscarriage, and her marriage dissolved. She checked herself into a psychiatric hospital and declared her desire for pain control medications that would assist her to commit suicide by self-starvation.

Normally, such a request would be rejected out of hand; it would be deemed a cry for help, and medical professionals and other compassionate and involved persons would have attempted to help Bouvia find a reason to go on living. But some thought this case was different. Why? Bouvia's stated reason for wanting to die was that she had cerebral palsy and was quadriplegic.

Ignoring the profound emotional blows Bouvia recently had experienced, blows that individually and collectively could produce a desire for suicide in almost anyone, the American Civil Liberties Union took up her cause. The lead A.C.L.U. attorney in the case, Richard Scott, had been the first legal counsel of the Hemlock Society.[19]

The trial court refused Bouvia's request. She left the hospital, and after an unsuccessful trip to Mexico to seek aid in dying, she again began to eat.

Her suicidal impulse seemed to have abated, but it later returned. She again checked into a hospital and stopped eating, and attorney Scott returned to court. To keep her alive, the hospital put in a feeding tube.

The second trial judge again refused her request for assisted suicide. The A.C.L.U. appealed the decision. But a new era was about to arrive in the food and fluids front, and consistent with the emerging ethic, the California Court of Appeals judge saw Bouvia's case in a different light. It decided that this was not a matter of assisted suicide but of refusing medical treatment. In language dripping with the pervasive societal prejudice that death is better than disability, Judge Lynn Compton of the California Court of Appeals wrote:

> In Elizabeth Bouvia's view, the quality of her life has been diminished to the point of hopelessness, uselessness, unenjoyability, and frustration. She, as the patient, lying helplessly in bed, unable to care for herself, may consider existence meaningless. She is not to be faulted for so concluding. . . . We cannot conceive it to be the policy of this State to inflict such an ordeal on anybody.[20]

On the surface, Judge Compton's thesis may sound reasonable. But is it really? Anybody who wants to commit suicide believes that his or her life is "meaningless," "useless," and "hopeless," forever to be without joy. Otherwise, the person would not want to die. Yet when the cause of such despair is the end of a love affair, the death of a child, loss of reputation, etc., no court would rule (at least not yet) that the suicide wish should be accommodated because it is wrong for the "State to inflict such an ordeal on anybody." Solely because Bouvia's stated reason to die was her disability, she was viewed differently by the court: Of course she wanted to die. Who wouldn't? She was disabled; thus, her hopelessness and despair were perceived as permanent conditions, unlike feelings caused by the loss of career or death of a loved one.

Mark O'Brien, who has been a quadriplegic since early childhood because of a severe case of polio, lives in an iron lung. He has not only graduated from the University of California at Berkeley but is a published poet, a journalist, and an author; he is currently writing his autobiography. O'Brien says of the court's reasoning: "It is false to say quadriplegics can never have a meaningful life. [Bouvia] had more mobility than I do. To link disability with worthlessness and uselessness, as too many people do and as the court of appeals did, is pure superstition.

These attitudes are based on fears and false presumptions held by people who aren't disabled."[21]

Bouvia's life was clearly not foreordained to uselessness. She had lived on her own in an apartment and had attended San Diego State University.[22] She once volunteered as a social worker and might well have continued in that field to a paying position had she not quit college in a dispute over her studies, after which the college had refused to readmit her.[23]

Paul Longmore, who has written extensively on the Bouvia case, agrees with Mark O'Brien's assessment. "When we [in the disability rights community] tried to point out that Elizabeth's depression was caused in large part by society's unwillingness to give us the assistance that would allow us to live independently, to work, to be free from discrimination, we were contemptuously dismissed by the court and in the media. Yet, in the end, everything we said was right and everything the A.C.L.U. said was wrong."[24]

Longmore's point is this: Elizabeth Bouvia didn't die. Instead of killing herself, she chose to go on, and now, ten sometimes difficult years later, she is living independently, with the help of a personal assistant, in California. Ironically, it was her lawyer, Richard Scott, who committed suicide.

The Bouvia case was not unusual in its reasoning or result. Other disabled people have asked successfully for court help in committing suicide by starvation, usually because their aspirations for independent living have been blocked, not because of their physical limitations. Joseph Shapiro, in *No Pity,* wrote about a young man named Larry McAfee, disabled in a motorcycle accident, who wanted to die because "every day when I wake up, there is nothing to look forward to."[25] The court agreed that his disability made his life hopeless and not worth living and sanctioned pulling his feeding tube in 1989.

Shapiro convincingly demonstrates what the court seemed unable to grasp: McAfee felt useless because he was "being handled like a piece of radioactive waste," forced unnecessarily to live in nursing homes solely because of his quadriplegia while denied life-enriching opportunities for independent living.[26]

The story had a happy ending. Once McAfee's death desire made headlines he received assistance. He was given a computer, which he worked by using his head and which allowed him to pursue his interest in architecture and engineering. Then, when he finally had the opportunity to have attendants to assist him, people he hired and could fire, his spirits rallied, and he decided he definitely wanted to live. McAfee lived for several more years in a shared living arrangement with other disabled young men, until his death by natural causes in 1996.

Similar cases have not ended so well, however. Several people have been assisted in their self-starvation solely because they were disabled. Disability rights activists note that all had been denied access to independent living assistance that could have changed despair into hope, a choice for death into a desire for life.

What if euthanasia and assisted suicide were legalized for disabled people like Elizabeth Bouvia and Larry McAfee, who request "rational suicide" out of despair caused in large measure by societal discrimination and disdain? What if, rather than having to go through lengthy court proceedings, Bouvia and McAfee had been required only to wait fifteen days from their request before being given a lethal injection or poisonous potion? In such a world, both of these people would have been dead and buried long before their spirits rebounded and they moved on to the next phase of their lives.

A review of the professional literature supports the contention of disability rights activists that disability is more of an emotional problem for the general community than it is for most disabled individuals. One study, which compared the attitudes of disabled people to those of medical professionals, found that 86 percent of spinal cord–injured high-level quadriplegics rated their own quality of life as average or better than average, while only 17 percent of the doctors and nurses surveyed thought they themselves would have an average or better-than-average quality of life if they became disabled.[27] Interviews and tests administered to 133 persons with severe mobility disabilities revealed no differences between them and the nondisabled norm on psychosocial measures. Another study found no significant difference between persons with severe disabilities and persons with no disabilities on quality-of-life measurements.[28] Hospital personnel consistently overestimated their disabled patients' level of depression, whereas self-rating of depression by these patients found levels similar to that of the general population.[29]

We must thus ask ourselves: Would legalizing assisted suicide and euthanasia for disabled people—too many of whom are cared for in medicalized or nursing home settings that devalue their lives, and in a health-care system increasingly concerned about cost of care—truly be "compassionate"? Or would it be an expression of the general community's own fears, prejudices, and—Mark O'Brien's apt term—superstitions about disability? If it is indeed the latter, as many in the disability rights community strongly assert, wouldn't the facilitation of disabled persons' deaths actually be to abandon them? Calling such "chosen" deaths exercises in liberty or death with dignity would not change that reality.

The extent to which society accepts the belief that death is better than disability is aptly illustrated by the case of Dr. Gregory Messenger, a Michigan dermatologist who, fearing that his son Michael would suffer and be disabled because of being born prematurely, at twenty-six weeks, took him off a respirator with the intent that the boy should die. Dr. Messenger unilaterally took this deadly action, even though Michael had not been examined, even though necessary diagnostic tests to determine his likely prognosis had not been conducted, even though his wife's doctor estimated the chance of Michael's survival before the emergency birth at 30–50 percent, even though a significant number of babies born at twenty-six weeks survive, many without significant impairment.[30] Michael Messenger died at age eighty-two minutes.

Everyone can deeply sympathize with Dr. Messenger's grief, worry, and fear about his baby. But did that give him the right to end his baby's life before his son had a chance to fight for his own survival? According to the jury, apparently so. After only four hours' deliberation, they acquitted Dr. Messenger of manslaughter charges, a verdict some delighted bioethicists called a blow for parental rights.[31]

Compare Dr. Messenger's exoneration to what happened to the parents of Baby Terry and Baby Ryan. The father who took away his son's right to live was widely viewed as a loving and caring parent only trying to prevent his son's suffering. But parents who wanted to give their prematurely born children every chance for life were turned over to the authorities by doctors and hospital administrators as child abusers and, in the Baby Terry case, were stripped of parental rights. There is a paradox here—unless these cases are seen in the broader context of a culture increasingly looking to death as the answer to the medical difficulties and disability potential associated with premature birth. Then, all the pieces of the death culture puzzle fit snugly into place.

The Messenger case also has about it the noxious odor of the euthanasia advocate Peter Singer's theory, that parents and doctors should have the legal and ethical right to have doctors kill unwanted disabled infants, as currently exists in the Netherlands. Singer states in *Rethinking Life and Death* (a reiteration of the same thoughts that he has presented in other forums):

> *Both for the sake of "our children" [other healthy children, whether or not they have yet been born], then, and for our own sake, we may not want a child to start life's uncertain voyage if the prospects are*

clouded. When this can be known at a very early stage of the voyage . . . we can still say no, and start again from the beginning.[32]

In the aftermath of the not-guilty verdict, Gregory Messenger and his wife have filed a civil lawsuit against the hospital and doctors, charging them with medical malpractice for putting their boy on life support against their wishes—actions taken at the time to allow for medical tests in order to accurately judge the boy's prognosis. As of this writing, that case is pending.

The Antifamily Values of Euthanasia

Even the most loving and supportive families are plunged into emotional crisis when a family member becomes catastrophically ill or injured. Sadly, too many families approach health crises or tackle long-term-care challenges without adequate information about services and products that would materially assist them. For example, many people who care for elderly parents are unaware of the many social-service options that exist to help them, such as respite centers, adult day care, hospice, group homes, support groups, etc.

The national culture can also be a barrier to effective caregiving. Caregivers report that many people look askance at their friends and neighbors who sacrifice personal pursuits in order to give sick and dying loved ones the loving care they need and deserve. This sad truth was illustrated by Lucette Lagnado in a *Wall Street Journal* article titled "Mercy Living" in which she wrote about the reactions of her friends and acquaintances when she brought her elderly and disabled mother home rather than keep her in a nursing home. Noting that "mercy killing is increasingly de rigueur," Lagnado wrote, "In the two years I cared for Mom at my home, if friends didn't make me feel that I was somehow mishandling—even wasting—my life, then the 'professionals' did. . . . Forced to rely on a battery of neurologists, cardiologists, gastroenterologists and pulmonologists . . . I learned to steel myself for that cold look, the shake of the head that meant there wasn't much hope for her, so why bother?"[33] One doctor even yelled at Lagnado. "What was I doing keeping a sick mother at home, he thundered. Posing a question as loaded as it was insidious, he asked: 'Is she really alive?' "[34]

Lagnado's experience is not unique. Increasingly, caring for the elderly, the profoundly disabled, the ill, is seen by many as a burden or an affliction that wastes time and resources that would be better spent "productively." This message is delivered throughout society, in personal conversations, in the attitudes of the youth culture, in the media, sometimes even in advocacy for the "right to die," in which dependency and disability are commonly likened to a lack of dignity and human worth.

This milieu of fractured communities, of societal indifference, of isolation, of many families shredded by dysfunction, of widespread ignorance about the ins and outs of caregiving, of ill or disabled loved ones receiving inadequate treatment for pain or depression, of patients worrying about being burdens is the one in which families would face "rational" decision making about euthanasia and assisted suicide. Even in the best of families, those with only loving and altruistic motives, such "crisis atmospheres" would not be conducive to reasoned decision making about killing as a perceived answer to difficulty. If legalized euthanasia were brought as a "solution" into a family crisis among people who are not loving or mutually supportive, or where there was substantial money at stake, the lethal danger to the ill and vulnerable is hard to overstate.

The tragic assisted suicide of the author and editor Myrna Lebov is a case in point. Myrna Lebov was disabled by multiple sclerosis. She committed suicide on July 4, 1995, at the age of fifty-two, with the active assistance of her husband, George Delury, a former editor of the *World Almanac* who was soon charged in her death.

As soon as the news broke about Lebov's death and Delury's arrest, many in the death-on-demand movement rushed to his support. The Hemlock Society created a legal defense fund for Delury. William Batt, chairman of the New York chapter, expressed confidence that Lebov had not been coerced, since most people would want to die if they were in her condition.[35] The case was widely seen by assisted-suicide advocates as a breakthrough that would move their cause forward.

Most of the media reports of Lebov's death as usual accepted at face value Delury's claim that he was merely a compassionate husband doing what his totally debilitated and suffering but courageous wife desperately wanted. The *Charleston Daily Mail,* for example, reported: "She knew her future was without hope. Instead of withering in a nursing home, Lebov, fifty-two, swallowed pills and died in her Manhattan apartment."[36]

But then the *Forward,* a Jewish weekly, reported that all was not as Delury wanted it to seem. For example, he claimed publicly that Lebov's life had been reduced to the merely "biological" by her disease. Yet only a week before she died, Myrna had swum twenty-eight laps with the help of a therapist.[37] The paper also discovered that Delury had convinced Lebov to accept a buyout of her monthly disability insurance payments by accepting a check for $50,000, which he then cashed against her express wishes.[38] Lebov's sister, Beverly Sloane, appalled at the sympathy and support she perceived her former brother-in-law was receiving among the public and in the press, publicly countered Delury's characterizations of Lebov's final months, describing her sibling as engaged in life, albeit struggling against depression caused, in part, by an emotionally unsupportive husband.

The lid blew off Delury's claim of selfless altruism when the New York district attorney's office released the contents of his diary. It revealed that Lebov did *not* have an unwavering and long-stated desire to die, as he had alleged. Rather, her moods waxed and waned, one day suicidal, the next day wanting to engage in life. Moreover, the diary clearly demonstrated that it was Delury, not Lebov, who had the unremitting suicide agenda.

Delury admitted that he encouraged his wife to kill herself, or as he put it, "to decide to quit." He researched her antidepressant medication to see if it could kill her, and when she took less than the prescribed amount, which in and of itself could cause depression, he used the surplus to mix the poisonous brew that ended her life.

But he went further than that. He helped destroy her will to live by making her feel worthless and a burden on him. Beverly Sloane says, "There was definitely psychological coercion involved [in Lebov's death]. He was telling her in front of others, including my daughter, . . . that she was exhausting, she was a burden, that in two years he would be dead [from taking care of her]."[39] Delury's own diary supports Sloane's recollections. On March 28, 1995, Delury wrote in his diary of his plans to tell his wife the following:

> I have work to do, people to see, places to travel. But no one asks about my needs. I have fallen prey to the tyranny of a victim. You are sucking my life out of my [sic] like a vampire and nobody cares. In fact, it would appear that I am about to be cast in the role of villain because I no longer believe in you.[40]

Delury later admitted on the NBC program *Dateline* that he had shown Lebov this very passage.[41]

That Delury wanted Lebov to kill herself cannot be disputed. On May 1, he wrote:

Sheer hell. Myrna is more or less euphoric. She spoke of writing a book today. [Lebov was a published author, having written Not Just a Secretary *in 1984.] She's interested in everything, wants everything explained, and believes that every bit of bad news has some way out. . . . It's all too much. I'm not going to come out of this in one piece with my honor. I'm so tired of it all, maybe I should kill myself.*[42]

On May 27, Delury wrote:

Myrna's mood was erratic today. Subdued in the morning, focused and realistic in the afternoon, rather more assertive in the evening—all definitely forward looking and without any indication that she wants to die. On the contrary, this evening she suggested that I was the only one who wanted her to die.[43]

On June 10, Delury's diary entry described an argument with Lebov that started after she left a message to her niece that "things are looking splendid":

I blew up! Shouting into the phone that everything was just the same, it was simply Myrna feeling different. I told Myrna that she had hurt me very badly, not my feelings, but physically and emotionally. "Now what will Beverly think? That I'm lying about how tough things are here." I put it to Myrna bluntly—"If you won't take care of me, I won't take care of you."[44]

July 3, the day before Myrna's death, Delury wrote:

Myrna is now questioning the efficacy of solution, a sure sign that she will not take it [the overdose] tonight and doesn't want to. So, confusion and hesitancy strike again. If she changes her mind tonight and does decide to go ahead, I will be surprised.[45]

Finally, on July 4, Delury got what he wanted. After postponing an earlier suicide date that her husband had advocated, the couple's anniversary, Lebov swallowed the overdose of antidepressant medicine that her husband prepared for her, and died. George Delury did not wait for her death by her bedside, but according to his diary, went into another room and went to sleep. The next morning he wrote, "Slept through the alarm. It's over. Myrna is dead. Desolation."[46]

In an interview with *Dateline,* Lebov's swimming therapist disclosed that she had indeed discussed suicide with her during their therapy sessions, although she subsequently told the therapist that she had decided to live. Lebov's self-described reason for wanting to self-destruct on July 4, Independence Day, was that she wanted to give her husband, George Delury, *his* deeply desired independence.[47] As one police official put it, George Delury put Myrna Lebov out of *his* misery.

And how has this man—a man who emotionally abandoned his nonterminally ill, disabled wife, a man who did nothing to seek treatment for his wife's intermittent suicidal thoughts, a man who helped push her into choosing an early grave—been treated? Delury has become the new hero of the euthanasia movement. He has signed a book deal; he has already been a featured speaker before the American Psychiatric Association, where he appears to have been warmly received despite his suggestion that "hopelessly ill people or people past the age of sixty should be able to just apply for a license to die . . . with or without assistance. I think that such a license should be granted on request, without examination by doctors, without securing the permission of any professional experts."[48] Despite this view, which he also expressed in somewhat different terms when he appeared on the *Charles Grodin Show,* Mr. Grodin lauded Delury as a "remarkable figure" who should "not be going to jail."[49] It is quite likely that Beverly Sloane is correct when she says that Delury will soon be making a "new career" out of his wife's suicide.[50]

Similar dynamics can be seen at work in a case that made national headlines and was featured on *60 Minutes.* Dr. Gerald Klooster is a retired physician from Castro Valley, California, who has Alzheimer's disease. When Klooster's son, Gerald (Chip) Klooster II, learned in August 1995 that his mother was about to take his father to Jack Kevorkian, he immediately flew to Florida, where his parents were visiting friends, and quickly whisked his father to safety. Chip then moved Gerald into his own home in Michigan, and after a psychiatric examination showed that Gerald was medically incompetent, he sent the finding to Kevorkian through his attorneys, pleading, "Please *do not* harm my father, he definitely does not want to end his life."

Chip then obtained temporary guardianship in his home state of Michigan and sought permanent custody of his father in a court battle that pitted him against his mother and siblings. Michigan Judge Richard Mulhauser heard five days of testimony: Gerald's wife, Ruth, took the Fifth Amendment, and testimony was presented that Gerald was not in pain, that he enjoyed his family, and that he had years left to live. Moreover, according to witnesses, Gerald repeatedly expressed a desire to live, not die, a statement he repeated on *60 Minutes* on February 25, 1996.[51]

At the end of the five-day trial, Judge Mulhauser granted temporary custody of his father to Chip, ruling that "there is overwhelming evidence in the record of this case that Ruth intended to pursue the ending of Gerald Klooster's life through either the use of fatal drugs . . . or by taking him to Dr. Kevorkian in Michigan"; that "Ruth's children, except son 'Chip,' proved incapable of protecting Gerald"; that "it must be presumed that Ruth still intends her husband's suicide"; that "Ruth was on a mission and that mission was the end of her husband's life because she believed it was the right thing to do"; and that "Chip likely saved his father's life."[52] In other words, according to the judge, Gerald's hastened death was Ruth's agenda, not Gerald's. She was the one who contacted Kevorkian and made arrangements to bring her husband to him, a visit that would probably have been a one-way trip.

The Klooster case soon turned into a bitter interstate custody struggle between Chip, in Michigan, and his siblings and mother, in California. In Alameda County, California, Judge William McInstry, who had not heard the evidence presented to Judge Mulhauser, granted custody of Gerald to Chip's sister, Kristen Hamstra, and ordered Gerald returned to California, threatening Chip with jail and a $500-per-day fine. Meanwhile, Chip was ordered by Judge Mulhauser to keep Gerald in Michigan. The interstate battle soon ended in federal court, where a mediator helped the family reach a settlement, in which Gerald was returned to his home in California after Chip's mother and siblings specifically agreed in writing that Gerald would not be euthanized or assisted with suicide, even if such practices become legal. Ruth also agreed to counseling to help her cope with her husband's ailment. Chip's sister, Kristen Hamstra, was named as her father's conservator.

Gerald lived with Kristen for several months. Then, over Chip's strenuous objections, Judge McInstry allowed Gerald to live with Ruth, who solemnly promised there would be no attempt to hasten the death of her husband.

A few months later, Chip's worst fears were realized. Gerald lay in a hospital near death from an overdose of alcohol and sleeping pills. The police treated the case as an "attempted suicide with suspicious circumstances," in part because Ruth had attempted to prevent resuscitation by paramedics after she called 911 and because of the family history.[53] After a hearing, Judge McInstry returned custody of Gerald to Kristen, ignoring

Ruth's pleas that she "would never hurt Gerald."[54] As this is written, Gerald has recovered from the overdose. On February 7, 1997, Judge McInstry granted Ruth's request that her husband live with her after she hired a live-in helper and took other court-requested actions designed to protect Gerald's safety. (The police investigation was unable to determine whether there was wrongdoing involved in Gerald's near-fatal overdose.)

These last two chapters demonstrate a disturbing truth: Legalized euthanasia would be a volatile, dangerous, and toxic social policy, rather than the compassionate, "last resort" beneficence imagined by euthanasia ideologues. In the real world, doctors routinely undertreat pain and fail to diagnose clinical depression in their dying, chronically ill, and disabled patients. In the real world, managed-care doctors are under tremendous financial pressures that can result in inadequate care and could lead to killing as a means of protecting their pocketbooks. In the real world, chronic inequalities and animosities within our society—racism, sexism, ageism, homophobia, prejudice against disabled people—affect the delivery of medical care as much as they impact other areas of society. For example, African Americans are less likely to receive adequate cancer pain control and have higher cancer death rates than whites. In the real world, people without private health insurance, such as the unfortunate Kevorkian victim Rebecca Badger, are driven to suicide by suffering caused by inadequate medical care. In the real world, relatives abandon their ill loved ones, have venal motives, or crack under the pressure of providing care. In the real world, as illustrated by the Klooster and Delury cases, vulnerable catastrophically ill and disabled persons are easily manipulated into a hastened death not necessarily of their own choosing.

If we want to avoid these tragedies in the future, we must, as Chip Klooster puts it, "throw the whole idea of euthanasia out the window."[55] Then, we must get on to the important task of finding truly humane ways out of the health-care dilemmas we face without resorting to killing the dying, ill, and disabled among us.

CHAPTER 8

Commonly Heard Arguments
for Euthanasia

Public policy controversies are a bit like the music business: Just as some songs are played so often that they become standards, some arguments made in political debates are so ubiquitous that they too can be called standards. This is certainly true in the euthanasia debate. Raise the issue, and usually sooner rather than later, one or more of the euthanasia standards will be played. For example, a talk-show caller may assert, "We put our animals to sleep when they get sick; don't humans deserve the same humane treatment?" Or a euthanasia proponent in an Internet chat-room debate may write, "The only reason to oppose euthanasia is religious. Laws opposing legalization violate the separation of church and state." Or a television interviewer may ask, "If abortion is legal, shouldn't euthanasia be legal? After all, both are about 'choice.' "

The reason music standards endure is that people like them. Similarly, euthanasia standards are perennial favorites because they represent ideas and concerns that normal people who are not euthanasia activists or death-culture ideologues respond to and take very seriously. Since it is real people, and not activists, who will ultimately decide whether the country adheres to the equality of life ethic or discards it in favor of the death culture, these common opinions, thoughts, feelings—and, yes, passions—about euthanasia need to be carefully and respectfully addressed.

Euthanasia Standard No. 1: Euthanasia Is a Religious Issue

"There are no grounds for denying euthanasia other than religion," the Dutch doctor Pieter Admiraal, who has personally killed more than a hundred patients, told me. "But I am not a believer, so what do they have to tell me?"[1] Similarly, proponents of Measure 16 painted opposition to the initiative as religious oppression and accused their political adversaries of seeking to impose sectarian religious beliefs on the people of Oregon. Jack Kevorkian and his representatives always label their opponents "religious fanatics" and accuse them of engaging in Salem-style "witch-hunts" when efforts are made to enforce the law against assisted suicide. (Kevorkian has also said that the only way he will be stopped is by being "burned at the stake," an unsubtle allusion to the Spanish Inquisition and the religious intolerance that that historical event represented.) Derek Humphry, Peter Singer, and others have all claimed the crown of rationalism for euthanasia, in contrast to their opponents' supposed religiosity.

It is true that many, although certainly not all, religious groups—including many Christian churches, representatives of Orthodox Judaism, Islamic groups, Buddhist organizations, and others—have issued policy positions opposing euthanasia. But these same religious groups supported the civil rights movement, oppose legislation or laws they consider anti-environment, take strong public-policy stands on immigration issues, and express opinions on many other controversial public-policy issues, such as welfare reform, without being accused of imposing religious hegemony over the land. As Rita Marker, director of the International Anti-Euthanasia Task Force, notes, "Legislation that prohibits sales clerks from stealing company profits also coincides with religious beliefs, but it would be absurd to suggest that such laws be eliminated because they conflict with the separation of church and state."[2]

This constant sectarian refrain by euthanasia advocates is as inaccurate as it is smart. "Proponents try to paint euthanasia as an issue of religious belief because they perceive accurately that most people don't want to be told what to do by churches," says the noted civil libertarian thinker and writer Nat Hentoff, who writes syndicated columns in the *Village Voice* and *The Washington Post*. "In that way, they hope that people won't look to the substance of the issue but rather, will accept euthanasia as a means of opposing church-state involvement."[3]

This tactic is very reminiscent of the 1960 presidential campaign, in which some political opponents of John F. Kennedy, well aware that most Americans strongly supported the separation of church and state, sought to create a rift between non-Catholic voters and Kennedy by claiming the Pope would call the shots if J.F.K. were elected. It wasn't true—but truth wasn't the point; politics was. The same is true in the euthanasia debate and should be dismissed as inconsequential now, just as voters did then.

There are myriad reasons to oppose legalizing euthanasia. "The euthanasia debate is about what will happen to all of us, sooner or later," says Hentoff. "It's a moral issue, an ethical issue, an issue involving medical ethics and managed care. It is a political issue about who has power and who does not, who is expendable and who is important. It is an issue about protecting the most weak and vulnerable among us. When you are near death, that is when you are the most vulnerable to coercion, intimidation, and to powerlessness. Allowing euthanasia would victimize the poor, the uneducated, minorities, and anyone without the ability or support to insist on receiving the best of medical care."[4]

Hentoff has it exactly right. Euthanasia is not a religious issue, it is a vital public-policy issue. At stake are our most fundamental mores and ethical concepts and determining what policy best promotes the highest good for individuals and society. That is why most of the prominent opponents of euthanasia, regardless of their individual religious beliefs or lack thereof, base their opposition to legalization on secular reasoning. These include Dr. Herbert Hendin, psychiatrist and director of the American Foundation for Suicide Prevention; the legal scholar Yale Kamisar, a "fervent agnostic"[5] who first wrote against legalizing euthanasia in 1958, an opposition based specifically on nonreligious concepts;[6] Diane Coleman, a disability rights activist and cofounder of Not Dead Yet; Rita Marker, director of the nonprofit and nonreligious educational organization the International Anti-Euthanasia Task Force; and of course the writer Nat Hentoff, just to name a few. Indeed, when I asked Nat Hentoff about this facet of the debate, he laughed and told me, "I can't base my opposition to euthanasia on religion. I am an atheist!"[7]

Euthanasia Standard No. 2: Guidelines Can Prevent Abuses

This book documents the many dangers, abuses, and opportunities for oppression inherent in legalizing and legitimizing euthanasia and assisted suicide. Euthanasia advocates recognize these concerns and have a facile answer: "We'll enact strict protective guidelines to protect against abuse."

A look at the record reveals that these assurances are hollow. Everywhere euthanasia or related policies have been instituted, in every country in which they have been tried, the result has been the same:

Germany

As we have seen, both in the pre-Nazi era and during Hitler's rule the Germans assured themselves that "protective guidelines" would prevent euthanasia abuses. Indeed, the medical profession, the driving force behind euthanasia in prewar and wartime Germany, established the policy under supposedly rigorous guidelines. But the guidelines, such as they were, soon broke down, leading to "wild euthanasia," where doctors killed any disabled patient they wanted to kill—even though the euthanasia policy had been canceled by Hitler, even though their activities violated previous methods of determining who received "treatment," and eventually, even though the war had ended.

The Netherlands

The Netherlands is the antithesis of Nazi Germany, particularly in the 1990s, a time of general peace. Yet in this historically rational, liberal, and humane nation, euthanasia guidelines are routinely ignored by Dutch doctors without consequence.

The findings of the Remmelink Report are worth reiteration: Physician-induced death (both voluntary and involuntary) accounts for nearly 9 percent of the 130,000 annual deaths in the Netherlands and more than 11 percent of deaths in which end-of-life medical decisions had to be made. In 1990,

- 2,300 people died as the result of doctors killing them upon request (euthanasia).[8]

- 400 people died as a result of doctors providing them with the means to kill themselves (physician-assisted suicide).[9]

- 1,040 people (an average of approximately 3 per day) died from involuntary euthanasia, meaning that doctors euthanized these patients *without the patients' knowledge or consent.*[10] Of the last group, 14 percent were fully competent,[11] 72 percent had never given any indication that they would want their lives terminated,[12] and in 8 percent of the cases, doctors performed involuntary euthanasia despite the fact that they believed alternative options were still possible.[13] Moreover, in 45 percent of cases involving hospitalized patients who were involuntarily euthanized, the patients' families had no knowledge that their loved ones' lives were deliberately terminated by doctors.[14]

• Another 8,100 patients died as a result of doctors deliberately giving them overdoses of pain medication, not for the primary purpose of controlling pain but with the specific intention of *causing* these patients' deaths.[15] In 61 percent of these cases (4,941 patients), the intentional overdose was given without the patient's consent.[16]

The above statistics indicate that Dutch physicians deliberately and intentionally ended the lives of 11,840 people by intentional lethal overdoses or injections in 1990. The figures also indicate that the majority of all doctor-induced deaths in the Netherlands are involuntary.

These statistics are most likely conservative. Dutch euthanasia guidelines require doctors to report all euthanasia and assisted-suicide deaths to local prosecutors. But in the overwhelming number of Dutch euthanasia cases, in order to avoid duplicate paperwork and the scrutiny of authorities, doctors deliberately falsify patients' death certificates, stating that the deaths are from natural causes.[17]

Since their first creation, the Dutch "guidelines" have been continually expanded and loosened by Dutch courts. As interpreted by judicial rulings, the guidelines now permit the killing of patients by doctors because of depression, even in the absence of organic disease, as well as infanticide that is based on "quality of life" considerations.

The United States

U.S. euthanasia advocates blithely assure us that this country will learn from the Dutch mistakes so that such abuses never happen here. There's only one problem with that assurance: Violations of euthanasia-type guidelines have already happened here.

In 1986 and again in 1992, the American Medical Association's Council on Ethical and Judicial Affairs issued ethical opinions designed to define the circumstances under which terminally ill and permanently unconscious patients could ethically be starved and dehydrated. These guidelines permitted "technologically supplied" food and fluids to be withdrawn from terminally ill people "whose death is imminent" and from unconscious patients whose coma or persistent vegetative state is "beyond doubt irreversible."[18]

Despite these easily understood restrictions, people who were *not* terminally ill nor unconscious have also had their "medical treatment" of food and fluids withheld. This expanded practice has even received the approval of some courts. The A.M.A. then expanded the guidelines to comport with actual clinical practice.[19]

Jack Kevorkian has also stated that he operates using strict "guidelines." He and a small group of doctors formed a group they call Physicians for Mercy. The group published a set of protective guidelines under which it claims to operate; they say they require, for example, that people who wish to die because of a specified disease consult with a specialist in that condition prior to their life destruction, and that if pain is an issue in the desire for suicide, the person must be directed to a pain-control specialist. Yet when Rebecca Badger wanted to kill herself because her purported multiple sclerosis pain was so severe she wanted to die, no news account, public statement by Kevorkian or his attorneys, or comment by Ms. Badger's children makes any mention of his referring her to a pain-control specialist or even to a specialist who treats the neurological disease.

Protective guidelines give the appearance of normalcy and protection while offering no actual shelter from abuse. Worse, they act subversively to hide the truth about the victims of euthanasia. In short, guidelines serve no useful purpose other than to provide false assurances to the public.

Euthanasia Standard No. 3: Euthanasia Would Be Only for the "Hard Cases"

The "hard cases," those in which a patient's pain is resistant to effective alleviation, or in which a patient is suffering so much that he or she is literally begging to die, are the people around whom the euthanasia debate often swirls. Proponents use the sympathy and compassion we all feel for seriously ill people, and our own fears of being similarly situated, as their foot-in-the-door toward a broad permissiveness regarding euthanasia. At the same time, euthanasia opponents occasionally act as if hard cases don't really exist. So the question has to be asked: What do we do about the hard cases?

"When any person is suffering, that's a hard case for that individual and the family," Rita Marker, the director of the International Anti-Euthanasia Task Force, says. "We simply must work harder to let people know that not only *can* something be done to alleviate suffering, but that it is the responsibility of the medical profession to do so."[20]

Marker also notes that the widespread but erroneous belief that suffering cannot be ameliorated can in and of itself lead to a suicidal desire. "There's often a mistaken perception that nothing can be done. This can lead to people feeling trapped into 'choosing' assisted suicide [as the only way out]. The tragedy is that the activities and attitudes of euthanasia activists make the news, eclipsing the realistic message of hope and caring that people want and deserve."[21]

Medical experts verify Marker's statement. Dr. Cicely Saunders, who established the model hospice St. Christopher's in London in 1967 and who has supervised the treatment of thousands of dying people in the last thirty years, points out that "the alternatives for the dying patient are not inevitable pain or a quick lethal injection," as is often asserted by euthanasia advocates. Rather, Dr. Saunders asserts, "If a patient asks to be killed, someone has failed him."[22] Dr. Ira Byock, president of the American Academy of Hospice and Palliative Medicine, agrees with this great hospice pioneer, adding that the reason there are "hard cases" at all is because "undertreatment and maltreatment at the end of life is endemic. It is the exception rather than the norm for dying patients to receive good care at the end of life, to have their physical symptoms adequately addressed and their human needs met. Given the decay in the social fabric that provides even basic care, including shelter, nutrition, assistance with bowel and bladder functions, we must be extraordinarily cautious in responding to the resulting suffering in any class of people by eliminating sufferers."[23] In other words, the hard cases exist primarily because we *allow* them to exist.

Dr. Linda Emanuel, the American Medical Association's vice president for ethics standards and the director of its Institute for Ethics, also sees the problem as one of inadequate care. She told *The New York Times Magazine*, "I simply have never seen a case nor heard of a colleague's case where it [euthanasia] was necessary. If there is such a request, it is always dropped when quality care is rendered."[24]

The pain-control specialist and hospice medical director Dr. Eric Chevlen says, "The hard cases by definition are hard. But that does not make them impossible. It is these very hard cases that require an experienced clinician, knowledgeable in the management of the physical symptoms of advanced illness." Chevlen adds, "It is striking that so many people are ready to cross the country for a lethal injection and yet will not put out that same effort to take their loved ones to one of the many world-class pain clinics associated with university hospitals across the country."[25] Often, this is because people are unaware that such clinics exist.

It is our lack of knowledge that suffering can be substantially alleviated that causes cases to harden. "A century ago, *all* the cases were hard cases," Dr. Chevlen notes. "And there was little outcry for euthanasia then. Yet now, when truly hard cases are growing fewer and fewer, there is less reason . . . for euthanasia than ever before in history. The hard cases are the pretext, not the reason, for legalization."[26]

A classic example of this systemic failure can be seen in the undertreatment of the pain caused by AIDS, an affliction that can lead to neuropathy (nerve pain), terrible headaches, and severe abdominal cramps, among other painful conditions. (I recall visiting an AIDS patient whom I had to hold in my arms to keep him from pounding his head into a wall, his head hurt so badly. Yet his doctor had prescribed only mild medication for his pain. Not coincidentally, this patient had little formal education, was living in a single-room occupancy hotel, and had no family, no assets, and no private health insurance.)

Despite the suffering AIDS pain causes, AIDS patients' pain is notoriously underpalliated. A recent report at the Eighth World Congress on Pain disclosed that 80 percent of AIDS patients receive inadequate analgesia (nonnarcotic pain-control agents). Only 6 percent of AIDS patients experiencing severe pain receive a strong opioid, often necessary to control pain that analgesics don't alleviate. Women patients and those with less education are the most likely to be undertreated.[27]

The pain associated with AIDS is often pointed to by euthanasia advocates as a reason to legalize assisted suicide. Yet, as these appalling statistics demonstrate, inadequate pain control is the source of a tremendous amount of suffering that could be alleviated. Obviously this needs to change. The question is: Will this situation change if killing becomes just another form of "comfort care"? Considering that killing is far cheaper and quicker than providing adequate medical treatment, and in light of the widespread marginalization and isolation of AIDS victims by society, it seems *less likely* that this profound medical failure to adequately treat AIDS pain will be corrected if euthanasia is legalized. Legalizing euthanasia does not solve the problem of suffering, but surrenders to it.

Sadly, there are a very few among the dying for whom no palliation effort sufficiently eases agony—but that does not mean that they must continue to suffer. For these patients, sedation throughout the balance of the dying process is a viable solution.

If people accept sedation as an acceptable answer to the very few cases of irremediable suffering that exist, the euthanasia movement will deflate. This is why euthanasia advocates brand sedation as unacceptable and somehow less dignified than euthanasia. But how is entering a state of deep sleep any less dignified than being killed by poison? Indeed, sedation has all of the "benefits" of euthanasia—an end to individual suffering—without any of the dangers inherent in the death culture. That so many euthanasia proponents disdain this very real and available beneficence of last resort and favor killing suggests that establishing the values of the death culture, rather than actually ending suffering, may be their primary goal.

Euthanasia Standard No. 4: We Put Suffering Animals to Sleep, So Why Not People?

Another argument one occasionally hears is that since we routinely put ill and dying dogs, cats, and other animals to sleep out of compassion, we owe human beings the same consideration. It seems to me that when we say that we should put humans to sleep as we do ill dogs and cats, what we are really proposing is that we treat people in the same way we treat animals. This euthanasia standard assumes an equivalency between the moral value of the life of an animal and that of a human being.

Most dogs and cats that are put to sleep are not killed because they are sick, but because they are abandoned. Thousands of pets are euthanized each year simply because they are unwanted. To follow this euthanasia argument to its logical conclusion, then, would be to countenance the mercy killing of despairing homeless people because society is unwilling to care for them—a ridiculous notion. Similarly, a horse can be shot legally when it breaks a leg, but to say that a similarly injured human could be killed to put him or her out of misery would never be accepted. Dogs and cats—as wonderful, delightful, and loving as they are—are not people. They are animals, and in the end, society permits them to be treated like animals.

Few people believe that animal deaths are the moral equivalent of human deaths. That is the reason society permits animals to be killed, whether for food, sport, purposes of population control, or, at times, out of compassion. While most pet lovers who have put a beloved sick or injured pet to sleep have done so because they didn't want their beloved friend to suffer, many have also chosen euthanasia for their animal because they didn't want to spend the time, effort, and money to provide their ill pet with curative treatment, pain control, and/or palliation that would materially reduce their suffering without killing them. Others euthanize pets when they cease to be loving as a result of illness or incontinence. Others have animals killed just because they don't want them anymore.

Interestingly, a few death fundamentalists, most notably Peter Singer, the author and philosopher who argues that infanticide is ethical, do not accept any moral distinction between human life and animal life. In addition to being a euthanasia advocate, Singer is one of the world's most preeminent animal rights activists. He believes that "species membership alone, is not morally relevant," in determining rights, including the right to live.[28] He believes that some "nonhuman animals," his misanthropic term designed to create a moral equivalency between humans and animals—specifically, pigs, dogs, cats, dolphins, and elephants—are "persons" and should have the same "rights" currently reserved for humans. At the same time, he proposes that some humans—newborn infants, cognitively disabled people, those diagnosed as permanently unconscious, etc.—be denied personhood status and the rights attendant thereon. Singer writes, "Since neither a newborn human infant nor a fish is a person, the wrongness of killing such beings is not as great as the wrongness of killing a person."[29] In other words, to Singer, a newborn child is the moral equivalent of a tuna, and killing a pig is more wrong than killing a human infant.

Singer is not alone in his misanthropy. Some prominent death fundamentalists who wrote favorable reviews of Singer's book *Rethinking Life and Death,* in which he expresses his animal rights philosophy throughout the text, demonstrated an astonishing lack of critical thinking, either by not criticizing these bizarre and radical notions or in some cases actually praising them. For example, the book review in the Hemlock Society newsletter, *Hemlock TimeLines,* approved Singer's thesis, stating, "Mr. Singer's new ethic is built [among other "cornerstone" concepts, such as euthanasia] with enlightening discussions of *speciesism* and the ongoing argument about differences between human life and all other life" (italics in original).[30]

The humane and proper treatment of animals is an important subject, worthy of our time, attention, and consideration. But to create an implied or explicit moral equivalency between animal lives and human lives is, in my view, to engage in a dangerous sophistry that devalues the lives of those true persons (humans) among us who are in need of our loving and compassionate care. Singer's classic book supporting euthanasia is an attack on the equality-of-human-life ethic that undergirds our society.

Euthanasia Standard No. 5: There Is No Difference Between "Choice" in Abortion and "Choice" in Euthanasia

Euthanasia advocates take every possible opportunity to identify their cause with that of the pro-choice* side of the abortion debate. They believe that by coupling euthanasia as the caboose to abortion's locomotive, they can benefit the euthanasia cause and gain the same public acceptance for euthanasia that they perceive currently exists for the right of a woman to terminate her pregnancy.

Many supporters of the pro-choice position who are convinced that maintaining the legality of abortion is essential to women's freedom have fallen for this gambit. For example, the National Organization for Women supports legalizing euthanasia, ignoring the sexism within the medical system that sometimes causes women to receive inadequate care, a key issue in the euthanasia debate. Officials of Planned Parenthood have likewise stated that "choice is choice," accepting a moral equivalency between abortion and being personally killed by a doctor. The media often feed this misperception by portraying euthanasia opponents as "pro-lifers," a group whom pro-choice advocates almost reflexively oppose, regardless of the topic under discussion.

The euthanasia issue and abortion are different. Certainly there is substantial opposition to euthanasia among pro-lifers. But there is also opposition to euthanasia among pro-choicers. In fact, opposition to euthanasia is one of the few places where many pro-choice and pro-life advocates can agree.

Linkage of the two issues is a legal fiction, according to the University of Michigan law professor Yale Kamisar, one of the nation's most renowned legal scholars and a strong supporter of *Roe v. Wade* and abortion rights. Kamisar has written:

> *In* Roe v. Wade, *the Court cleared the way for its ultimate holding [finding a right to abortion] by rejecting the argument that a fetus is "a person" within the meaning of the Constitution. . . . But terminally ill persons, for example, a cancer patient who despite our best medical*

---

* I use the terms each side of the abortion debate uses for itself: "pro-choice" for those who are in favor of abortion rights, and "pro-life" for those who favor significant legal restrictions on abortion.

efforts, is likely to die in four or five months, is incontestably a "person" or "human being."[31]

In other words, a primary legal justification for the legal right to abortion is that the act, unlike euthanasia or physician-assisted suicide, is not the taking of a human life (a presumption rejected by pro-life proponents but accepted by most in the pro-choice camp). Therefore, for those who accept the right to an abortion, the procedure differs little, at least in the earlier months of gestation, from any desired surgery. Those who are both pro-choice and anti-euthanasia believers also note that the courts permit states to significantly restrict late-term abortions because the fetus is then able to live independently outside the womb, which changes the moral issues involved, giving greater weight to the moral value of fetal life. Thus, for anti-euthanasia–pro-choice advocates, there is no inconsistency between supporting the right to an abortion and opposing euthanasia. The two issues are separate and distinct.

Kamisar also notes that legal scholars who do view the fetus as a "person" but who think there is a right to abortion anyway have "maintained that the right to abortion is grounded on principles of sexual equality, rather than due process or privacy,"[32] an issue not involved in the euthanasia controversy. As for *Planned Parenthood v. Casey* (see page 136), which confirmed the right of states to restrict abortion but not to limit it, a case relied upon by the Ninth Circuit's decision in *Compassion in Dying v. The State of Washington* to justify overturning laws against assisted suicide, Kamisar points out, as did the Michigan Supreme Court in the *Kevorkian* case, that a major legal underpinning for the *Casey* decision was a desire not to expand the right of privacy but rather to preserve the vitality of precedent. In other words, the *Casey* court was bent on "bringing an old constitutional war [over abortion] to an end—not getting ready to fight a new one."[33]

For pro-choice advocates there is also a tactical problem in linking abortion rights with euthanasia. The liberal *Washington Post* columnist E. J. Dionne notes that linking euthanasia and abortion tends to highlight some of the very arguments anti-abortion advocates have made over the years about the societal impact of accepting legalized abortion. "The pro-choice movement should be very wary of embracing physician-assisted suicide," Dionne says. "Right-to-lifers have always argued that there is a slippery slope between abortion rights and euthanasia. By accepting the same arguments for both issues, pro-choicers could give philosophical validation to what their opponents have claimed all along."[34]

The abortion debate divides this country like no issue since the war in Vietnam. Mention the topic and people immediately go to their usual corners, the bell rings, and the fighting begins. Euthanasia is similarly emotional and divisive, but unlike abortion, public opinion is fluid and still forming. That is why euthanasia advocates want people to see their cause as the identical "choice" issue as abortion; they believe it will create unthinking support among pro-choice supporters for euthanasia and thereby save them from having to deal with the substance of the issue.

Euthanasia is a policy that should be decided on its own merits and/or demerits, regardless of one's opinion about abortion. One can be pro-choice and still oppose euthanasia. Indeed, it is an issue around which pro-choicers and pro-lifers can find desperately needed common ground.

Euthanasia Standard No. 6: The Polls Show That People Support Euthanasia, So Legalization Is Inevitable

Many have argued on the basis of polls that euthanasia and assisted suicide enjoy wide support in the United States, and that it is foolish to resist legalizing a practice that the people want. The evidence that doctors are kindly disposed in favor of euthanasia is extremely thin (see Chapter 6), so it should come as no surprise that the proof of widespread popular support for the practice is also flimsy.

With the exception of the sparsely populated Northern Territory of Australia, euthanasia is already universally outlawed. (Even though accepted in practice, euthanasia remains against the law in the Netherlands.) Here in the United States, only Oregon has legalized physician-assisted suicide, a law now being tested in the courts. The criminalization of these forms of killing throughout most of the Western democracies, and throughout the world, reflects the near universal recognition that euthanasia and assisted suicide substantially undermine the equality-of-human-life ethic and endanger vulnerable populations.

Some recent public opinion polls seem to show widespread support for legalization of assisted suicide and/or euthanasia, often in the 70 percent range, at least for the terminally ill. But the various polls that have been taken on the issue sometimes disagree. For example, an October 1996 Gallup Poll that asked 1,007 adults "Should it be legal for a physician to participate in assisted suicide?" found that support and opposition to legalization are narrowly divided, with 50 percent in favor and 41 percent opposed. (The margin of error was plus or minus 3 percent.)[35]

Some of the support for legalization has to do with confusion over terms. Many people confuse refusing unwanted treatment—"pulling the plug"—with active killing. Some confusion may also have to do with the way the polls are conducted. Poll questions about legalizing euthanasia often start with the false premise of the dying person's being in unrelievable agony, and then ask whether that person should have the "right to die."

Regardless of the reasons for current poll results, concrete evidence indicates that popular sentiment in favor of euthanasia is probably loosely held rather than deeply ingrained. When a concrete opportunity to officially sanction euthanasia occurs, support for legalization generally plummets. This is illustrated by the several attempts to legalize euthanasia or assisted suicide by means of ballot referendums over the last decade:

	THE PROPOSAL	THE OUTCOME
1988, California	To legalize active euthanasia of the terminally ill	Insufficient signatures obtained to qualify initiative for the ballot
1991, Washington State Initiative 119	To legalize active euthanasia of the terminally ill	Initial polls showed more than 70% support. Referendum lost, 54% to 46%
1992, California Proposition 161	To legalize active euthanasia of the terminally ill	Initial polls showed more than 70% support. Referendum lost, 54% to 46%
1994, Michigan	Jack Kevorkian and associates attempted to legalize euthanasia for the terminally ill and the disabled	Insufficient signatures obtained to qualify initiative for the ballot
1994, Oregon Measure 16	Proposal to permit doctors to issue lethal prescriptions for the terminally ill	Began with a nearly 70% approval in the polls. Won, 51% to 49%

What do the differing polls and the outcome of these legalization attempts teach us? That rather than being overwhelmingly supportive of legalization, the public is profoundly ambivalent and deeply divided. Indeed, if actual legal change is any indication, Americans oppose legalization. Three states—Iowa, Louisiana, and Rhode Island—have banned assisted suicide since the passage of Measure 16, and no other state has legalized it. If left to democratic processes, legalization is anything but a sure bet.

Euthanasia Standard No. 7: Euthanasia Is Needed to Prevent Doctors from Keeping Patients Alive for Too Long

One of the driving forces behind the euthanasia movement is the conviction by many people that modern medicine is too impersonal, too technologically driven, more interested in keeping the body's biological functions operating than in treating patients as people. This belief is emotional but not irrational. Too many people have seen their loved ones "hooked up to machines" against their will, treated as if they were slabs of meat, and otherwise chewed up and spit out by an unresponsive medical system.

Euthanasia advocates are well aware of these fears. Indeed, they take every opportunity to exploit the anger and worry of patients and families regarding unwanted medical treatment and twist it into an argument for euthanasia by falsely accusing euthanasia opponents of being "vitalists," extremists who insist that doctors should do everything that can be done in every case to keep people alive for as long as possible, regardless of the suffering the procedures cause or of the patient's desires.

That charge, often made, is absolutely untrue. "No one should be forced to accept unwanted medical treatment," says Rita Marker, the director of the International Anti-Euthanasia Task Force. "Insisting that death be postponed by every means available is not only against current laws and practice, it is also cruel and inhumane. Patients have a right to say, enough is enough, and to refuse curative medical treatment they don't feel is appropriate."[36]

But saying that one has a right to refuse care is one thing; actually getting it done in the clinical context is too often a different matter. Even for heretofore healthy patients, many medical situations and procedures that begin benignly or with a positive prognosis do not end that way. If a patient is in an accident, or unforeseen or unlikely medical complications arise, families and doctors may be faced with situations that require split-second decisions about treatment options where the patient's desires are unknown. That is why all states permit patients to prepare written legal documents known as advance directives. The most common of these are "durable powers of attorney for health care" and "living wills."

With an advance directive, all competent adults can leave instructions about their future medical care—whether they want treatment or not and under what circumstances—for use in the event they become incapacitated and therefore unable to give informed consent. (Informed consent is the right of the patient to accept or refuse medical treatment on the basis of adequate information provided by the doctor.)

Advance directives have the potential to be a positive antidote to overzealous doctors keeping patients alive by rendering undesired treatment. (Although with the new financial imperatives of managed care, the danger is greater that desired treatment will be withheld.) Unfortunately, proponents of the death culture use advance directives to promote their agenda. In the discussions about advance directives, the only choice generally discussed or promoted is the termination or withholding of life-saving treatment. The desire to fight for life—as legitimate as the decision to allow nature to take its course by not forcing life to be artificially prolonged—almost always receives short shrift or goes completely unmentioned.

Evidence of this agenda can be seen in the advance directives themselves, which are drafted to make refusing treatment easy. Some "form" advance directives only permit one choice: nontreatment. On others, all you have to do is check a box if you don't want treatment. But if your decision is to fight for life, it can get complicated, often requiring you to create your own detailed treatment instructions—a daunting task.

Even more worrisome is that many health-care professionals appear to be confused about the legalities surrounding advance directives, sometimes leading to misapplication of the directive and the denial of care to people with *treatable* medical conditions. One such case was that of Martha Musgrave, a seventy-three-year-old woman who in 1993 decided to undergo a hip replacement. After being discharged from the hospital and upon being admitted to an interim-care facility, she was given a form advance directive to sign along with the other usual admission documents. Musgrave either did not know what she had signed or thought so little about it that she didn't even mention the fact to her daughter, Phyllis Robb, of Fort Wayne, Indiana, with whom she shared every important decision.[37]

Musgrave seemed well on the road to recovery, then she suffered a cardiac arrest caused by an unexpected embolism, a complication of her surgery. Rather than attempt to save her (she was not otherwise terminally ill), the staff assumed that because she had signed a living will, she wanted to die if faced with a grave medical condition. Thus, Musgrave was given no medical assistance whatsoever. The hospital staff just stood there and watched as she died, a process that took about twenty minutes. Her daughter was not even notified of the problem or asked for permission to "do nothing." The first she found out about her mother's crisis was when she was informed of her mother's death.[38]

Another case involves a nursing-home resident from Washington State who was accidentally given the wrong medication by a staff nurse. Though the mistake was quickly discovered, the patient was not advised of the mishap, even though she was mentally competent. Why? She had signed a living will instructing that she not be resuscitated if she suffered a cardiac arrest. It was thus assumed she would not want to be treated for a condition that might (and did) lead to her death, even though she was capable of making that decision herself.[39]

Even more disturbing are the "gotcha" cases, where people who have signed living wills were not allowed to explicitly or implicitly change their minds about refusing care. One such case is that of Marjorie Nighbert. Nighbert had signed a durable power of attorney (see page 241 for a discussion of the durable power of attorney) giving her brother Maynard the authority to make her health-care decisions should she become incapacitated. While visiting her family in Alabama, Nighbert had a stroke, which caused some disability. After she was stabilized, she seemed well enough to benefit from rehabilitation.[40]

Nighbert was transferred to the Crestview Nursing and Convalescent Home in Florida, where doctors attempted to teach her techniques used by stroke patients to eat and drink. Unfortunately, she had difficulty with the technique. Worried that she would aspirate and die, doctors performed the minor surgery of placing a gastrostomy (feeding) tube in her abdomen so she could be safely nourished. (Feeding tubes are commonly used for people who have difficulty eating. Rose Kennedy at age ninety-four had a gastrostomy tube inserted "to correct a nutritional problem," which aided her for the last ten years of her life.)[41]

This presented a problem for Nighbert's brother. Although she had not said so in her power of attorney granting him authority to make her medical decisions, Nighbert had previously stated in conversations that she would not want to use a feeding tube. Thus, even though she was not terminally ill, her brother asked the doctors to cease all food and fluids, a request to which they consented.

Twenty days later she should have been dead. But she wasn't—members of the staff were apparently sneaking food to her. "She was saying things like, 'Please feed me,' 'I'm hungry,' 'I'm thirsty,' and 'I want food,' " says attorney William F. Stone, who later became Marjorie's guardian ad litem when her case went before a judge.[42] In response to Nighbert's utterances, staff members were feeding her, ignoring a doctor's order to dehydrate her to death.

The pressure of feeding Nighbert in the face of the doctor's order eventually was too much for one distraught staff person (who remains anonymous). This person blew the whistle, leading to a state investigation and a temporary restoration of nutritional support. (One person at the Crestview Nursing and Convalescent Home was later fired as a result of the Nighbert case.)

Stone was appointed Nighbert's temporary guardian by Okaloosa County (Florida) Circuit Court Judge Jere Tolton, who gave him only twenty-four hours to conduct an investigation into the matter. Stone was unable to explain the need for the rush. "My authority was limited to determining whether she had the legal capacity to revoke her durable power of attorney," Stone told me. "I stayed up until after four A.M. trying to interview all involved." After his rushed investigation Stone reported back to Judge Tolton that Nighbert did not *at that time* "have the capacity to revoke her advanced medical directive" (in other words, to ask for the "medical treatment" of food).[43] Stone also specifically noted that he was unable to determine what her capacity had been before she was malnourished for twenty days. Furthermore, in the brief time he had to issue his report to the court he was unable to determine what, if any, financial issues might have been involved in the decision to dehydrate Nighbert, who had once been the head of the Cincinnati Chamber of Commerce, or whether any conflict of interest might exist, for example, with regard to inheritance. Stone did tell me that Nighbert's brothers were emotionally distraught over their sister's impending death.[44]

With Stone's report in hand, Judge Tolton ordered the starvation to continue. Stone considered an appeal but before he could determine the legal and ethical issues, Nighbert died, on April 6, 1995.

"I was disturbed by Marjorie's case," Stone says now. "I had no problem with the judge's ruling concerning her then legal capacity, because at the time I did my investigation [after twenty days of undernourishment] she didn't have capacity to revoke her advance directive. I did feel, however, from a public policy point of view, that the issues I raised were not adequately addressed by the court."[45] Stone was convinced that the decisions implementing Marjorie's advance directive did not comply with Florida law.[46]

The case has also changed Stone's approach to his own legal practice. "It has made me change the way I prepare advance directives," Stone says. "There are difficult moral and practical issues involved. I have told my mother and father not to sign advance directives supplied to them at hospitals upon admission. People need to think carefully about these issues in advance and realize their seriousness and what they might actually mean."[47]

Marjorie Nighbert imagined that she would not want a feeding tube. But when the time came, even though she *specifically* asked for food and water, at a time in which she might very well have been legally competent (not that strict legal competence should matter if someone asks to be fed), her currently expressed wishes to be nourished were ignored because she had made contrary statements in the past. Her earlier expressed sentiments ended up costing the nonterminally ill Nighbert her life.

A similar controversy ensnared a Colorado woman named Mary Theresa Corrao, age fifty-nine, and her family. Mary, a breast cancer patient, was placed in the Hospice of Metro Denver by her doctors, having signed an advance directive that she did not want medical treatment once she entered the dying stage of her illness. Later, her brothers Paul (a board-certified pathologist) and Marc, Mary's designated health-care decision makers, decided that her advance directive had been misapplied because she was not actually in the final, dying stage of her condition. They were also upset that at the hospice Corrao developed a kidney infection and a very large bedsore and, they claimed, was overmedicated.

Paul and Marc Corrao, as Mary's duly designated health-care decision makers, insisted that she be returned to the Columbia Aurora Presbyterian Hospital for further treatment. (The hospital and Mary Corrao's insurance company are owned by the for-profit Columbia/HCA Health Care Corp., the largest in Colorado and one of the largest in the country.) Mary improved under the treatment she received at Columbia Aurora Presbyterian, becoming alert and interactive. She then decided to accept curative medical treatment and eschew further hospice care, a sentiment she later reiterated in the media.[48]

But the hospital and Mary Corrao's doctors disagreed. Doctors conceded that Mary's immediate condition had materially improved. Indeed, her cancer had not grown or progressed since January 1995. They also conceded that she had changed her mind about wanting hospice care and refusing curative treatment. However, they contended that her mental capacities were so reduced that she was incapable of making such a "complex decision." They also insisted that she be transferred back to the hospice or to a nursing home so that her hospital bed could be saved for a "salvageable case."[49] In other words, they wanted to hold her to her previous advance directive instructing doctors not to provide curative treatment, even though that was no longer her desire.

The fact that Mary had signed a new advance directive containing a "presumption for life" and requiring ongoing treatment made little difference to the hospital or her doctors. They claimed she remained incompetent to make medical decisions and they were bound and determined to hold her to her previous directive for withholding curative treatment. Columbia Aurora Presbyterian decided to make an example of Mary and her brothers. With vastly superior financial resources, they sicced their corporate lawyers on the family and filed a lawsuit that requested, among other things, that Paul and Marc Corrao be stripped of their rights as medical decision makers for their sister, and/or that the hospital be allowed involuntarily to discharge her back into the hospice or a nursing home. Adding to the pressure on the Corraos, the insurance company then sent a notice that it would pay for only six of seventy-eight days of hospitalization, presenting the family with financial ruin.

Not coincidentally, a member of Columbia's Colorado Division Ethics Committee is the medical futilitarian Dr. Donald J. Murphy, of the Colorado Collective for Medical Decisions. Dr. Murphy urged Columbia Aurora Presbyterian onto the legal battlefield, saying, "This conflict could be a landmark in medical history. This case has the potential to affect much of what we do, if it gets solved."[50] The court appointed Susan Fox-Buchanon, the legal counsel for Dr. Murphy's C.C.M.D., as Mary Corrao's guardian ad litem—hardly a likely candidate to make objective decisions about her care. (The Corraos' lawyer had stipulated that Fox-Buchanon could serve as guardian ad litem, apparently not knowing of her C.C.M.D. affiliation. When the Corraos learned of her connection with C.C.M.D., they asked her to step aside. But Fox-Buchanon refused to recuse herself, despite the apparent conflict of interest.)

If Mary Corrao's newly desired treatment did not medically require acute hospitalization for its safe and effective delivery, the hospital was within its rights to request that she be discharged to a more appropriate setting for her continued care, paid for by her health insurance. As the controversy unfolded, there was discussion of moving her to a ward within the hospital that provided less acute care, since her bedsore still required treatment. But if the hospital and/or insurance company sought to bind Mary to the terms of her former advance directive—as appeared to be the case, despite her obvious change of mind—or if the hospital and/or insurance company took action successfully to preclude further medical treatment on the basis of their value judgments about her life, the Corrao case would be a profoundly dangerous watershed event. If the hospital and doctors could refuse legally to provide treatment that Mary Corrao desired, it would become difficult for health-care consumers to have their desires for treatment heeded if they sign an advance directive eschewing care but later change their mind after they become seriously ill. Such a precedent would threaten the very purpose for which advance directives were created, gutting the value of patient autonomy that the documents are supposed to protect. Postscript: The Corrao matter was never resolved legally. Mary Corrao died in September 1996 after surgery to treat her bedsore. As of January 1997 the cause of her death has not been determined.

Euthanasia Standard No. 8: Only Conservatives Oppose Euthanasia

Many so-called progressive supporters of legalizing euthanasia try to make the case that this issue is one that liberals must embrace as they embraced the civil rights movement and the pro-choice view in the abortion issue. With euthanasia, however, the usual liberal-conservative paradigm does not apply. The controversy cuts a diagonal swath across the usual political differences, sometimes making for some strange political bedfellows. Thus, people on the "religious right" generally oppose euthanasia—and so, too, do many on the "secular left." On this issue (and perhaps only this issue), the Republican Pat Buchanan agrees completely with the Democrat Bill Clinton: Euthanasia should not be legalized. Democrat Mario Cuomo, the former governor of New York, agrees with the Republican 1996 presidential candidate, former senator Bob Dole. The left-wing political commentator Nat Hentoff, who writes for *The Washington Post* and the *Village Voice,* agrees with the *Post*'s right-wing pundit, Charles Krauthammer, when it comes to euthanasia.

The nationally syndicated *Washington Post* columnist E. J. Dionne told me why he, a liberal, opposes euthanasia and assisted suicide. "Above almost everything else, liberals are supposed to be allied with the powerless, the disabled, the poor, the infirm, and the dying, and it is the powerless who could be victimized by euthanasia. We are also supposed to understand how individual decisions can be less than free if they are made under unfair or unreasonable constraints. Considering the growth of managed care, legalizing physician-assisted suicide would place people in the weakest and most vulnerable positions under excruciating pressures to do things they don't want to do and shouldn't be asked to do."[51]

Add in other such liberal voices as those of Matthew Rothschild, the editor of *The Progressive,* Donna Shalala, the secretary of health and human services, and this author, a supporter of Ralph Nader—to name just a few—and it can be safely said that opposing euthanasia is neither a "liberal" nor a "conservative" position; it is a human position.

Euthanasia Standard No. 9: There Is No Difference Between Pain-Control Treatment and Euthanasia

One of the more disturbing standards sung by euthanasia advocates rests on the "double-effect" scenario in pain control. Pain control, which often requires powerful drugs, can have the effect not only of controlling pain but also—sometimes—of hastening death. Thus, euthanasia proponents argue, since death might be hastened by the use of pain control, and since euthanasia is designed (they allege) to reduce suffering, there is no difference between aggressively applied pain palliation and intentionally hastened death.

This is an intentional misapplication of the principle in ethics called the "double effect": There are occasions when a person may intend to do a good thing, recognizing that a bad result *might* occur instead, despite his good intentions. Even if the bad outcome actually occurs, so long as the intention was for good, then the action is morally acceptable.

In order for the double-effect principle to apply—meaning an act that produces a bad result is still considered to be ethical—four conditions must be met:

1. THE ACTION TAKEN (IN THIS CASE, TREATING PAIN) IS "GOOD" (THE RELIEF OF SUFFERING) OR MORALLY NEUTRAL.
2. THE BAD EFFECT (IN THIS CASE, DEATH) IS NOT INTENDED.
3. THE GOOD EFFECT (IN THIS CASE, THE RELIEF OF SUFFERING) CANNOT BE BROUGHT ABOUT BY AN ACT DESIGNED TO INTENTIONALLY CAUSE THE BAD EFFECT (DEATH).

4. THERE IS A SUFFICIENTLY GRAVE REASON TO PERFORM THE ACT (IN
   THIS CASE, THE PRESENCE OF SEVERE PAIN).

If properly applied pain control accidentally hastens death, the palliative act remains ethical on the basis of the principle of double effect, since
the bad result, death, was not intended. Euthanasia fails the third requirement that the hoped-for good, relief of suffering, was accomplished by intentionally causing the bad effect, death. As the pain-control expert Dr.
Eric Chevlen notes, "Euthanasiasts have tried to stand the concept of double effect on its head, arguing that the killing of the patient is done with the
intention to relieve suffering, and that therefore it is morally acceptable
under the doctrine of double effect. This is casuistic nonsense. When a
doctor purposely kills a patient, the fact that the doctor liked the patient
and didn't want him to suffer does not change the fact that he has acted
wrongly. Only if the bad outcome is *possible* and *undesired* rather than
certain and *intentional* does the doctrine of double effect come into play.
Sadly, in the hands of euthanasiasts, the only thing certain is that there will
be one more corpse by the end of the day."[52]

Although the use of pain-control drugs such as morphine, like surgery
or most other medical treatments, can have serious side effects, including
death, pain control, if *properly applied,* rarely hastens death; in any event,
it is in no way akin to intentional killing. "Effective application of pain control is not euthanasia," says the Oregon hospice physician and pain-control
expert Gary Lee, M.D. "People receiving pain control at the very end of
their lives to preserve comfort are in the dying process. As folks relax, and
there is less drive to breathe and fight the pain, they fade off. That happens
in the natural course of dying anyway. People become weak or drowsy; because of their advanced disease they cough less and develop pneumonia
and die. From a practical standpoint, you can't really tell if the patient died
earlier because of the pain control or not." Dr. Lee adds, "We don't see respiratory depression in patients not on the brink of death already, unless
the intent is to cause respiratory depression. That is what euthanasia advocates are interested in. Causing these effects 'earlier' than they would
occur in the natural processes, including when they would happen even
with the proper application of proper pain control techniques."[53]

Dr. Chevlen agrees. "Certainly, the doctor prescribing morphine must
be knowledgeable about its safe use to avoid adverse effects. But fortunately, patients become tolerant to the respiratory effects of morphine.
Those patients who have been taking the drug for a fair while experience
very little, if any, suppression of respiratory drive on the doses of mor-

phine needed to control pain, which can be increased as time goes on. When morphine is used properly in the last hours of life, it eases the anxiety and discomfort the patient might otherwise have, but it does not hasten death."[54]

Euthanasia advocates seek to justify killing by hiding behind the double-effect principle of ethics. But, like many of the notions they use in their efforts to blur vital distinctions and distort accepted definitions, the double effect simply does not apply to intentional killing. Pain control is not a subtle form of euthanasia and euthanasia is not a synonym for pain control.

Another aspect of the false pain control–euthanasia equation is that many well-meaning and compassionate people accept the legalization of euthanasia because they believe that killing patients is sometimes the only way to alleviate suffering. This is a false premise. There are abundant opportunities for compassionate and empowering caregiving. If these were fully accessed and competently implemented, human suffering would be alleviated significantly. This in turn would allay the public's fear of dying in agony—perhaps the primary reason many reluctantly support legalizing doctor-induced death. These important issues will be addressed in the last chapter.

CHAPTER 9

Hospice or Hemlock:
The Choice Is Ours

Euthanasia is on the cutting edge of 1990s social trends. This is not surprising. Few other issues so perfectly reflect the public gestalt of our times: Euthanasia is justified by claims of compassion, appeals to raw emotionalism, and paeans to "choice." But in light of the consequences that could flow from the legalization and legitimization of euthanasia, we should all think deeply about what accepting the values of the death culture would really mean for our country.

Social libertarians argue that the state has no interest in preventing suicide, because each person's body is exclusively his or her own. Therefore all of us must be free to do exactly as we please with our own body—even destroy it if that is what we want. Reasonable people can differ on that. But do we really want to live in a country whose public policy would require authorities to stand back and watch deeply depressed persons jump off a bridge or shoot themselves in the head?

Some would say that legalizing physician-assisted suicide (P.A.S.) and euthanasia wouldn't prevent police from stopping bridge jumpers who want to die. It would, however, prevent us from stopping doctors from killing patients who want to die. But what is the difference between a jump off a bridge and a lethal injection? In both cases, the despairing person wants to die, for reasons that are compelling at that moment. It thus seems to me that if we are to create a noninterference policy toward the one, we must also stand back and permit the other: If we stand back to let a physician kill, then we must stand back to let a person kill himself.

That being said, suicide per se is not the issue. Jumping off a bridge or turning on a car engine in a closed garage to kill oneself by carbon monoxide poisoning is an individual act. Being killed by a doctor or committing P.A.S. is a joint endeavor between two or more people. The point at issue is not the propriety of suicide itself, but whether we should have the legal right to have ourselves killed by another person. Looked at from another angle, the question before us is whether the broad prohibition against killing by private persons, self-defense and defense of others being the exceptions, should be discarded so as to permit third parties to collaborate and participate in the deaths of sick and disabled people and those who are incompetent, and this on the basis of beliefs that certain lives are not worth living.

This question is of monumental importance. If we remain the society of "ordered liberty" envisioned by the Founders, a nation created to promote the greatest common good while allowing for as much individual liberty as practicably consistent with this broader purpose, we will reject euthanasia and assisted suicide as a danger to vulnerable persons, as a threat to basic institutions, and as a dangerous frayer of the social fabric.

If, on the other hand, our nation is above all else a radical personal-autonomy state, existing primarily to maximize individual behavioral license regardless of the overall impact such conduct has on the whole, if the state's primary raison d'être is merely to prevent one autonomous individual's proverbial fist from punching another autonomous individual's proverbial nose, then legalized euthanasia makes sense. But, as Charles Krauthammer of *The Washington Post* has warned, if choosing to be killed by others is a matter of individual liberty, then what "private" activities are there that can be proscribed? If individuals cannot be prevented from arranging their own killing, then how can we logically outlaw a pregnant woman taking crack cocaine? What could possibly be more personal than what one chooses to put into one's body? What is more intimate than one's chosen state of consciousness? Similarly, if we accept euthanasia as a basic liberty interest the state cannot proscribe, would the laws that prohibit the selling of human organs for transplants fall too? Such a policy could easily fall into the "choice" category as well as fit into the increasing commercialism of our culture; it is also likely such a policy would create a marketplace in human organs leading to the catastrophic exploitation of the poor and to a medical system where transplants would go to the highest bidders. But this prospect would be of no concern—after all, "true freedom" has its costs.

In a very real sense, how we decide the euthanasia controversy will determine the kind of society we live in and the one we will create for our children as we enter the next century. Seen in this light, the issue transcends what may or may not be good or bad, right or wrong, for individuals. It literally defines who and what we are as a society, a culture, and a people.

Change isn't necessarily progress. As the victims of the French and Russian revolutions discovered to their dismay, change can be violent and/or culturally destructive. Since we are dealing with the most fundamental issue, life and death, we should not make changes lightly or base them on emotionalism or sound-bite rationales and slogans. Legalizing euthanasia would cast aside 2,500 years of accumulated wisdom, ethics, and morality, and dramatically burden our culture with foreseen and unforeseen consequences. We only should risk such consequences if it is rational to do so.

I propose a three-pronged test to judge the rationality of creating a "right to die":

- Is there a deep and abiding need for this proposed revolutionary change that cannot be met through other means?

- Are the expected benefits of the change worth the foreseeable risks of the change?

- Would the change be progress?

I believe that a rational analysis of the euthanasia issue demonstrates that the answer to all three questions is a resounding no.

Is There a Deep and Abiding Need to Legalize Euthanasia?

Pain Can Be Controlled

The most emotionally compelling arguments in favor of euthanasia are that euthanasia is needed to help relieve human suffering caused by illness, that euthanasia is necessary to safeguard the human right to refuse unwanted medical treatment in favor of death with dignity, and that euthanasia is preferable to living with certain disabilities. I do not find these arguments persuasive.

Advocates of euthanasia assert that legalization is necessary to make available through killing the relief of otherwise unrelievable suffering and pain. This is a false premise. It is certainly true that far too much pain and suffering go unrelieved, not because we can't provide relief but because we don't.

The difference between "can't" and "don't" is a vital part of this analysis. If relief of agonizing pain and suffering is the overarching purpose for legalizing assisted killing, and if medical science has the wherewithal to relieve pain and significantly reduce suffering, then there is no real need to legalize euthanasia. Rather, there is a need to make the currently available relief universally accessible.

In fact, nearly all pain can be effectively treated and controlled, including pain associated with arthritis, cancer, AIDS, and multiple sclerosis. Regardless of the cause of pain, severity of condition, or type of disease or affliction, with proper medical treatment nearly every patient can exercise "power over pain," adding tremendously to the quality of his or her life and even its length. The beneficent potential of pain control and relief through palliative care of other symptoms such as itching, constipation, and nausea cannot be overstated.

Of course, some conditions are more difficult to palliate than others. For example, one of the most painful diseases known to medicine is bone cancer. The pain can be excruciating, unbearable. Bones grow brittle and break easily. The patient may be unable to bear simply being touched. But even this pain can be significantly relieved. It isn't easy. It takes multiple strategies and hard work and concerted effort by dedicated doctors.

Dr. Robin Bernhoft, a Washington surgeon, has seen such an effort succeed in his own family. That is one of the reasons he opposes euthanasia. Dr. Bernhoft told me the following story:

> *People who say bone cancer pain cannot be relieved are mistaken. My brother died of multiple myeloma [a bone-marrow cancer] when he was forty-one. His cancer destroyed his spine and ribs. He had fractures all over his chest which moved when he breathed. It was as painful a case of cancer as I have seen since I became a surgeon in 1976. But Larry was lucky. He was at the Mayo Clinic, where doctors knew how to take care of such horrible pain, even back in 1981. Throughout his illness, he remained very comfortable, and very alert, because they knew how to treat such pain. Pain can almost always be controlled—and without putting people into a drugged stupor. Pain medicine—even morphine—goes straight to the pain. If the dosage is properly controlled, the patient will not feel drunk, drugged, and most importantly, will not be in pain.*[1]

The bad news, of course, is that too many patients are not given the proper treatment that Larry Bernhoft received. We have a choice: Do we improve the training of doctors in the areas of pain, depression, disability, and the needs of the dying, and demand that their professional performance meet the highest standard, or do we lower our medical standards to, in Dr. Bernhoft's words, "veterinary levels" and allow doctors off the hook by permitting them to kill?

If we want the former, we have a lot of work to do. When it comes to pain control, doctors are notorious underachievers. As discussed earlier in the book, in the United States alone tens of millions of people—cancer patients, AIDS patients, M.S. patients, rheumatoid arthritis patients, and others—receive inadequate pain relief, causing unnecessary suffering and giving impetus to the euthanasia movement. According to medical literature, there are several reasons for this failure of modern professional medicine:

- Too many doctors did not receive sufficient training in pain control in medical school and have not pursued the subject since graduation. As a consequence, they don't even know about the newest pain-control techniques, thus depriving their patients of relief that should be theirs.

- Too many doctors fear that pain medicine will cause drug addiction. This is a false fear. When used appropriately for pain control, and when applied properly, narcotic agents are virtually never addicting. That means that narcotics can be used liberally, relieve pain and suffering, and not add to the country's drug abuse problem.

- Pain control is often an innocent casualty of the war on drugs. Many state laws designed to curb drug abuse instead make it difficult or inconvenient for doctors to effectively treat their patients' pain.

- Too many doctors are excessively concerned about side effects that sometimes occur with pain control, such as constipation. Yet, like pain, these side effects can almost always be controlled.

- Too many doctors believe that only the severest pain requires treatment, thereby abandoning many chronic pain sufferers to their misery.

- Too many doctors treating patients for painful conditions do not take the time or effort to reevaluate their patients' pain on a regular and continuing basis. Some doctors never even ask their patients about their pain.[2]

Patients also know too little about the benefits of pain control. They and their loved ones do not know that they are suffering unnecessarily, and consequently they may come to believe that death is the only way to obtain relief. Like doctors, patients sometimes eschew pain control for fear of becoming addicted to drugs. It needs to be reiterated: Morphine and other pain-control agents, when used in appropriate doses to stop or prevent actual pain, do not cause addiction. Nor, again assuming proper application, do they usually cause mental confusion, pronounced drowsiness, personality change, or stupor.

For more information on cancer pain control, see "Resources," page 253.

Hospice Care Already Provides "Death with Dignity"

Many dying people who consider assisted suicide are afraid of future pain, abandonment, and/or a "medicalized" death hooked up to machines in a cold, sterile institutional setting. While some patients do still die this way, dying does not have to be so impersonal and burdensome.

Over the last few decades the hospice movement has slowly reversed the overmedicalization of death. Hospice is less a place than a concept. According to the *Harvard Health Letter,* "The hospice philosophy is that dying should be accepted as a unique part of life, not resisted with every weapon in medicine's armamentarium. When nothing more can be gained from [curative] treatment, hospices focus on making people as comfortable as possible."[3]

The goal is to provide whatever care patients need to enable them to die naturally, in peace, and with dignity. This means that no efforts are made to extend the patient's life. Instead, the focus is on providing whatever treatment is necessary to control pain and alleviate symptoms, while at the same time taking a holistic approach by providing emotional support for the patient and the family.

Hospice uses a team approach to better ensure that all of the patient's and family's needs are met. A typical team includes a physician, such as the hospice physicians interviewed for this book, Drs. Eric Chevlen, Ira Byock, and Gary Lee. But the doctor is only the beginning. Hospice nurses make house calls to check on patients and provide needed medical services. Social workers are available to assist the patient and family and assess their needs. Psychological therapists and bereavement counselors provide valuable grief counseling and emotional support. Volunteers work creatively to fill caregiving niches for the benefit of patient and family. Respite care is also available to aid families needing a short break from the intense effort of caregiving. Since most hospice care occurs in the home (although there are hospice facilities), once a patient enters hospice, usually when the prognosis is life expectancy of six months or less, he or she can say good-bye to the impersonal hospitals and being "hooked up to machines" that so many of us fear during the dying process.

The beneficence of hospice, for those patients who desire to cease curative or life-prolonging medical treatment and transition peacefully into death, cannot be overstated. "Hospice is often misunderstood as limited to controlling a dying person's symptoms," says Dr. Ira Byock. "Symptom control is the first priority of hospice, but it is not the ultimate goal. The fundamental purpose of hospice is to enhance the quality of life for the dying individual and the family, to give the opportunity for the patient to live as fully as possible in community with his or her friends or family, to get affairs in order, to deepen and complete relationships. Hospice is about the completing of a life, and in that context, it is . . . wonderfully human."[4]

Euthanasia advocates usually give lip-service support to hospice but contend that hospice providers should also be in the business of hastening their patients' deaths—called by the euthanasia advocate Lonny Shavelson "hospice and hemlock."[5] This idea is anathema to most hospice professionals as the antithesis of the hospice philosophy.

The message of hospice is that each patient is valuable and important, that dying is an important stage of life that is worth living through and growing from—until death comes through natural processes. The euthanasia philosophy is just the opposite. By definition, euthanasia is a statement that life is not worth living, that the answer to dying, disability, or other "hopeless illness" is to artificially induce death and "get it over with."

Dr. Carlos F. Gomez, assistant professor of medicine at the University of Virginia School of Medicine and a hospice physician of national repute, firmly opposes mixing hospice with hemlock as an easy way out of truly caring for dying patients. He told a congressional committee looking into the assisted-suicide issue: "We now have it well within our technical means to alleviate, to palliate and comfort and control the worst symptoms of those of our fellow citizens who are terminally ill. The question before . . . the country at large is whether we have the heart, the courage, and the will to make it so, or whether we will opt for expediency and call it mercy."[6]

Dr. Gary Lee also strongly opposes mixing hospice with hemlock. "I am there to take care of the patient," he says. "You can't move the line in hospice to allow the killing of patients. It would destroy the line." Dr. Byock puts it even more succinctly: "The hospice focus is on life and the alleviation of suffering," whereas "the goal of assisted suicide and euthanasia is death."[7]

From this perspective, euthanasia threatens the hospice movement. "Hospice commits to the patient and the family that we will take care of them, to nonabandonment," says Dr. Lee. "But if euthanasia becomes a standard of practice, too many times there would be a real incentive to do it. There are some patients whose proper care requires time and effort, professional services that aren't necessarily paid for by insurance companies. I might say, 'There has to be an easier way.' I could too easily find myself seeing euthanasia as the simple answer; one that is less time-consuming and the least expensive. If accepted, euthanasia could very easily take the place of proper patient care."[8]

The Dutch experience with hospice lends credence to Dr. Lee's concerns. Studies show that hospice-style palliative care "is virtually unknown in the Netherlands."[9] There are very few hospice facilities, very little in the way of organized hospice activity, and few specialists in palliative care, although some efforts are now under way to try and jump-start the hospice movement in that country. One reason for the lack of hospice opportunities in the Netherlands is the general-practitioner style of medical delivery, in which doctors make house calls and care for citizens from birth until death—a hands-on approach to medicine that the hospice movement is reintroducing to American health care. However, the widespread availability of euthanasia in the Netherlands may be another reason for the stunted growth of the Dutch hospice movement. As one Dutch doctor is reported to have said, "Why should I worry about palliation when I have euthanasia?"

Hospice can be provided in the home, in a nursing home, or in a hospice facility. The cost of hospice treatment is covered by Medicare and most health insurance policies.

For more information on hospice, ask your physician, look in your local Yellow Pages under "Hospices," or contact one of the hospice resources listed on page 255 of "Resources."

Independent Living Eliminates Despair by Empowering Disabled People

As we have learned from people such as Paul Longmore, Diane Coleman, and Carol Gill, disabled people usually seek out assisted suicide because they have suffered the kind of life crisis that can afflict anyone—divorce, the death of a loved one, career crisis, financial collapse, etc.—or because their desire to live freely and independently has been needlessly stymied, leading to feelings of despair and hopelessness. As with untreated pain and undesired medicalized dying, this need not be so. Increasingly, the disability rights and independent-living movement works on behalf of disabled people and their families to help overcome hurdles that needlessly interfere with the living of full and productive lives. The movement provides disabled people with personal assistants who help them learn independent-living skills and help perform tasks their disabilities prevent or make difficult. It also provides other forms of peer counseling and deals with issues of housing advocacy, disability rights advocacy, transportation, and most important of all, information and referral. By law, the centers for independent living must have at least 51 percent control by people with disabilities, ensuring that the perspective of disabled people is amply considered in decision making. There are independent-living centers all around the country.

Independent living makes a tremendous difference in so many lives. Take Mark O'Brien, the Berkeley, California, journalist-poet described earlier in the book. O'Brien contracted polio at the age of six and has been a complete quadriplegic for forty-one years. The polio so profoundly disabled his musculature that he is dependent on an iron lung, rarely leaving the machine other than for a few hours a month when he is able to survive in a supine position on a ventilator, which allows him to be wheeled outside for an hour or so and to make personal appearances at lectures near his home in Berkeley. Otherwise, almost his entire life is spent inside his yellow iron lung, which dominates the small living room–kitchen of his one-bedroom loft apartment.

Jack Kevorkian has said that those among us who have significant physical impairments, people such as O'Brien, are "certifiably pathological" if they are not in despair.[10] Nothing could be more wrong. He is not in despair and he is definitely not "certifiable." While he faces some considerable challenges, he enjoys life and lives it to the fullest—in large part because of the independent-living movement. "Before I lived on my own," O'Brien told me, "I was afraid my life wouldn't amount to anything, that I couldn't do anything, that I would never be able to contribute to society. But because of independent living, I now have my own career, work at it, and live my own life. Because of independent living, I paid income taxes for the first time in my life last year. Most disabled people could achieve at least partial self-sufficiency with the appropriate services made available to them."[11]

According to O'Brien, "The idea of disabled people being stuck in nursing homes for life is not only wasteful of resources, it is wasteful of people, and little better than slavery. We know how to assist people to live independently, it is cheaper than warehousing people, we are just not doing it sufficiently to be of assistance to most disabled people. I consider the cause of independent living to be the moral equivalent of the civil rights movement of the 1960s."[12]

Another example of the difference that independent living can make for even the most profoundly disabled was brought to my attention by an attorney named Beth Roney Drennan, of Baraboo, Wisconsin. Drennan was appointed guardian ad litem for David W. Domenosky, a young man whose brain was injured in an auto accident. Domenosky awakened from a six-month coma with total quadriplegia. Despite his medical records' showing that he has no intellectual impairment, and despite his being able to communicate by blinks and stares, Drennan was shocked to learn that doctors had discussed withholding antibiotics from Domenosky should he develop an infection. His parents refused to authorize discontinuing treatment for their son.

When Drennan asked about this, one of Domenosky's nurses nonchalantly admitted that the idea was for him to die if he should ever develop pneumonia.[13] When Drennan asked a supervising nurse at a different facility (where she was thinking of placing Domenosky) her views on this matter, the woman asserted that she too believed treatment should be withheld from Domenosky because he "is no longer experiencing life." The nurse then asked Drennan, "Do you want your tax dollars supporting people like this forever?"[14]

Appalled at what she considered a cavalier attitude about Domenosky's life on the part of some of his professional caregivers, worried that "David would be killed without his mother being consulted"[15] (as we have seen, this is not an unreasonable fear), and believing firmly in her client's right not only to live but to thrive, Drennan spent more than a year, in her words, "fighting blindly" to get Domenosky out of the nursing home and into a better placement.[16]

Eventually, Drennan's care for Domenosky and her innate tenacity led her to a disability rights group committed to the independent-living concept. With the group's help, she has overcome "budget cuts, recalcitrant bureaucrats and overburdened case workers," and placed David into his own apartment.[17]

Domenosky's release from the nursing home is only the beginning of Drennan's plans for her friend and client. "David will get communication therapy," Drennan says excitedly. "He will receive vocational training so he can work or otherwise involve himself in projects, plus, he will receive physical therapy to improve his physical abilities." According to Drennan, Domenosky is almost as charged about his upcoming new life as she is. "He is most excited about 'getting back into the culture,' " Drennan says. "He can hardly wait to listen to his own style of music, watch current movies on video, create a new life for himself outside of a nursing home setting."[18]

This success story needs multiplying. "David's life has gotten much better," Drennan says. "And so have the lives of the people with which he has come into contact simply because they have gotten to know him."[19]

Compare Drennan's understanding of human compassion to the mindsets of so many others—doctors, euthanasia advocates, well-meaning relatives of disabled people—who proclaim that some lives are simply not worth living, that for the good of the patient, to ease the burden on the patient's family and relieve society of a financial burden, disabled people like Domenosky can ethically be dehydrated to death, assisted with suicide, or, indeed, fatally injected. To this Drennan responds:

> In our culture, I think that many people see affection as something that occurs post hoc, ergo propter hoc [after something and therefore because of it]. They believe there must be a "cause" for affection, that the cause comes first. If there is enough cause then the effect follows— that if the person is deserving or has certain attributes, then that is a cause for having affection for them. But I believe that real affection for each other is inherent in our natural state, and that if we do nothing to block that affection, it will flow through us toward others, at least in some degree. No cause is required, no attributes of mind or body, not earned by conditions but not lost by them either. Not even old age, loss of teeth, loss of hair, loss of physical beauty, or ability to move the body due to quadriplegia, can make the affection go away. Those of us who have affection for David, see the beauty and infinite value of his life—and that affection is not conditioned on the state of David's body. David is wonderful, just as and because he is.[20]

Mark O'Brien, David Domenosky, and so many disabled people like them are "cases" of "suffering" that pro-euthanasia types would consider "hopeless conditions," people who, in Jack Kevorkian's words, are "pathological" if they are not in despair and whose killing should therefore be deemed "rational" and, again in Kevorkian's words, "a standard medical service."[21] Yet, given appropriate access to independent living rather than abandoned to "warehousing," most disabled people lose any desire to die, much less to be killed, and instead get about the adventure of life.

Is the Expected Benefit of Euthanasia Worth Its Considerable Risks?

Euthanasia is akin to "destroying the village in order to save it." There are far better ways to serve people in need, care opportunities that dramatically reduce suffering and pain while simultaneously increasing the sense of personal dignity and self-worth in virtually all ill or disabled people. If we applied these treatment and caregiving strategies universally, people's fear of suffering, the driving force behind the advance of the idea of euthanasia, would virtually disappear. At this juncture in the debate, death fundamentalists will usually say, "But what about the few who, despite the best of care, would still want euthanasia rather than to await a natural death or live a life with the limitations of disability, or chronic disease? Shouldn't they be given the opportunity to have their lives ended as they choose?"

Again, that depends on what one believes the purpose of society to be, as expressed through its public policy. Is it to best serve the forest or is it to make sure that each tree has maximum autonomy? In the latter case there isn't really a forest, but merely a bunch of trees in close proximity to each other. Should the morality, ethical concepts, and laws that protect and benefit the many be cast aside because a relatively small group of people do not want to abide by them?

Certainly, there are times when the rights of even one person override the views of the rest of society. One of the genius-points of our system is that at such times, special legal niches can be created to accommodate and protect the rights of small groups. For example, the law in most states requires universal education to age sixteen or so. Yet Amish parents have the legal right to remove their children from public school years before they reach sixteen, owing to the special nature of the Amish subculture.

The niche created to accommodate the Amish has little if any impact on the general society. Nor does it endanger non-Amish children. The same cannot be said of euthanasia. As we derive rights from our community, so too we bear responsibilities. That is what it means to be part of a community. Even though a few people would undoubtedly wish to hasten their deaths despite receiving the best medical treatment and care that exists, asking to be killed should be viewed in the same way as someone threatening to jump off the Golden Gate Bridge: as a request for help. The compassionate answer must be to render assistance, not give the suicidal person a "helpful" push off the rail. Legalization would be a step backward, not forward.

The history of the West in general, and this nation in particular, has been largely about the epic struggle to transform the equality-of-human-life ethic from hoped-for future ideal into present-day reality. Equality requires us to shed our social smallness and distance ourselves from past and present discrimination based on race, creed, gender, physical ability, religious beliefs, sexual orientation, and status of health. Toward that end great strides have been made, profound evils have been overcome. Yet for many, true equality remains an elusive dream.

As long as some remain on the outside looking in, the struggle will continue. How can it not? Equality is the bedrock foundation of our culture. But as this vital work continues, as we rid ourselves of false concepts and phony distinctions, let us not make the mistake of replacing current groups of oppressed people with a new collection of "others"—this time based on our fears and prejudices about health, age, disability, and death. As we eschewed Jim Crow, let us also reject the inherent discrimination of futilitarianism. As we open our arms to those whom we have traditionally rejected, let us not turn our backs on the dying, the disabled, and the chronically ill. In short, as we painfully climb the mountain toward true equality, let us not jump back off the cliff by countenancing the killing of the weakest and most vulnerable among us.

Would the Change Be Progress?

I believe it is fair to assert that this book has demonstrated that legalizing euthanasia would not be a step forward for society but rather a giant leap backward in our desire to serve and assist those among us who have had their lives impacted by a terminal diagnosis, disability, chronic pain, the debilitation of advanced years, the despair of depression—indeed, everyone and anyone experiencing what euthanasia advocates call "hopeless illness." It would be to countenance their killing, in essence to legalize murder. It would inevitably lead, as it has in the Netherlands, to involuntary euthanasia. This is especially dangerous for those among us who are less powerful: African Americans and other minorities who too often receive lower standards of health care, such as the poor and the uneducated, those with little understanding or ability to assert their rights to quality health care in an increasingly commercialized medical milieu. It would be to make a virtue out of abandonment and accelerate the country's tendency to isolate those most in need of community.

This last point was brought home to me in a forceful manner recently in my work as a hospice volunteer. One of my hospice friends has A.L.S., which has left him almost entirely paralyzed. Bob and I have spent many hours discussing his feelings about dying, about becoming disabled, indeed, about the purpose and meaning of life. Our many conversations have been deep, profound, inspiring, and rewarding. "For the first two and a half years after my diagnosis I wanted to kill myself," Bob told me early in our relationship. "It wasn't the illness so much that depressed me but the reaction of the people around me. First they stopped visiting, then they stopped calling to speak to me, then they stopped calling. I found myself completely isolated. I felt like a token presence in the world."*

Jack Kevorkian was first making headlines during this time and Bob took acute notice. He told me that he listened to the newscasts carefully and that they definitely impacted his thinking about suicide. "During my worst moments, the idea of a quick demise had an appeal," he recalls. "I didn't want to be a burden and I figured it would be the best thing for everyone." If Kevorkian didn't plant the suicide seeds in Bob's consciousness, his activities and their coverage certainly watered the sprouts.

Suicide thoughts and Bob eventually parted company as he, his wife, and their children pulled together and kept on going through the difficulties caused by his inability to work and the distress caused by his weakening condition. When he joined the Mormon church he found a new community whose members rallied to his side. Church members visit Bob every day. Two and a half years after his diagnosis he "came out of the fog." He discovered that life held a very special meaning for him, and that for as long as nature permitted, he deeply wanted to live.

Now, three years after Bob was expected to die, he spends his days relishing life, thinking, pondering, feeling, growing, loving his family, watching his children mature and thrive. "Believe it or not, this has been a

* My conversations with Bob were private and not undertaken for inclusion in this book. I have placed them here with Bob's express permission because I think they demonstrate an important point.

blessing," he told me. "I have grown. I have come into my own. I know my-self better than I ever thought I would. I understand more about life than I ever thought I could. I am living more intensely than I ever have. I wouldn't have missed the last several years for anything in the world."

Had Bob requested assisted suicide during his years of depression, death fundamentalists would have considered the request "rational." They would have labeled his illness "hopeless." They would have believed, on the basis of their own fears and prejudices, that the quality of his life was not and would never again be good enough for his life to be worth living. They would have readily granted his request for a hastened death, thinking they were being oh so compassionate. (In fact, A.L.S. has become some-thing of the poster disease for the entire euthanasia movement.) What they would not have considered was that by acceding to his suicidal desire, they actually would have been robbing him of some of the best and most important years of his life. And no one would have ever known because those years would have been lost to Bob forever.

In this regard, the words of Dennis Brace, of Youngstown, Ohio, should also be heeded. Brace, forty-two, was told more than four years ago that his inoperable colon cancer would kill him within a few months. Sev-eral doctors told him there was virtually no point in fighting, since his can-cer had spread to his muscle tissues.[22]

According to Brace, one of the greatest emotional burdens he faces in combating his malady are attitudes like those expressed by Jack Kevor-kian, Judge Stephen Reinhardt, Dr. Timothy Quill, and other euthanasia proponents, who in their different ways send the message that his life is as good as over. "What am I supposed to think when the government or the courts or society says it is okay to snuff people out like me because we are sick?" Brace angrily asked. "If you wanted to push me into giving up, that is how to do it. Any kind of negativism from the outside is devastating to a person in my position. This euthanasia stuff is the opposite of compassion and support. It is saying to me that no one cares."[23]

Creating a Culture of Compassion

Rejecting the death culture does not mean we should accept the status quo. Quite the contrary. Euthanasia, like a fever, is a symptom, not the un-derlying disease. To eradicate the symptom, we will have to cure the un-derlying unhealthy societal conditions that cause it and take needed steps.

We Must Overcome Our National Death Phobia

"People routinely think that doctors know how to prognosticate, how to mitigate pain, and generally how to serve dying persons," Dr. Joanne Lynn told the Senate Finance Committee. "Nothing could be further from the truth. This culture has been so thoroughly death-denying that we have not even described our course to death nor developed professional skills in service of the dying, except for the development of hospice services. . . . We do not know how to see to it that most who die get excellent care, shaped to their needs, and responsive to their symptoms."[24]

"By any standard one chooses," it has been observed, "medical schools in the United States fail to provide even adequate education in the care of the dying."[25] Only 5 of 126 medical schools in the United States offer a separate required course in the care of the dying. According to the A.M.A., as of 1995 only 26 percent of residency programs offered a course on the medico-legal aspects of end-of-life care as a regular part of the curriculum. A national survey of accredited residency programs in family medicine and internal medicine/pediatrics, the specializations from which primary-care physicians come, revealed that 15 percent of these programs offer no formal training in terminal care and that residents in the majority of these programs coordinated the care of ten or fewer terminally ill patients throughout the course of their studies. Only 17 percent of these programs use hospice rotations, despite the widespread availability of hospice programs that could be served by the residents and that could teach them. The report summarized this and other data to state that the evidence reveals a "well-established pattern of neglect of medical education in the care of the dying."[26]

People who are dying, disabled, or seriously ill are often abandoned by friends and are isolated by a culture that celebrates youth and vitality and that often places cosmetic values ahead of human values. We treat those among us with disabling conditions as unwelcome reminders of our ultimate lack of control over life and of the fact that someday we too will come face to face with our own mortality. This needs to change.

The good news is that calls for more humane treatment of dying people are finally being taken seriously. For example, the Ethics Committee of the American Geriatric Society has produced a nine-point plan to improve the care of the dying, including renewed focus on respecting patient values in treatment decisions; the creation of multidisciplinary teams to treat dying people; more attention to the relief of symptoms with emphasis on pain control; better reimbursement policies for providers of palliative care; and education of doctors and patients on the desirability of a peaceful and natural death when this is desired by the patient rather than a drive for curative care until shortly before death.[27] Those are good suggestions, and hopefully the medical profession will listen and act upon them.

The current and future dying people of America also need to change our attitudes toward death. We should strive to ensure that no one is left to face death alone. Rather than shy away from dying people, as many of us do, we should embrace them, let them know we love and care for them, and that we will be with them to the end. We need to stop avoiding visiting those we know who are ill or dying and should volunteer with hospice or other beneficent organizations that succor the ill and assist the needy.

To give ourselves peace of mind about our own end-of-life care, every adult should create an advance directive stating our preferences about desired medical treatment should we become incapacitated. A caveat is in order here. Advance directives should not be taken lightly. As we have seen, once you fill one out, you may get what you ask for—like it or not. Too often people wait until an advance directive form is given to them by a hospital admissions clerk before considering these important issues. Federal law requires that every new patient to a hospital or nursing home be provided an advance directive form to sign, if the patient so desires.

The time to consider your preferences is before incapacitating illness or injury strikes. This brings us back to the concept of informed consent. As we have discussed previously, in our health-care delivery system patients make health-care decisions, not doctors. Under the law of informed consent, the doctor is charged with fully advising the patient of the pros and cons of treatment or nontreatment, testing, and the like, and charged with giving opinions. The patient is then free to accept or refuse a doctor's recommendation or get a second opinion or even a different doctor, if that is what the patient desires. This provides a valuable check on the power of doctors, who sometimes make mistakes, and it allows patients to pursue treatment or nontreatment as best fits their personal values and ethical systems.

There are two primary kinds of advance directive, generally known as the "living will" and "durable power of attorney for health care" (sometimes called a health-care proxy). Living wills negate informed consent. Since no one knows the future, by definition their care or noncare instructions must generally be written. Thus, when an incapacitation occurs, the patient's feelings and desires about this specific circumstance may not be known. The living will puts tremendous power into the hands of doctors, who are empowered to decide whether and when the living will takes effect, when treatment should be withdrawn or withheld. Moreover, the decision regarding the type and extent of medical intervention to be withheld is the doctor's. And this power isn't restricted to "extraordinary care" such as ventilators to assist with breathing, but to any medical intervention—from not treating a curable bacterial infection to withdrawing food and fluids so that the patient starves and dehydrates to death. Thus, with a living will, the check of informed consent is surrendered to medicalized decision making—especially dangerous in H.M.O. settings where doctors may have potent financial incentives to withhold care.

In contrast, on the other hand, with a durable power of attorney for health care (DPAHC) the right to informed consent is substantially retained. Why? Rather than appoint a doctor as decider, the DPAHC appoints an "attorney in fact" to be the patient's health-care decision maker should he or she become incapacitated. The attorney in fact, also known as an agent or a proxy, for all intents and purposes steps into the shoes of the patient and decides issues of treatment or nontreatment as the patient would were he or she able to do so. Like the patient, the proxy can ask questions, request second opinions, disagree with the doctor's recommendation, etc. The DPAHC also permits people to opt in favor of life-prolonging care, an option often unavailable in the language of living wills.

Living wills are analogous to the used car advertised as a cream puff that is really a lemon. In a world of assembly-line medicine where many patients have little interaction with their doctors, isn't it better to eschew a doctor-empowering living will in favor of a patient-empowering durable power of attorney? It's not as catchy a name but it is a much better document, one that may make the difference between suffering a premature death and receiving personal health-care decision making, which everyone deserves.

If people are to become confident in the use of advance directives, laws need to be drafted to avoid the problem of denying people requested care if they become technically incompetent, when they have previously written an advance directive in which they refuse care. Michigan already has just such a law. "Under Michigan statutory law, the benefit of the doubt is given to providing lifesaving treatment if there is any expressed desire to receive it," says attorney John Hess, who represented Michael Martin's mother and sister and saved the disabled man's life (described in Chapter 2). "Even if you are incompetent and, secondly, even if you are unable to participate in general with your own health care decisions, as long as you have the ability to communicate a desire to live, it must be honored under the law, regardless of what a previously executed writing says."[28] The Michigan statute is a good model for the rest of the country.

Those who view advance directives as a vehicle for ending the lives of seriously ill or disabled people sooner rather than later might squawk that such a law interferes with the purpose for which these legal documents were created. But the purpose of advance directives is not to get sick people to check out, but rather to give them a tool to control their own destinies. People are far more likely to prepare advance directives that request nontreatment (assuming that is their desire) if they know that, in the event that they change their minds, there won't be a futilitarian or H.M.O. executive opposing their newly expressed desire to fight to live.

One last point about advance directives. Most advocacy about signing these important documents stresses refusing care. The option of accepting care is rarely discussed, much less encouraged. (This isn't surprising. Choice in Dying, the nation's foremost promoter of advance directives, was first formed as the Euthanasia Society of America, a euthanasia advocacy organization.[29] From time to time, Choice in Dying's leaders still advocate legalizing hastened death in the media.) That doesn't mean you have to go along with the nontreatment agenda. When preparing your advance directive, it is important to remember that you can opt for continued treatment.

Exert Better Control over H.M.O.s

Health care isn't just another industry, like manufacturing and selling cars, computers, or shoes. While the forces of the "invisible arm of the marketplace" might be the best way to assure the manufacture of quality goods at fair prices, it is not necessarily the best way to assure access to quality health care, and it can be extremely dangerous for patients—especially if euthanasia and futilitarianism ever become legal.

This book has only touched upon the dangers facing patients in the emerging profit-driven H.M.O. health-care financing system. In the long run, a system that is open and accessible to everyone, whether through government involvement or the private sector, is a moral and ethical imperative. That may involve a government-financed "single payer" system, which exists in every other Western democracy in the world, including South Africa. It may require enacting controversial proposals such as means testing of Medicare, taxing Social Security as income, ending all corporate welfare and tax loopholes, even truly triaging the federal government, reducing its activities to genuinely vital national functions.

At best, these necessary reforms are years away. For now we are stuck with the managed-care system that is developing. There is no doubt that for the next several years for-profit H.M.O.s will increasingly dominate health care, bringing with them increased centralization and forcing amoral marketplace values and mores onto the practice of medicine. This will increasingly affect nonprofit organizations as well, forcing them to adapt and struggle to keep pace so as to remain competitive in the marketplace. As a consequence, patients and doctors will increasingly be caught in a terrible vise, with insurance executives having untoward control over the kind of care patients receive and the workings of the physician-patient relationship.

A good model for reform of the H.M.O. industry is the Patient Protection Act, an initiative in California known as Proposition 216. The proposal, backed by Ralph Nader and written by the California Nurses Association in affiliation with Nader's colleague Harvey Rosenfield, provides important patient protections, including the following:

- Ending arbitrary denials of care so common to managed care by requiring a second opinion from a qualified health-care professional before coverage for treatment recommended by a patient's doctor can be denied.

- Preventing insurers and H.M.O.s from giving bonuses and other financial incentives to doctors and nurses for withholding care, improperly limiting hospitalization, refusing referrals to specialists, not writing needed prescriptions, etc. It is especially imperative that capitation contracts requiring doctors to pay for patient-specialized care out of their own pockets be banned.

- Requiring safe staffing levels at all health-care facilities.

- Providing whistle-blower protection for doctors, nurses, and other H.M.O. employees, contract service providers, and other H.M.O.-affiliated caregivers, so that they can report abuses without fear of job sanction.

- Prohibiting mandatory arbitration clauses that bar wronged H.M.O. members from taking their cause to the courts.

- If a physician commits malpractice as a result of pressure from H.M.O. policies, allowing the H.M.O. to be a defendant in the case.

- Guaranteeing patients full access to information about their medical care by prohibiting gag rules that prevent doctors from telling the truth about their financial arrangements with the patient's H.M.O., from criticizing the H.M.O., or from discussing care that the H.M.O. might not wish to pay for.

- Creating nonprofit, H.M.O. member–controlled consumer advocacy groups to serve as H.M.O. watchdogs.

- Setting a standard of care such that ninety cents out of every health-care dollar be spent on patient care rather than on H.M.O. bureaucracies, marketing, profits, or bonuses.

The civil justice system should also be utilized to deter improper H.M.O. practices. The fear of loss of money can be a great deterrent to improper behavior. If H.M.O.s could be sued for punitive damages (money above and beyond the actual level of damages caused) in cases of egregious and willful wrongdoing, the likelihood of their intentionally sacrificing patients to the bottom line would be greatly reduced. Federal legislation may be required to overcome a U.S. Supreme Court decision that prohibited beneficiaries from collecting punitive damages against wrongdoing by health insurance companies if the insurance was received by the employee as an employment or union benefit.

Consumers and business and union executives in charge of negotiating health insurance contracts for employees or members need to use the power of consumerism to punish "bad" H.M.O.s—those that sacrifice quality of care for profits and/or put the desires of investors before the health-care needs of patients—by withholding their business. On the other hand, "good" H.M.O.s that put patient care first should be rewarded with patronage, even if the premiums cost a bit more.

Make Pain Control More Accessible

If we want to create a truly humane health-care system that cares for people rather than killing them, pain control must be made universally available. Toward that end, physicians who treat patients in the clinical setting should be required by medical associations and state law to educate themselves on pain-control techniques and other palliative protocols. For pain that average doctors cannot overcome, all H.M.O.s must be required to make referrals to board-certified pain-control experts readily available to plan members without arbitrary restriction, on an as-needed basis. In that way, suffering people such as Rebecca Badger, Jack Kevorkian's thirty-third victim, who stated in a presuicide television interview that she would prefer to live if she could escape the pain, would be able to obtain relief without resorting to death peddlers.[30]

We also need to stop making pain sufferers the victims of the war on drugs. Too many states place burdens in the way of doctors in providing adequate pain treatment. For example, many states have rules that require triplicate prescription forms for the dispensation of certain medications, and some state authorities even harass physicians deemed to be too liberal in prescribing certain controlled substances.

One suggestion that requires reasoned consideration is the legalization of marijuana for medicinal purposes. Supporters of legalizing cannabis for medicinal purposes claim that the drug smoked in its natural state (instead of taken as a pill) can ease the suffering of patients with AIDS, cancer, glaucoma, M.S., and other afflictions. Since morphine and other drugs are legalized for medicinal purposes, there is little reason to ban marijuana from being prescribed if appropriate. Controlled medical studies should be undertaken to determine marijuana's palliative effects on extreme pain associated with different illnesses. This research should be authorized by the government as soon as possible so that an appropriate public policy can be fashioned.

Improve Hospital Ethics Committees

Hospital ethics committees have tremendous power in today's health-care delivery system. Yet their membership is anonymous and their meetings are held in secret, leaving tremendous potential for abuse and decision making based on prejudice or incomplete information, as occurred in the Michael Martin and Robert Wendland cases.

"There are no unified standards and no regular performance reviews applied to ethics committees," says Lance K. Stell, M.D., Ph.D., a medical ethicist with the Department of Internal Medicine at the Carolinas Medical Center in Charlotte, North Carolina, and chairman of the Philosophy Department at Davidson College, Davidson, North Carolina. Dr. Stell observes, "It is amazing how often ethics committees make judgments without even seeing the patient or discussing the patient with all concerned parties, including the nursing staff and other caregivers. More than once I have seen a decision made to stop treating a patient and then when I have gone to see the person, I have been appalled."[31]

Dr. Stell tells of one case he personally witnessed where a daughter requested that her mother be taken off a ventilator. Yet when Dr. Stell went to see the patient, the woman "vigorously nodded her head" when he explained her treatment and asked whether she wished to continue indefinitely with assisted breathing. "It turned out the daughter had financial problems and needed money and so she decided the time had come to get her mother out of the way," Dr. Stell told me. "If our ethics committee had been a rubber stamp, and if the surgeon hadn't vigorously opposed the idea, the patient's life might well have been ended. Some ethics committees are rubber stamps, and some doctors are very compliant in these cases."[32]

With such potential for abuse, serious thought must be given to the workings of these committees as well as their makeup. What kind of training should ethics committee members receive? It should definitely be broader and more well rounded than "right-to-die" seminars funded by health-care foundations! Should certifications be required? Should the proceedings of the committees be formalized and subject to review? These are important thoughts for future consideration.

There is something that can be done now. Every ethics committee should take the advice of Diane Coleman, an expert on independent living and a disability rights activist: Hospitals, H.M.O.s, and other health-care organizations should make every effort to have substantial representation on their ethics committees of people who are disabled and who are knowledgeable about the independent living movement and other care options for disabled people, which have such power to improve lives. In that way, fear, prejudice, and ignorance about life with disability will be far less likely to be the basis of ethics committees' decision making.

Commit to Community

In the end, we will only have as compassionate a society as we, the people, decide individually and collectively to make it. The American people are a woefully undertapped resource in the care equation. There are so many ways to serve one another: as hospice or hospital volunteers, in a service organization that has outreach to marginalized people, through local churches, and individually and as neighbors as needs are identified. If each of us would commit to finding service opportunities and helping fill each other's needs, the feeling of abandonment, hopelessness, despair, and isolation that fuels the euthanasia movement would materially slacken, and with it the temptation to set foot on the slippery slope.

Losing Our *Ubutu*?

Once, when I was recounting some of the events I have written about in this book to my best friend, Arthur Cribbs, he shook his head and said to me, "Man, we are losing our *ubutu*." Art, an African American, explained to me that *ubutu* is a Zulu word he picked up from a friend who has traveled extensively in Africa. The concept of *ubutu* has no exact English counterpart—the term "soul" is inadequate—but can be roughly translated as being all of the attributes that go into that exquisite spark that makes humankind special and unique in the known universe.

When we shrug off the Kevorkian-facilitated deaths of desperate and depressed people, whose suffering could have been substantially alleviated with proper medical treatment and humane care, we are losing our *ubutu*. When the euthanasia policies of the Netherlands are perceived by many as "enlightened" and a model for our own health-care system—even though they include infanticide and involuntary killing—we are losing our *ubutu*. When we stand by and watch desperately needed health-care dollars transferred from health-care delivery into the pockets of profiteers, threatening the well-being of patients, we are losing our *ubutu*. When "philosophers" such as Peter Singer equate the moral value of the life of a fish with the moral value of the life of a human infant and are not hooted out of town, we are losing our *ubutu*. When courts send messages through their rulings and decisions that death is preferable to disability and that the lives of dying, chronically ill, and disabled people are not as worthy of state protection as are the lives of those among us who are young, healthy, and vital, we are losing our *ubutu*. When the "right to die" has more resonance among much of the public than protecting the right to live, we are, without doubt, losing our *ubutu*. When a radio station auctions Kevorkian's cardigan sweater and a Kevorkian-signed imitation death certificate as a charity fundraiser, and it is seen as all in good fun, we are losing not only our *ubutu* but also our senses of propriety and decency.[33]

And yet . . . our *ubutu* may be leaking but it is not yet lost. We remain a caring and compassionate people. Indeed, those very attributes are exploited by death fundamentalists. And it will be these attributes—essential ingredients of *ubutu*—that will, in the end, restore us to a more humane and enlightened course.

A good step toward reclaiming *ubutu* is the Missoula Demonstration Project, the brainchild of Dr. Ira Byock, in Missoula, Montana. Under the direction of its executive director, the gerontologist Barbara K. Spring,

Ph.D., the project is actively restoring community to people approaching the end of their lives. "People who are dying tend to become isolated," Dr. Byock says. "We are changing that. We are committed to restoring a sense of belonging."

The project is involving the whole city in a nonmedical approach to these important issues. Under the direction of the project, workers are setting up intergenerational programs such as combining day care for children with care for the elderly. Discussions are held in schools, churches, among civic groups, and in health-care facilities to teach people that dying is a natural part of living, and that caring for terminally ill people is a life-enhancing experience.

Dying people also receive the message that they are important members of the community. Their life histories are recorded and the tapes are available in the local library. They are helped to come to terms with their fears with support groups and innovative approaches such as art therapy.

"The intent behind the project," Dr. Byock says, "is to show America what truly 'dying well' can mean and to demonstrate that one's life is not over because a terminal prognosis is given. Dying is a very scary, extraordinary time of life that requires adjustments and changes in expectations. But so do other times of change, such as marriage, having a child, or losing a spouse. What I have seen and know to be true is that people can exert a sense of mastery over this stage of life."[34]

Can dying really be a meaningful time in life, as Dr. Byock asserts? Dr. Maurice Victor certainly believes that such a time of life has tremendous meaning: "Once pain and depression are treated," he says, "there is gratification to be obtained simply from living. I have talked with survivors of concentration camps who experienced as extreme suffering as can be imagined. One woman put it very well: Life matters. Just to have the opportunity to spend a boring evening at home is worth everything. There is so much pleasure to be gotten merely from the simple routines: getting coffee in the morning, reading the morning paper, planning the little errands of the day, so much pleasure to be derived from the most inconsequential type of things, from what some call a boring life. It comes from within."[35] That is exactly how life has become for my friend Bob.

Dr. Victor sees euthanasia as antithetical to living a meaningful life in its end stage. "I am dreadfully offended by the whole notion," he says. "Euthanasia replaces the importance of life and replaces it with an impersonal, crass discarding of sick people on the ash heap. It is anathema to true compassion and care."[36]

Let us wish the Missoula Project and its blend of hospice, community education, and outreach well, and hope that it serves as a guide in transforming dying from the too often lonely and isolated experience it is now into an event centered in the love and involvement of the entire community, the way it should be. If we care enough about each other to accomplish this task, we will have transformed isolation into inclusion, abandonment into an embrace, indifference into love—dying into an event steeped in *ubutu*. Do that, Dr. Byock firmly believes, and we will make assisted suicide and euthanasia superfluous, whether legalized or not.

We don't have to be part of the hospice movement or engaged in the euthanasia debate to make a real difference in the lives of suffering and dying people. We have that opportunity even with virtual strangers. I recall my former law partner, Jack A. Rameson III, of Woodland Hills, California, who many years ago taught me a lesson in compassion and dignity that I have never forgotten. Jack is an estate planner. We went out to a hospital to visit a woman who was dying of brain cancer, so she could sign her will.

As Rameson was explaining the will-signing process to her, she suddenly became ill. Now, there are those who would say throwing up in front of strangers is undignified. But dignity depends, does it not, on how others react to the afflicted person? In this case, Rameson transformed what could have been a disturbing and perhaps humiliating moment for our client into one overflowing with *ubutu*. He immediately ran to her side, gently held her head as she was in the act of being sick, so she would not soil her bedclothes. When she was finished he took a damp cloth, wiped her face and brow, gave her a cup of water, and, when she felt better, we went on with our business as if nothing had happened.

That kind of outreaching love is the essence of community. It erases indignity. It welcomes those in need of assistance as vital parts of the community's life, as people of inherent value and worth.

Then there is the kind and loving care shown by my friend Tom Lorentzen as he intimately participated in his mother's death, not by mixing her a poison brew and hastening her end, but as a loving and caring son who valued and welcomed her in each moment of her natural life. And in that caring he found himself comforted and transformed:

> *In July of 1990, my mother was diagnosed with early-stage kidney failure. I said, "Mom, I hope you will be okay." She responded by saying, "If I need you, I know you will know what to do." This statement*

was different from anything she had ever said to me before. I sensed change and I shed a tear.

In November 1991, Mom's condition worsened and she was placed in the hospital. I left Washington, D.C., my job, my girlfriend, and my dog behind, and rushed to her side. I sensed that my life had taken a dramatically different path, that I would not be soon in returning.

During the next seven months, I took care of my mother at home, cooking her meals, doing laundry, cleaning house, working at a job I was fortunate to obtain in San Francisco during the day. Leaving home at six in the morning, I would call her during the day to make sure she was all right.

She was in and out of the hospital until June of 1992, when the doctor told me she was dying. Together, we informed her, as I sat on the bed holding her hand. I watched her eyes change as the message was received. She looked at me with an expression that only Shakespeare could adequately describe. She then turned to the doctor, and with her New York sense of humor, said, "Thanks a lot!"

We revisited the possibility of kidney dialysis with the doctor. She asked two questions: Would it hurt? The doctor said there would be some discomfort and explained why. She then asked, "Will it give me strength?" The doctor explained that it would for a day or so, and then she would have to undergo another treatment.

With that, she gently shook her head and said, "No." I saw tears form in the doctor's eyes.

For ten days I stayed in the hospital room with her, leaving only to shave, shower, and change clothes. At night, I would sleep on the bed with her, holding her in my arms. During that time I smelled the aroma of her hair and daydreamed about what her life had been like from the time she was born. A strange and comforting sense of peace dominated my essence, as I held her like a child in my arms.

As my mother was traveling through the dying process, the intimacy of death became shared between us. She shared her love with others who visited the room.

As the end grew very near, gangrene began to set in, caused by her kidney failure. Mom required morphine to ease the pain, which she received during the last two to three days. At one point, I said to the doctor, "I can't believe I am saying this, but I hope she dies sooner rather than later." He and I agreed that we would do nothing to prolong her dying and that no treatment would be given to keep her going. We also agreed that she would receive sufficient pain medication to ensure that she felt no discomfort. I told him that I hoped she would die in my arms.

On the tenth day of her hospitalization, I awoke at four A.M. and noticed my mom fixing her hair. I moved to the reclining chair and awoke at six-thirty. Mom was lying quietly in bed. As I stirred, she asked, "Tom, are you still here?" I said, "Yes, Mom. Don't worry. Everything is all right." "Okay," she said—her last words.

A little while later, I looked down at her as the morning sun was beginning to illuminate the room. Her breathing was barely observable. I laid on the bed and took her in my arms. As I did, her breathing gently stopped.

Tears immediately covered my face. In addition, two feelings simultaneously dominated my being. The most powerful was a sense of loss. Immediately overriding it, however, was a sense of enrichment. We had done everything we could to save her life. I had done everything I could to take care of her and give her life value, and to make sure that she was cared for and loved during her dying, temporarily giving up on my life to take care of her when she needed me most. My wish had been granted that she die in my arms.

My reward was a deepening of our love and a tightening of our friendship. I knew that I had gained the greatest wealth that can be achieved in life. By participating in the natural dying process with a loved one in the most intimate, loving, and caring manner possible, I had become enriched beyond anything I ever expected in life. What I am now, what I will always be, will stem from this experience. I am a very fortunate and lucky person.[37]

A Time to Choose

As we come to the end of the millennium, we are at a crossroads that forces us to choose between two mutually exclusive value systems. Will we remain on the trail that leads ultimately to the full realization of the equality-of-human-life ethic and with it, the tremendous potential for the creation of a true community, or do we take a hard turn down the slippery slope toward a coarsening of our views of the afflicted, the dying, the chronically ill, the disabled, and those in pain or depression to the point where we feel they have a duty to die and get out of the way? To put it more bluntly: Will we choose the road of inclusion and caregiving for all, including the weakest and most vulnerable among us, or that of exclusion and ever-expanding killing opportunities? More simply yet: Will we choose to love each other or abandon each other? The bottom line: Will we keep or lose our *ubutu*?

The two paths that lie before us, the death culture or the struggle toward a truly caring community, lead to dramatically different futures. The choice is ours. So will be the society we create.

Resources

Sources of Information About Euthanasia from an
Opposition Standpoint

International Anti-Euthanasia Task Force

P.O. Box 760
Steubenville, Ohio 43952
(614) 282-3810
Home page: http://www.iactf.org
(800) 958-5678 to order PMDD or other IAETF material (see below)

The International Anti-Euthanasia Task Force (IAETF) is the primary international source of information and background material on euthanasia and assisted suicide. Among its ongoing activities, the IAETF

- Provides background materials and information for radio, television, and print journalists

- Maintains an extensive and up-to-date library devoted solely to the issues surrounding euthanasia

- Upon request, prepares analyses of pending legislation

- Analyzes the probable impact of policies considered and/or adopted by medical, legal, and social work organizations

- Provides speakers for local and national radio and television programs, and for major international bioethical conferences

- Files amicus curiae briefs in major "right-to-die" cases

- Publishes position papers and fact sheets on euthanasia-related topics

- Prepares and provides specialized materials for health-care professionals, attorneys, ethicists, and for students ranging from middle school through graduate school

- Conducts training in effective communication of issues related to euthanasia, assisted suicide, death, and dying

- Provides information and assistance to individuals and groups regarding resources for medically vulnerable individuals and their caregivers
- Publishes the bimonthly *IAETF Update*
- Networks with individuals and organizations from five continents
- Publishes Protective Medical Decision Document (PMDD) (see page 258).

Individuals and groups who network with the IAETF have a common concern about the threat of euthanasia but hold widely differing views on other public-policy issues.

American Medical Association (A.M.A.)
515 N. State St.
Chicago, Ill. 60610   (312) 464-5000

American Foundation for Suicide Prevention
120 Wall St.
New York, N.Y. 10005   (888) 333-2377

The Compassionate Health Care Network
P.O. Box 62548
12874 96th Ave.
Surrey, B.C.,   (604) 582-8687
Canada   e-mail: chn@intergate.bc.ca
The CHCN is a group based in Canada that is opposed to euthanasia and assisted suicide.

National Conference of Catholic Bishops
Attn: Richard Doerflinger, Associate Director for Policy Development
Secretariat of Pro-Life Activities
211 4th St., N.E.
Washington, D.C. 20017   (202) 541-3070

New York Task Force on Life and the Law
5 Penn Plaza
New York, N.Y. 10001-1803   (212) 613-4303
To obtain copies of When Death is Sought, *the New York State Task Force's report on legalizing euthanasia or P.A.S., contact:*

Health Research Inc.
Health Education Services
P.O. Box 7126
Albany, N.Y. 12224   (518) 439-7286

Pain Control and Palliation

Agency for Health Care Policy and Research (AHCPR)
Executive Office Center, Suite 501
2101 E. Jefferson St.
Rockville, Md. 20852   (800) 358-9295 to order publications
This agency of the Department of Health and Human Services publishes many patient guides on topics of pain control and palliation that are available free of charge.

National Academy of Hospice Physicians
P.O. Box 14288
Gainesville, Fla. 32604-2288   (904) 377-8900

National Cancer Institute's Cancer Information Service
Office of Cancer Communications, Building 31, Room 10A24
Bethesda, Md. 20892   (800) 422-6237 (4CANCER)
Provides information for patients and families, health-care professionals, and the public about pain control and other topics related to cancer.

National Chronic Pain Outreach Association
7979 Old Georgetown Rd., Suite 100
Bethesda, Md. 20814-2429   (310) 652-4948
This organization offers information and pamphlets for patients, information about chronic-pain support groups, and referrals to pain-management specialists and clinics.

The National Hospice Organization
1901 N. Moore St., Suite 901
Arlington, Va. 22209   (800) 658-8898
Home page: http://www.nho.org
Offers information and referral services.

Wisconsin Cancer Pain Initiative
4720 Medical Science Center
University of Wisconsin Medical School
1300 University Avenue
Madison, Wis. 53706   (608) 262-0978
Offers information about pain relief for cancer patients.

Disability Issues

Amyotrophic Lateral Sclerosis (A.L.S.) Association
21021 Ventura Blvd., Suite 321
Woodland Hills, Calif. 91364   (800) 782-4747
Provides education, information, and referral services to assist A.L.S. patients and their families.

Independent Living Resource Utilization Training Center
2323 S. Shepherd, Suite 1000
Houston, Tex. 77019   (713) 520-0232
Offers information about the independent-living movement, and provides the addresses and phone numbers of an independent-living center near you or one you love.

National Multiple Sclerosis Association
733 Third Ave.
New York, N.Y. 10017   (800) LEARNMS (532-7667)
Information for patients and families about M.S.

National Spinal Cord Injury Association
600 W. Cummings Park, Suite 2000
Woburn, Mass. 01801   (617) 935-2722
National Spinal Cord Injury Hotline
(800) 526-3456
Offers information about spinal cord injury and referral services and access to support groups.

United Cerebral Palsy Foundation Association
1522 K St., N.W., Suite 1112
Washington, D.C. 20005   (800) 872-5827
Offers a referral service and information about interventions, patient and family support, assisted technology, and employment.

Books

These books are excellent resources for those who wish to learn more about the topics discussed in this book.

Ira Byock, M.D. *Dying Well: The Prospect for Growth at the End of Life.* New York: Riverhead Books, 1997.

This moving and important book, written by the president of the American Academy of Hospice and Palliative Medicine, illustrates the beneficence of hospice and the quality of life available for dying people when they are properly cared for and valued. If all dying persons were as well cared for as were the patients whose stories are recounted in this book, the assisted-suicide movement would quickly wither on the vine.

Hugh Gregory Gallagher. *By Trust Betrayed: Patients, Physicians and the License to Kill in the Third Reich.* Arlington, Va.: Vandamere Press, 1995.

An excellent source for anyone interested in the German euthanasia policies and the part they played in the Holocaust. (See also Lifton, *The Nazi Doctors.*)

Herbert Hendin, M.D. *Seduced by Death: Doctors, Patients and the Dutch Cure.* New York: W. W. Norton, 1997.

A detailed and disturbing account by the head of the American Foundation for Suicide Prevention of what has gone wrong with Dutch medical ethics as a result of the acceptance of euthanasia. A clarion warning for the United States.

Jack Kevorkian, M.D. *Prescription Medicide: The Goodness of a Planned Death.* Buffalo, N.Y.: Prometheus Books, 1991.

Learn the truth about the sick philosophy of Jack Kevorkian in his own words.

Robert Jay Lifton. *The Nazi Doctors: Medical Killing and the Psychology of Genocide.* New York: Basic Books, 1996.

An excellent source for learning about the participation of many German physicians in the Holocaust.

Rita Marker. *Deadly Compassion: The Death of Ann Humphry and the Truth About Euthanasia.* William Morrow, New York, 1993.

This book, by the executive director of the International Anti-Euthanasia Task Force, recounts the tragic story of the Hemlock Society's cofounder Ann Wicket Humphry: how she was abandoned by her husband, Derek Humphry, when she was diagnosed with breast cancer, and the reasons she turned against the death culture before committing suicide.

New York Task Force on Life and the Law. *When Death Is Sought: Assisted Suicide and Euthanasia in the Medical Context.* New York: New York Task Force on Life and the Law, 1994.

This vital study of the topic clarifies many issues. After more than a year of intensive investigation, in a unanimous vote the task force recommended against legalizing assisted suicide for reasons that are both compelling and pragmatic.

Joseph P. Shapiro. *No Pity: People with Disabilities Forging a New Civil Rights Movement.* New York: Times Books, 1993.

An excellent account of the prejudice faced by people with disabilities and the empowering potential of the independent-living movement.

Peter Singer. *Rethinking Life and Death: The Collapse of Our Traditional Ethics.* New York: St. Martin's Press, 1994.

Singer is more candid than most euthanasia advocates about where the death culture would take us. He promotes the destruction of the "sanctity of life" ethic in favor of a "quality of life" ethic in which euthanasia, assisted suicide, and infanticide would play a vital part.

Advance Medical Directives

For a detailed discussion of advance directives, see page 240.

The American Medical Association, the American Bar Association, and the American Association of Retired Persons worked together to create a very detailed power of attorney that covers just about all circumstances, including whether you want food and fluids under specified conditions. To obtain the A.M.A./A.B.A./A.A.R.P. Durable Power of Attorney for Health Care, write:

American Association of Retired Persons
601 E St., N.W.
Washington, D.C. 20049

The International Anti-Euthanasia Task Force (address on page 253) publishes a power-of-attorney form it calls the Protective Medical Decision Document (P.M.D.D.), which empowers a health-care proxy to make treatment and nontreatment decisions while prohibiting the proxy from agreeing to medical actions that are directly intended to cause death. The proxy you name in your P.M.D.D. has the authority to make the same medical treatment decisions that you could have made if you were able to do so. For example, after consulting with your physician, your proxy may determine that continued attempts to cure a condition should be stopped and that you should receive comfort care and pain relief only. Your proxy may also approve a D.N.R. (do not resuscitate) order or a "no aggressive treatment" order. He or she may determine that surgery, ventilator support, or other interventions should be provided, withheld, or withdrawn. However, the P.M.D.D. specifically denies your proxy the authority to approve any *direct and intentional* ending of your life. For example, your proxy may not direct that you be given lethal drugs or a fatal injection (should that become legal), and your proxy may not direct that you be denied food or fluids for the purpose of causing your death by starvation or dehydration.

Like a will or a trust, an advance directive is a legal document and should be treated as such. The laws of each state regarding their preparation and contents differ. As of spring 1997, a few states—California, Ohio, Texas, and Vermont—require specific language not used in the forms mentioned here. It is a good idea to have your attorney review any advance directive you sign, or prepare yours on the basis of your instructions and desires.

To find an attorney who knows the ins and outs of the laws concerning advance directives, contact your local bar association and ask for a lawyer who specializes in "elder law." Or contact:

National Academy of Elder Law Attorneys (NAELA)
1604 Country Club Rd.
Tucson, Ariz. 85716   (520) 881-4005

Notes

Introduction

1. Wesley J. Smith, *The Senior Citizens' Handbook* (Los Angeles: Price, Stern, Sloan, 1990).
2. American Foundation for Suicide Prevention, *Suicide Facts* (New York: American Foundation for Suicide Prevention).
3. Ibid.
4. "Suicide Rate Among Elderly Climbs by 9% over 12 Years," *New York Times,* Jan. 12, 1996.
5. "A Peaceful Passing," *Hemlock Quarterly,* no. 30 (Jan. 1988).
6. Ibid., p. 7.
7. Ibid., p. 6.
8. Ibid., pp. 4–5.
9. Derek Humphry, "Self-Deliverance with Certainty," *Hemlock Quarterly,* no. 30 (Jan. 1988).
10. Ibid., p. 4.
11. "Suicide Rate Among Elderly."
12. Wesley J. Smith, "The Whispers of Strangers," *Newsweek,* June 28, 1993.
13. Ibid.
14. Personal correspondence, June 24, 1993.
15. Personal correspondence, June 30, 1994.
16. Personal correspondence, June 29, 1993.
17. Personal correspondence, June 24, 1993.
18. Personal correspondence, Aug. 23, 1993.
19. Personal correspondence, June 29, 1993.
20. Personal correspondence, June 23, 1993.
21. Personal correspondence, July 7, 1993.
22. Personal correspondence, June 29, 1993.
23. Personal correspondence, June 24, 1993.
24. Smith, "Whispers of Strangers."
25. Ann Landers, "One 85-Year-Old's Old-Age Solution," *St. Louis Post-Dispatch,* Oct. 3, 1993.
26. Margaret E. Hall, ed., *Selected Writings of Benjamin Nathan Cardozo* (New York: Fallon Publications, 1947), p. 388.

Chapter 1: Death Fundamentalism

1. Stephanie Gutmann, "Death and the Maiden," *New Republic,* January 24, 1996, p. 24.
2. "Kevorkian Patient Was on Halcion," *Detroit News,* Nov. 3, 1991.
3. "Attitudes Toward Euthanasia Sharply Divide, Survey Finds," Reuters, June 29, 1996.
4. Andrew Coyne, "The Slippery Slope That Leads to Death," *Globe and Mail* (Toronto), Nov. 21, 1994.

5. Derek Humphry, Letters to the Editor, *New York Times Magazine,* Aug. 11, 1996.

6. James L. Wert, Jr., B.S., and Debra C. Cobia, Ed.D., "Empirically Based Criteria for Rational Suicide: A Survey of Psychotherapists," *Suicide and Life Threatening Behavior* 25 (Summer 1995).

7. Arthur Caplan, "System Messed Up, Hands Down," *Oakland Tribune,* May 31, 1996.

8. Jack Lessenberry, "Physican Assisted Suicide Is a Constitutional Right," in Carol Wekesser, ed., *Euthanasia: Opposing Viewpoints* (San Diego: Greenhaven Press, 1995), p. 91.

9. Matthew Rothschild, interview with author, June 6, 1996.

10. Dr. I. van der Sluis, interview with author, Oct. 14, 1995.

11. Paul Longmore, interview with author, June 3, 1996.

12. Derek Humphry and Lonny Shavelson, *Self-Deliverance from an End-Stage Terminal Illness by Use of a Plastic Bag.*

13. Richard Leiby, "Whose Death Is It Anyway?" *Washington Post,* Aug. 11, 1996.

14. Mark Hosenball, "The Real Jack Kevorkian," *Newsweek,* Dec. 6, 1993.

15. Jack Lessenberry, "Death Becomes Him," *Vanity Fair,* July 1994, p. 106.

16. Hosenball, "The Real Jack Kevorkian."

17. Jack Kevorkian, M.D., *Prescription Medicide: The Goodness of a Planned Death* (Buffalo: Prometheus Books, 1991), p. 211.

18. Ibid., p. 243.

19. Ibid., p. 214.

20. *Report of the University of Rochester Medical Center Task Force on Physician-Assisted Suicide* (Rochester, N.Y.: University of Rochester, 1993), p. 5.

21. "Wait—An Alternative to Assisted Dying," *Patient Care,* May 30, 1994.

22. Andrew Solomon, "A Death of One's Own," *New Yorker,* May 22, 1995.

23. "Kevorkian Aid Ruled Homicide," *Boston Globe* (Reuters), Sept. 4, 1996.

24. Dr. Eric Chevlen, interview with author, Sept. 6, 1996.

25. Lonny Shavelson, *A Chosen Death: The Dying Confront Assisted Suicide* (New York: Simon & Schuster, 1995).

26. Ibid., p. 75.

27. Ibid., p. 92.

28. Ibid., p. 93.

29. Ibid., p. 94.

30. Ibid., pp. 93–94.

31. Lonny Shavelson, interview with author, June 19, 1996.

32. Lonny Shavelson, personal communication, at the studio of KQED-FM, San Francisco, March 14, 1996.

33. Shavelson, *A Chosen Death,* p. 94.

34. Lonny Shavelson interview.

35. Peter Singer, *Rethinking Life and Death: The Collapse of Our Traditional Ethics* (New York: St. Martin's Press, 1995).

36. Ibid., pp. 213–14.

37. Daniel J. Kevles, "We All Must Die; Who Can Tell Us When?" *New York Times,* May 7, 1995.

38. Scott Judd, book review of *Rethinking Life and Death,* by Peter Singer, *Hemlock Time-Lines,* May–June 1995, p. 10.

39. Ralph Mero, "Executive Director's Report," *Compassion in Dying Newsletter,* no. 4 (1995), p. 2.

40. Singer, *Rethinking Life and Death,* book jacket biography.

41. Jack Kevorkian, quoted in Hosenball, "The Real Jack Kevorkian."

42. Kevorkian, *Prescription Medicide,* p. 201.

43. "About the Patients," *Detroit Free Press,* Aug. 29, 1996.

44. Gutmann, "Death and the Maiden," p. 21.

45. Kevorkian, *Prescription Medicide*, p. 33.

46. Ibid., p. 24.

47. Mike Martindale, "Kevorkian Says He May Assist in 21st Suicide," *Detroit News*, March 29, 1994.

48. Emilia Askari and Mike Williams, "Doctors Wanted to Help," *Detroit Free Press*, Nov. 29, 1994.

49. Ibid.

50. "Arthritis Foundation Statement About Planned Death," Arthritis Foundation, Michigan Chapter, press release, March 29, 1994.

51. Dr. Randolph B. Schiffer, interview with author, Sept. 14, 1995.

52. Lisa Belkin, "There's No Such Thing as a Simple Suicide," *New York Times Magazine*, Nov. 14, 1993. Cited hereafter as "No Simple Suicide."

53. Ann Landers, "When Taking Your Own Life Makes Sense," *San Francisco Examiner*, Feb. 6, 1994.

54. Ibid., p. 53.

55. Herbert Hendin, "Selling Death and Dignity," *Hastings Center Report*, May–June 1995, p. 22.

56. Ibid.

57. Belkin, "No Simple Suicide," p. 74.

58. Ibid.

59. Ibid., p. 75.

60. Ibid., pp. 63, 74.

61. Ibid., p. 50.

62. Ibid., pp. 50–51.

63. Hendin, "Selling Death and Dignity," p. 22.

64. On June 10, 1996, I telephoned the Washington State office of Compassion in Dying seeking comment from Ralph Mero about "No Simple Suicide" and my criticisms of him, based on Belkin's story. I was informed by Barbara Coombs Lee that Mero was no longer with the organization and that she was acting as the interim director. (Lee is an author of Oregon's Measure 16, a 1994 effort to legalize physician-assisted suicide.) I asked where I could contact Mero; she refused to tell me and asked why I wished to speak with him. I told her, and she promised to pass on the message. I repeated this request in a fax to Compassion in Dying on June 18, 1996, and also requested an interview with Lee or another representative of Compassion in Dying and informed her that to ensure that she was quoted accurately I would tape-record the interview. No representative of Compassion in Dying has contacted me.

CHAPTER 2: Creating a Caste of Disposable People

1. Sharon S. Orr, interview with author, April 2, 1996.

2. Medical records of Robert Wendland, a nurse's note dated July 25, 1995.

3. *In re Conservatorship of Robert Wendland* (Case no. 65669, Superior Court of California, County of San Joaquin), testimony of Rose Wendland, Sept. 5, 1995.

4. Jon Dann, producer, "A Matter of Life and Death," KRON-TV (San Francisco) news, aired Nov. 6, 1995, and Jan. 5, 1996.

5. *In re Conservatorship of Robert Wendland*, testimony of various witnesses, Sept. 5, 1995.

6. Ibid.

7. Ibid., testimony of Florence Wendland, Sept. 5, 1995.

8. Janie Hickock Siess, interview with author, June 23, 1996.

9. *In re Conservatorship of Robert Wendland*, petition for appointment of probate conservator, August 8, 1995.

10. Margaret Goodman, San Joaquin County ombudsman assigned to Robert Wendland, interview with author, Sept. 5, 1995.

11. *In re Conservatorship of Robert Wendland,* testimony of Margaret Goodman, Sept. 5, 1995.

12. Ibid., testimony of Dr. Ronald Kass, Sept. 5, 1995.

13. Janie Hickock Siess interview.

14. *In re Conservatorship of Robert Wendland,* testimony of Rose Wendland, Sept. 5, 1995.

15. Richard John Neuhaus, "The Return of Eugenics," *Commentary,* April 1988, p. 19.

16. No one would argue that indisputably dying patients who, on the brink of death, cannot assimilate food and fluids should be given them anyway. That would be pointless and cruel. Under discussion here is the provision of food and fluids that effectively nourish the body but that are removed for nonmedical reasons.

17. American Medical Association Council on Ethical and Judicial Affairs, "Opinion 2.15," 1986.

18. See, for example, Geoffrey E. Pence, *Classic Cases in Medical Ethics,* 2nd ed. (New York: McGraw Hill, 1995), p. 17.

19. *Cruzan v. Harmon and Lampkins,* Case No. CV384-9p, Circuit Court of Jasper County, Missouri, transcript for March 9, 1988.

20. Rita Marker, *Deadly Compassion* (New York: William Morrow, 1993), p. 43.

21. *Nancy Beth Cruzan v. Robert Harmon et al.,* 760 SW 2nd 408, Nov. 1988.

22. *Cruzan v. Director, Missouri Department of Health,* 110 Supreme Court, 2841, 1990.

23. Diane M. Gianelli, "Major Figure in Right-to-Die Debate Dies," *American Medical News,* Sept. 2, 1996.

24. Scott Canon, "New Right-to-Die Case Goes to Court," *Kansas City Star,* Jan. 6, 1991.

25. Ibid.

26. Sharon Orr interview.

27. Theresa Tighe, "State Releases Videotape of Busalacchi, Patient Appears to Be Responsive," *St. Louis Post-Dispatch,* Feb. 5, 1991.

28. Dann, "A Matter of Life and Death."

29. Wesley J. Smith, "Creating a Disposable Caste," *Open Forum,* Dec. 8, 1995.

30. *In re Conservatorship of Robert Wendland,* transcript of deposition of Ronald Cranford, M.D., May 7, 1996, p. 48.

31. American Medical Association Council on Ethics and Judicial Affairs, "Opinion 2.20," 1994.

32. Dr. William Burke, interview with author.

33. *In re Conservatorship of Robert Wendland,* transcript of deposition of Dr. Ronald Cranford, May 7, 1996, p. 48.

34. Dr. Vincent Fortanasce, interview with author, Jan. 9, 1995.

35. My experiences as an anti-euthanasia advocate provide much anecdotal support for Dr. Fortanesce's statement. Whenever I appear on talk radio discussing euthanasia, invariably at least one caller will share a sad story about a loved one, newly unconscious because of a stroke or injury, whose doctors urged the family to withhold all life support, including nutrition, within days or even hours of the event. I also receive such calls at my office on a regular basis.

36. Dr. Vincent Fortanasce interview.

37. *In re Correan Salter,* Case no. CV-94-160, Circuit Court, Baldwin County, Alabama.

38. This depiction is based on Ron Comeau's medical records, deposited with the court, which the author reviewed, and on interviews with most of the participants in the Comeau case.

39. Amy Swisher, interview with author, Jan. 11, 1994.

40. *In re Guardianship of Ronald Comeau,* Bennington Probate Court, 1993, Findings and Order of the Court, court transcript, Aug. 17, 1993.

41. Joseph Schaaf, interview with author, Jan. 11, 1994.

42. Ronald Comeau's medical records.

43. Ibid.

44. Joseph Schaaf interview.

45. Ronald Comeau's medical records.

46. Dr. Peter Zorach, interview with author, Jan. 12, 1994.

47. Stephen L. Saltonstall, interview with author, Jan. 14, 1994.

48. *In re Guardianship of Ronald Comeau,* Findings and Order of the Court, court transcript, Nov. 9, 1993.

49. Reverend Mike McHugh, interview with author, Jan. 10, 1994.

50. Ibid.

51. Stephen Saltonstall interview.

52. "To Live or Die," editorial, *Rutland Herald,* Nov. 18, 1993.

53. Jack Hoffman, "Vermont Press Fails to Take a Stand," *Rutland Herald,* Nov. 18, 1993.

54. John Howland, Jr., "Wonderful or Ruthless: Some Question Motives That Guide Michael McHugh," *Burlington Free Press,* Nov. 22, 1993.

55. Mike Donoghue, "Dad: Keep Comatose Son Alive," *Burlington Free Press,* Nov. 19, 1993.

56. Renald Comeau, interview with author, Jan. 14, 1994.

57. Frederick Beaver, "Family Rallies Around Comeau," *Bennington Banner,* Nov. 20, 1993.

58. Patricia Comeau, interview with author, May 9, 1996.

59. Joseph Schaaf interview.

60. Renald Comeau interview.

61. Medical records of Michael Martin, New Medico Neurological Center of Michigan, Speech-Language Pathology Daily Treatment Notes, Dec. 7, 1992.

62. Ibid.

63. Medical records of Michael Martin, New Medico Neurological Center of Michigan, Augmentation Evaluation Summary, April 19, 1992.

64. Ibid.

65. *In re Michael Martin,* Michigan Court of Appeals, Docket No. 161431, Judge Grieg's Observations of Michael Martin, as attached to appeal brief, court transcript, pp. 12–16.

66. John H. Hess, J.D., "Looking for Traction on the Slippery Slope," *Issues in Law and Medicine* 11, no. 2: 105–122. Hess and his brother were lawyers for Michael Martin's mother and sister.

67. Butterworth Hospital Ethics Committee, correspondence to Mary Martin, Jan. 15, 1992.

68. Hess, "Looking for Traction," pp. 107–8.

69. *In re Michael Martin,* 504 NW 2d, 917 (Michigan Appellate, April 1993).

70. "Mary, Mary, Quite Contrary, How Was I to Know? Michael Martin, Absolute Prescience, and the Right to Die in Michigan," *University of Detroit Mercy Law Review* 27 (1996): 828.

71. Ibid., p. 832.

72. Kenneth F. Schaffner, M.D., Ph.D., "Recognizing the Tragic Choice: Food, Water, and the Right to Assisted Suicide," *Critical Care Medicine,* October 1988.

73. Helga Kuhse, "Ethics Panel: The Right to Choose Your Death—Ethical Aspects of Euthanasia," Sept. 21, 1984, as quoted in Marker, *Deadly Compassion,* p. 94.

74. Peter Singer, *Rethinking Life and Death: The Collapse of Our Traditional Ethics* (New York: St. Martin's Press, 1995), p. 80.

75. *Cruzan v. State of Missouri.*

76. *Compassion in Dying v. State of Washington,* Case no. 94-35534, U.S. Court of Appeals for the Ninth Circuit, 79 F.3d 790 (9th Cir. 1996).

77. *Quill v. Dennis C. Vacco,* U.S. Court of Appeals for the Second Circuit, April 2, 1996, 80 F.3d 716 (2nd Cir. 1996).

CHAPTER 3:   Everything Old Is New Again

1. "A New Ethic for Medicine and Society," editorial, *California Medicine* 113, no. 3 (Sept. 1970), pp. 67–68.

2. Peter Singer, *Rethinking Life and Death: The Collapse of Our Traditional Ethics* (New York: St. Martin's Press, 1995).

3. Hugh Gregory Gallagher, *By Trust Betrayed: Patients, Physicians, and the License to Kill in the Third Reich* (Arlington, Va.: Vandamere Press, 1995), p. xiv.

4. Robert Jay Lifton, *The Nazi Doctors: Medical Killing and the Psychology of Genocide* (New York: Basic Books, 1986), p. 14.

5. Michael Burleigh, *Death and Deliverance: Euthanasia in Germany, 1900–1945* (New York: Cambridge University Press, 1994), p. 4.

6. Hugh Gregory Gallagher, interview with author, May 21, 1996.

7. Lifton, *Nazi Doctors*, p. 48.

8. Ibid., p. 46.

9. Quoted in Burleigh, *Death and Deliverance*, p. 13.

10. Ibid., pp. 13–14.

11. Ibid., p. 14.

12. Ibid., p. 15.

13. Karl Binding and Alfred Hoche, M.D., *Permitting the Destruction of Life Not Worthy of Life: Its Extent and Form* (Leipzig, Germany: Felix Meiner Verlag, 1920), reprinted in *Law and Medicine* 8, no. 2 (1992), pp. 231–65.

14. Lifton, *Nazi Doctors*, p. 46.

15. Gallagher, *By Trust Betrayed*, p. 60.

16. Binding and Hoche, *Permitting the Destruction*, p. 247.

17. Ibid., pp. 260–61.

18. Ibid., p. 249.

19. Ibid., p. 252.

20. Burleigh, *Death and Deliverance*, p. 15.

21. Adolf Hitler, *Mein Kampf*, quoted in Lifton, *Nazi Doctors*, p. 257.

22. Lifton, *Nazi Doctors*, p. 27.

23. Burleigh, *Death and Deliverance*, pp. 22–23.

24. *New York Times*, Oct. 8, 1933, as cited in Gallagher, *By Trust Betrayed*, p. 62.

25. As described in Lifton, *Nazi Doctors*, p. 49, and Gallagher, *By Trust Betrayed*, p. 61.

26. Lifton, *Nazi Doctors*, p. 50.

27. Burleigh, *Death and Deliverance*, pp. 95–96; Lifton, *Nazi Doctors*, pp. 50–51; Gallagher, *By Trust Betrayed*, pp. 95–96.

28. Quoted in Burleigh, *Death and Deliverance*, p. 100.

29. Ibid., p. 125.

30. Ibid.

31. Lifton, *Nazi Doctors*, p. 77.

32. For example, see the Hemlock Society cofounder Derek Humphry's essay "Nazi Germany and Its So-called 'Euthanasia Program,' " available in DeathNet on the World Wide Web.

33. Hugh Gregory Gallagher interview.

34. Ibid.

35. Ibid.

36. Quoted in Gallagher, *By Trust Betrayed*, p. 200, and Burleigh, *Death and Deliverance*, p. 178.

37. Ibid.

38. Michael Franzblau, M.D., "Investigate Nazi Ties of German Doctor," *San Francisco Chronicle*, Dec. 29, 1993.

39. *Buck v. Bell*, 274 U.S. 200.

40. Ibid.

41. "Three Generations of Imbeciles," editorial, *Detroit Daily News*, Dec. 16, 1992.

42. Rita L. Marker et al., "Euthanasia: A Historical Overview," *Maryland Journal of Contemporary Issues* 2 (Summer 1991), p. 276.

43. Ibid.

44. Cited in Rita Marker, *Deadly Compassion* (New York: William Morrow, 1993), p. 39.

45. Arthur Caplan, "The Relevance of the Holocaust to Bioethics Today," in John J. Michalczyk, ed., *Medicine, Ethics, and the Third Reich: Historical and Contemporary Issues* (London: Sheed & Ward, 1994), pp. 10–11.

46. Lifton, *Nazi Doctors*, p. 17.

47. Burleigh, *Death and Deliverance*, pp. 5–6.

48. Ibid. p. 6.

49. Ibid., p. 233.

50. *Compassion in Dying v. State of Washington*, p. 3117.

51. Binding and Hoche, *Permitting the Destruction*, p. 241.

52. *Compassion in Dying v. State of Washington*, p. 3135.

53. Binding and Hoche, *Permitting the Destruction*, p. 241.

54. *Compassion in Dying v. State of Washington*, n. 120, p. 3201.

55. Binding and Hoche, *Permitting the Destruction*, p. 241.

56. *Compassion in Dying v. State of Washington*, p. 3201.

57. Binding and Hoche, *Permitting the Destruction*, p. 242.

58. *Compassion in Dying v. State of Washington*, p. 3135.

59. Binding and Hoche, *Permitting the Destruction*, p. 265.

60. *Compassion in Dying v. State of Washington*, p. 3204.

61. Binding and Hoche, *Permitting the Destruction*, p. 261.

62. *Compassion in Dying v. State of Washington*, p. 3217.

63. Carol J. Gill, interview with author, Dec. 4, 1995.

64. Ibid.

65. Leo Alexander, M.D., "Medical Science Under Dictatorship," *New England Journal of Medicine* 241 (July 14, 1949); reprint, p. 8.

66. Ibid. p. 11.

CHAPTER 4:   Dutch Treat

1. Leo Alexander, M.D., "Medical Science Under Dictatorship," *New England Journal of Medicine* 241 (July 14, 1949); reprint, p. 9.

2. Ibid.

3. Dr. I. van der Sluis, interview with author, Oct. 13, 1995.

4. Penal Code of the Netherlands, Paragraphs 293 and 294.

5. "42 Million Lack Health Insurance, Study Concludes," *Oakland Tribune* (based on study by American College of Physicians and Surgeons), April 27, 1996.

6. Eugene Sutorius, interview with author, Oct. 17, 1995.

7. "Euthanasia Case Leeuwarden–1983" (excerpts from court decision), trans. Walter Lagerway, *Issues in Law and Medicine* 3 (1988), pp. 429, 439–42.

8. "Implications of Mercy," *Time*, March 5, 1973, p. 70.

9. Ibid.

10. Ibid.

11. Carlos Gomez, *Regulating Death* (New York: Free Press, 1991), p. 30.

12. "Dutch Parliament Approves Law Permitting Euthanasia," *New York Times*, Feb. 10, 1993.

13. Gomez, *Regulating Death*, p. 32.

14. Timothy E. Quill, M.D., "Physician-Assisted Death: Progress or Peril?" *Suicide and Life Threatening Behavior* 24, no. 4 (Winter 1994), pp. 315–25.

15. Ibid., p. 318.

16. Dr. K. F. Gunning, interview with author, Oct. 18, 1995.

17. Ibid.

18. J. Remmelink et al., *Medical Decisions About the End of Life,* in 2 vols.: *Report of the Committee to Study the Medical Practice Concerning Euthanasia; The Study for the Committee on the Medical Practice Concerning Euthanasia* (The Hague, 1991). Cited hereafter as Remmelink Report I/II.

19. Remmelink Report I, p. 14, n. 2.

20. Richard Fenigsen, M.D., Ph.D., "The Report of the Dutch Government Committee on Euthanasia," *Issues in Law and Medicine* 7, no. 3 (November 1991), p. 340.

21. Remmelink Report I, p. 13.

22. Ibid., p. 15.

23. Remmelink Report II, p. 49, Table 6.4.

24. Ibid., p. 50, Table 6.6.

25. Ibid., p. 58, Table 7.2.

26. This figure was arrived at by calculating 8.5 percent (the approximate percentage of all Dutch deaths that result from killing by physicians) of the total number of yearly U.S. deaths, which in 1985 was a little over 2 million (*New York Public Library Desk Reference,* 1989, p. 613).

27. "Dutch GPs Report Euthanasia as Death by Natural Causes," *British Medical Journal* 304 (Feb. 1992).

28. P. J. van der Maas, "Euthanasia and Other Medical Decisions Concerning the End of Life, *Health Policy Monographs* 2 (1992), p. 49.

29. Fenigsen, "Euthanasia in the Netherlands," p. 239; and "Special Report from the Netherlands," *New England Journal of Medicine* (Nov. 1996), pp. 1699–1711.

30. "Dutch Court Rejects Nurse's Defense in Euthanasia Case," Reuters, March 23, 1995.

31. Dr. K. F. Gunning interview.

32. Herbert Hendin, M.D., "Assisted Suicide, Euthanasia, and Suicide Prevention: The Implications of the Dutch Experience," *Suicide and Life Threatening Behavior* 25 (1) (Spring 1995), p. 202.

33. Ibid., pp. 201–2.

34. Herbert Hendin, M.D., "Seduced by Death: Doctors, Patients, and the Dutch Cure," *Issues in Law and Medicine* 10, no. 2 (Fall 1994), p. 137.

35. Ibid., p. 139.

36. "Choosing Death," *The Health Quarterly,* WGBH Boston, aired March 23, 1993.

37. Ibid.

38. "Choosing Death."

39. Hendin, "Assisted Suicide, Euthanasia, and Suicide Prevention," p. 197.

40. "Choosing Death."

41. Ibid.

42. Ibid.

43. Mark O'Keefe, "The Dutch Way of Doctoring," *The Oregonian,* Jan. 9, 1995.

44. Herbert Hendin, M.D., "Dying of Resentment," *New York Times,* March 21, 1996.

45. Ibid.

46. Dr. K. F. Gunning interview.

47. O'Keefe, "Dutch Way of Doctoring."

48. "CQ Interview: Arlene Judith Klotzko and Dr. Boudewijn Chabot Discuss Assisted Suicide in the Absence of Somatic Illness," *Cambridge Quarterly of Healthcare Ethics* 4, no. 2 (Spring 1995), p. 243.

49. Gene Kaufman, "State v. Chabot: A Euthanasia Case Note," *Ohio Northern University Law Review* 20, no. 3 (1994), p. 816–17.

50. Ibid., p. 817.

51. Eugene Sutorius interview.

52. Ibid.

53. "Choosing Death."

54. "Dutch Court Says Baby's Euthanasia Justifiable," Reuters, April 26, 1995.

55. "Choosing Death."

56. Fenigsen, "Euthanasia in the Netherlands," p. 240.

57. "Report of the Dutch Royal Society of Medicine: Life-Terminating Actions with Incompetent Patients," part I, "Severely Handicapped Newborns," *Issues in Law and Medicine* 8, no. 2 (1992).

58. Ibid., p. 173.

59. Fenigsen, "Euthanasia in the Netherlands," p. 240.

60. Ibid., p. 238.

61. "Dutch Pediatricians Move to Address Infant Euthanasia," *American Medical News*, Sept. 14, 1992, p. 6.

62. "Choosing Death."

63. G. G. Humphrey, Letters to the Editor, *Journal of American Medicine* 260 (1988), p. 788.

64. Royal Dutch Medical Association, *Vision of Euthanasia* (The Hague: Royal Dutch Medical Association, 1986), p. 14.

65. H. Jack Gleiger, M.D., editorial, "Race and Health Care—An American Dilemma?" *New England Journal of Medicine* 335, no. 11 (Sept. 1996).

66. W. C. M. Klijn, interview with author, Oct. 17, 1995.

67. Dr. Pieter Admiraal, interview with author, Sept. 14, 1995.

68. Hendin, "Seduced by Death," pp. 158–59.

69. Ibid.

70. Ibid.

71. Ibid.

72. "Helping a Man Kill Himself as Shown on Dutch TV," *New York Times*, Nov. 13, 1994.

73. Andrew Kelly (Reuters), "Audience Plays Solomon in Dutch Show," *Chicago Tribune*, Oct. 28, 1993.

74. Sarah Lambert, "Dutch Stand Idly By as Child Drowns," *San Francisco Examiner*, Aug. 28, 1993.

75. Ibid.

76. *Levenswens-Verklaring* (*Declaration on the Value of Life*), wallet card, distributed by Stichting Schuilplaats, Veenendaal, Netherlands.

77. Ibid.

78. Dr. Pieter Admiraal interview.

79. Eugene Sutorius interview.

80. Ploes Pijnenborg, *End of Life Decisions in Dutch Medical Practice* (The Hague: CIP-Gegevens Koniglijke Bibliotheek, 1995), p. 146.

CHAPTER 5:   Inventing the Right to Die

1. Jack Kevorkian, M.D., "Fail-Safe Model for Justifiable Medically Assisted Suicide ('Medicide')," *American Journal of Forensic Psychiatry* 13, no. 1 (1992), pp. 11–12.

2. Ibid., p. 22.

3. Dr. Ljubisa J. Dragovic, interview with author, Aug. 21, 1996.

4. Derek Humphry, "Oregon's New Assisted Suicide Law Gives No Sure Comfort to Dying," Letters to the Editor, *New York Times,* Dec. 3, 1994, p. 22.
5. Ibid.
6. *Lee v. State of Oregon* (Civil no. 94-6467-HO, U.S. District Court for the District of Oregon, 1994), opinion (equal protection) of Judge Michael Hogan, court transcript, pp. 5–6.
7. Transcript of "Yes on 16" advertisement aired on various stations, beginning Oct. 24, 1994.
8. Transcript of "Yes on 16" advertisement aired on various stations, beginning Oct. 12, 1994.
9. Interview with author (interviewee asked anonymity), Oct. 10, 1995.
10. Rita Marker, interview with author, June 13, 1996.
11. Oregon, Death with Dignity Act, Sect. 2.01.
12. Ibid.
13. Oregon, Death with Dignity Act, Sect. 3.01 et seq.
14. "No License to Kill," editorial, *The Oregonian,* Nov. 30, 1995.
15. Oregon, Death with Dignity Act, Sect. 1.01.
16. Dr. Gary L. Lee, interview with author, Nov. 30, 1995.
17. Dr. Ira R. Byock, interview with author, June 18, 1996.
18. Patrick O'Neill, "Suicide Aid Worries Oregon Doctors," *The Oregonian,* Feb. 1, 1996.
19. Carol Gill, interview with author, June 13, 1996.
20. Mark O'Brien, "Thoughts About 'Terminal Illness' from Inside an Iron Lung," *Oakland Tribune,* April 5, 1995.
21. Ibid.
22. Tom Bates, "Write to Die," *The Oregonian,* Dec. 18, 1994.
23. See, for example, New York State Task Force on Life and the Law, *When Death Is Sought: Assisted Suicide and Euthanasia in the Medical Context,* report (New York: New York State Task Force, May 1994).
24. Oregon Death with Dignity Act, Sect. 1.01.
25. Ibid.
26. Dr. Gary Lee interview.
27. *Lee v. Harcleroad,* Case no. 94-6467-TC, U.S. District Court, District of Oregon, 1994, Complaint for Declaratory and Injunctive Relief, civil rights.
28. Ibid.
29. *Lee v. State of Oregon,* 891 F. Supp., 1995, pp. 1421, 1438.
30. Ibid., pp. 1438–39.
31. Ibid., p. 1439.
32. "Federal Judge Refuses to Enforce Assisted Suicide Law," Associated Press, May 10, 1996.
33. Ibid.
34. Paul M. Barrett, "Federal Appeals Judge Embraces Liberalism in Conservative Times," *Wall Street Journal,* March 10, 1996.
35. *Compassion in Dying v. State of Washington,* Case. no. 94-35534, U.S. Court of Appeals for the Ninth Circuit, 79 F. 3d 790 (1994), p. 3131.
36. The other seven judges joining in the majority opinion were James R. Browning, Procter Hug, Jr., Mary M. Schroeder, Betty B. Fletcher, Harry Pregerson, Charles Wiggings, and David R. Thompson.
37. *Compassion in Dying v. State of Washington,* p. 3178.
38. *People of Michigan v. Jack Kevorkian et al.; Hobbins v. Attorney General of Michigan,* Case Nos. 99591-99674, 99752, p. 27.
39. *Compassion in Dying v. State of Washington,* p. 3178.
40. Dr. Ira R. Byock interview.
41. *Compassion in Dying v. State of Washington,* p. 3178.
42. Ibid., p. 3206.
43. Ibid., pp. 3188–89.

44. Ibid., p. 3190.
45. Ibid., p. 3201, n. 120.
46. Ibid., p. 3188.
47. Ibid., p. 3201.
48. Howard Mintz, "Dissenters Rip Right-to-Die Vote," *The Recorder,* June 13, 1996.
49. *Quill v. Dennis C. Vacco* (U.S. Court of Appeals for the Second Circuit, 1996), F.3d 49 (1995), p. 586.
50. Ibid., p. 12.
51. *In re Quinlan* (Supreme Court of New Jersey, 1975), N.J. 70, p. 10.
52. Diane Gianelli, "Karen Ann Quinlan's Family Remembers," *American Medical News,* Dec. 15, 1989, pp. 9, 49–50. Quinlan lived for ten years after her life respirator was withdrawn.
53. *Compassion in Dying v. State of Washington,* F. 3d 49 (1995), p. 586.
54. Ibid.
55. *Quill v. Koppell* (U.S. District Court, Southern District of New York, 1994), Civ. 94, p. 5321.
56. 1993 PA 3.
57. *People of Michigan v. Jack Kevorkian et al.; Hobbins v. Attorney General of Michigan,* Case Nos. 99591-99674, 99752.
58. Ibid., p. 33.
59. Ibid., p. 32.
60. Ibid., p. 33.
61. *Planned Parenthood of Southern Pennsylvania v. Casey,* U.S. Supreme Court, 1992, U.S. 505.
62. *Roe v. Wade,* U.S. Supreme Court, 1973, U.S. 410, p. 113.
63. *Michigan v. Kevorkian,* p. 35.
64. Ibid., p. 36.
65. Ibid., p. 42.
66. Ibid., pp. 42–43.
67. Ibid., p. 43.
68. Charles H. Baron et al., "Statute: A Model Act to Authorize and Regulate Physician-Assisted Suicide," *Harvard Journal on Legislation* 33, no. 1 (1996), p. 11.
69. Ibid., p. 15.
70. Timothy Quill, M.D., "A Case of Individualized Decision Making," *New England Journal of Medicine* 324 (March 1991), pp. 691–94. Reprinted in Quill, *Death and Dignity: Making Choices and Taking Charge* (New York: Norton, 1993), pp. 9–16.
71. Ibid., p. 15.
72. Quill, "Care of the Hopelessly Ill: Proposed Clinical Criteria for Physician-Assisted Suicide," *New England Journal of Medicine* 327 (Nov. 1992).
73. In several articles and in his book *Death and Dignity* (see n. 70), Dr. Quill urges that assisted suicide be made available for nonterminally ill people.
74. Quill, "Care of the Hopelessly Ill," p. 1382.
75. Ibid.
76. Ibid.
77. Ibid.
78. Timothy Quill, M.D., "Risk Taking by Physicians in Legally Gray Areas," *Albany Law Review* 57 (1994), p. 700.

CHAPTER 6: Euthanasia's Betrayal of Medicine

1. Timothy E. Quill, M.D., "Physician Assisted Death: Progress or Peril?" *Suicide and Life Threatening Behavior* 24, no. 4 (Winter 1994), p. 317.

2. Dr. Quill doesn't really mean it when he writes that hospice care must fail before assisted suicide can be considered. Later in the same article (p. 320), he writes that it should be considered if hospice is "unacceptable to the patient." Thus, in the world envisioned by Dr. Quill, a patient who could be effectively treated with comfort care but who wants to die immediately instead can receive assisted suicide. So much for "last resorts."

3. Jack Kevorkian, *Prescription Medicide* (Buffalo: Prometheus Books, 1991), p. 175.

4. Stephen Jamison, Ph.D., *Final Acts of Love: Families, Friends, and Assisted Dying* (New York: Putnam's, 1995), pp. 258–60.

5. Lonny Shavelson, *A Chosen Death: The Dying Confront Assisted Suicide* (New York: Simon & Schuster, 1995), p. 224.

6. Jack Kevorkian, interview, *Dateline*, NBC, Aug. 25, 1996.

7. New York State Task Force on Life and the Law, *When Death Is Sought: Assisted Suicide and Euthanasia in the Medical Context*, report (New York: New York State Task Force on Life and the Law, May 1994).

8. Ibid., p. ix.

9. Ibid., p. xiii.

10. Ibid.

11. Ibid.

12. Ibid., p. xv.

13. Ibid.

14. Ibid.

15. Ibid., p. xi.

16. *Report of the University of Rochester Medical Center Task Force on Physician-Assisted Suicide* (Rochester, N.Y.: University of Rochester, 1993), p. 4.

17. "When Will Adequate Pain Treatment Be the Norm?" editorial, *Journal of the American Medical Association* 274, no. 23 (Dec. 20, 1995).

18. "Painfully Clear," editorial, *American Medical News*, Sept. 26, 1994.

19. Ada Jacob, R.N., Ph.D., et al., "Special Report: New Clinical-Practice Guidelines for the Management of Pain in Patients with Cancer," *New England Journal of Medicine* 330, no. 9 (March 3, 1994).

20. Department of Consumer Affairs, State of California, *Summit on Effective Pain Management: Removing Impediments to Appropriate Prescribing*, report, Sacramento, March 18, 1994, p. 3.

21. "42 Million Lack Health Insurance, Study Concludes," *Oakland Tribune*, April 27, 1996.

22. Rachel L. Jones, "Health Plans Cover Fewer U.S. Children," *Philadelphia Inquirer*, Aug. 17, 1996.

23. Bruce Hilton, "Hospital Chains Are on a Buying Binge," *San Francisco Examiner*, Aug. 23, 1996.

24. Jeff Wong, "Woman Says She Would Seek Kevorkian's Help Days Before Death," Associated Press, July 10, 1996.

25. Richard Leiby, "Just How Sick Was Rebecca Badger?" *Washington Post*, July 29, 1996.

26. Dr. Ljubisa J. Dragovic interview.

27. Leiby, "Just How Sick."

28. John R. Cookson, F.S.A., and Peter F. Reilly, F.S.A., "National Health Expense Forecast," in *Milliaman & Robertson's Health Insurance Trend Model*, 1996, available from the publisher on the Internet, http://www.captive.com/service/m&r.html.

29. "Traditional Health Insurers Losing Ground to Managed Care," Reuters, May 13, 1996.

30. Ibid.

31. Ibid.

32. See, for example, Elisabeth Rosenthal, "Patients Say N.Y. HMOs Don't Deal Well with Complex Illnesses," *New York Times*, July 15, 1996.

33. Kurt Laumann, "How Restructuring Affects Patient Care," *San Francisco Chronicle,* April 5, 1995. Laumann is the president of the California Nurses Association.

34. Robert Pear, "Doctors Say H.M.O.'s Limit What They Can Tell Patients," *New York Times,* Dec. 21, 1995.

35. Stuart Auerbach, "Managed Care Backlash," *Washington Post,* June 25, 1996.

36. Rebecca Smith, "Doctors, Nurses Must Take Loyalty Oaths, Groups Say," *San Jose Mercury News,* July 17, 1996; Sabin Russell, "Put Company First, Hospital Handbook Tells Workers," *San Francisco Chronicle,* July 17, 1996.

37. "Kaiser Permanente Southern California Region Business Plan, 1995–97," Kaiser Permanente Corp., Los Angeles.

38. Ibid.

39. "Evaluation of Medicaid Managed Care," J. E. Sisk et al., *Journal of the American Medical Association* 276, no. 1 (July 1996).

40. Harris Meyer, "Quality Problems Could Spell Trouble for Medicaid HMOs," *American Medical News,* Jan. 23–30, 1995.

41. Daniel P. Salmasy, O.F.M., M.D., "Managed Care and Managed Death," *Archives of Internal Medicine,* Jan. 23, 1995, p. 134.

42. "When Doctors Become Subcontractors of Medical Care," *USA Today,* Jan. 22, 1996.

43. Ibid.

44. *In the Matter of the Accusation of the Commissioner of Corporations of the State of California v. TakeCare Health Plan, Inc.,* hearing before the Department of Corporations of the State of California, Nov. 17, 1994, File no. 933-0290.

45. Ibid., p. 7.

46. Ibid., p. 4.

47. Ibid., p. 5.

48. Ibid., p. 6.

49. Ibid., p. 12.

50. Robert Pear, "U.S. Shelves Plan to Limit Rewards to HMO Doctors," *New York Times,* July 8, 1996.

51. Ibid.

52. Auerbach, "Managed Care Backlash."

53. Rhonda L. Rundle, "Pacificare Health Agrees to Buy FHP International," *Wall Street Journal,* Aug. 6, 1996.

54. Based on disclosure statements on file with the office of the California attorney general.

55. Auerbach, "Managed Care Backlash."

56. *New York Times,* April 11, 1995.

57. Harvey Rosenfield, *Silent Violence, Silent Death: The Hidden Epidemic of Medical Malpractice* (Washington, D.C.: Essential Books, 1994), p. 9.

58. Charles B. Inlander, Lowell S. Levin, and Ed Weiner, *Medicine on Trial: The Appalling Story of Ineptitude, Malfeasance, Neglect, and Arrogance* (New York: Prentice Hall, 1988), p. 178.

59. T. A. Brennan, et al., *Patients, Doctors and Lawyers: Medical Injury, Malpractice Litigation, and Patient Compensation in New York,* Report of the Harvard Medical Practice Study to the State of New York (Cambridge: President and Fellows of Harvard University, 1990).

60. As described in Ralph Nader and Wesley J. Smith, *No Contest* (New York: Random House, 1996).

61. Inlander, Levin, and Weiner, *Medicine on Trial,* p. 178.

62. I interviewed several people in the spring and summer of 1996 who were close to the administrative and civil cases that resulted from this incident. Although several spoke freely about the facts of the case and all were in substantial agreement about them, none would permit me to use their names nor would they disclose the names of the principals.

63. "Review Process at UUCSF Regarding Withdrawal of Life Support Case," *UCSF News,* March 29, 1995.

64. Sarah Henry, "The Battle over Assisted Suicide," *California Lawyer,* Jan. 1996, p. 34.

65. O'Neill, "Suicide Aid Worries Oregon Doctors."

66. "Physicians 'Polarized' About Ethics of Helping Patients Die," *Physician's Management Newsline,* Oct. 1994.

67. National Hospice Organization, "New Findings Address Escalating End-of-Life Debate," press release, Oct. 3, 1996, describing N.H.O.–sponsored public opinion poll conducted by the Gallup Organization of Princeton, N.J.

68. O'Neill, "Suicide Aid Worries Doctors."

69. "Physicians 'Polarized.' "

70. "AMA Soundly Reaffirms Policy Opposing Physician-Assisted Suicide," American Medical Association, press release, June 25, 1996.

71. British Medical Association, *Euthanasia: Report of the Working Party to Review the British Medical Association's Guidance on Euthanasia,* 1988.

72. World Medical Association, "Statement on Physician-Assisted Suicide," adopted by the 44th World Medical Assembly, Marbella, Spain, Sept. 1992.

73. Allen J. Bennett, M.D., "When Is Medical Treatment Futile?" *Issues in Law and Medicine* 9, no. 1 (1993), pp. 40, 43.

74. Marcia Angell, M.D., "After Quinlan: The Dilemma of the Vegetative State," *New England Journal of Medicine* 330, no. 21 (May 1994), p. 1524.

75. Charles B. Clayman, ed., *The American Medical Association Encyclopedia of Medicine* (New York: Random House, 1989), p. 334.

76. Angell, "After Quinlan."

77. Thomas Marzen, attorney, interview with author, Nov. 14, 1995.

78. Madelaine Lawrence, R.N., Ph.D., "The Unconscious Experience," *American Journal of Critical Care* 4, no. 3 (May 1995).

79. Jeremy Laurance, "Vegetative State Diagnosis Wrong in Many Patients," *The Times* (London), July 5, 1996.

80. Margaret P. Battin, "Age Rationing of Health Care," *Ethics,* Jan. 1987, pp. 336–37.

81. Ibid.

82. Ibid., p. 340.

83. Derek Humphry, "Rational Suicide Among the Elderly," *Suicide and Life Threatening Behavior,* Spring 1992.

84. "Rationing Health Care: Will It Be Necessary? Can It Be Done Without Age or Disability Discrimination?" *Issues of Law and Medicine* 5, no. 3 (1989), p. 364.

85. Daniel Callahan, *The Troubled Dream of Life* (New York: Simon & Schuster, 1993), pp. 201–2.

86. Ibid., p. 217.

87. Donald J. Murphy, M.D., and Elizabeth Barbour, "GUIDe (Guidelines for the Use of Intensive Care in Denver): A Community Effort to Define Futile and Inappropriate Care," *New Horizons* 2, no. 3 (1994).

88. "Draft Guidelines Supported by CCMD," CCMD, May 17, 1996.

89. Ibid.

90. Murphy and Barbour, "GUIDe," Introduction.

91. Dr. Donald J. Murphy, interview with author, July 3, 1996.

92. Quoted in Nat Hentoff, "Death: The Ultimate in Managed Care," *Washington Post,* July 16, 1994.

93. Oregon, Department of Human Resources, *The Oregon Health Plan* (Salem, Ore.: Office of Medical Assistance Programs, 1995).

94. Ezekiel J. Emanuel, M.D., Ph.D., "Cost Savings at the End of Life: What Do the Data Show?" *Journal of the American Medical Association* 275, no. 24 (June 1996), pp. 1907–14.

95. Senate Finance Committee Hearings, "Advance Directives and Care at the End of Life," testimony of Joanne Lynn, M.D., M.A., May 5, 1994.

96. Ezekiel J. Emanuel, M.D., Ph.D., and Linda L. Emanuel, M.D., Ph.D., "The Economics of Dying," *New England Journal of Medicine* 330, no. 8 (Feb. 1994), p. 543.

97. Doug Bandow, "Dole's Military Card," *New York Times*, July 6, 1996.

98. *Knox-Keene Plan Expenditures Summary*, results of survey sponsored by California Medical Association, 1995. The CMA compiled the data based on information on file with the California Department of Corporations, the agency in charge of regulating H.M.O.s.

99. Ibid.

100. Report of the Illinois State Medical Society, *Illinois Health Maintenance Organizations*, November 1996.

101. Milt Freudenheim, "Health Chief's Big Paychecks for Chopping Costs," *New York Times*, April 11, 1995.

102. Hilton, "Hospital Chains Are on a Buying Binge."

103. Dr. Donald J. Murphy interview.

104. Ibid.

105. Maureen Dowd, "See Dick Run," *New York Times*, July 11, 1996.

106. Dr. Donald J. Murphy interview.

107. Ibid.

108. Alexander Morgan Capron, "Abandoning a Waning Life," *Hastings Center Report*, July–Aug. 1995, p. 24.

109. Ibid.

110. Ibid., p. 26.

111. Arthur Caplan, "Point Counterpoint: Should Physicians Be Allowed to Withhold CPR Unilaterally?" *Physician's Weekly* 6, no. 4 (Jan. 1989).

112. *In re Terry Achtabowski, Jr.*, Docket no. 93-1247-AV, Michigan Court of Appeals, 1994, Appellee's Brief, p. 2.

113. Sharon Andres Green, "Relatives Struggle over Disabled Baby," *Detroit Free Press*, Aug. 11, 1993.

114. *In re Ryan Nguyen*, Case no. 94-06074-5, State of Washington Superior Court, Petitioner Nguyen's Brief Supporting Motion for Injunction.

115. Washington, Department of Child Protective Services, Intake Summary Report for Referral, Nov. 23, 1994.

116. *In re Ryan Nguyen*, Sacred Heart Medical Center Brief.

117. Ibid., Declaration of Dr. Nancy Binder, Dec. 9, 1994.

118. Jeanette White, "Baby Ryan May Be Released from Hospital," *Spokane Review*, Jan. 8, 1995.

119. *Nghia Nguyen et al. v. Sacred Heart Medical Center*, Case no. 95-202095-4, State of Washington Superior Court.

120. Dr. Donald J. Murphy interview.

Chapter 7:   Euthanasia as a Form of Oppression

1. Paul Longmore, interview with author, July 13, 1996.

2. Evan Kemp, speech before Capitol Hill Club, Washington, D.C., Oct. 10, 1995.

3. Kathi Wolfe, interview with author, May 21, 1996.

4. Paul Longmore interview.

5. Carol Gill, interview with author, Dec. 4, 1995.

6. "Disability Rights and Assisted Suicide," *One Step Ahead,* Aug. 22, 1994.

7. "Advanced Directives and Disability," *One Step Ahead's Second Opinion* 2, no. 1 (Winter 1995).

8. William G. Strothers, "Death and Life—It's Time to Choose Up Sides," *Mainstream,* Feb. 1996.

9. Diane Coleman, interview with author, July 9, 1966.

10. Ibid.

11. Denny Boyd, "Where Were the Doctors When Robert Latimer Needed Them?" *Vancouver Sun,* Nov. 30, 1994.

12. *Latimer v. Her Majesty the Queen* (Court of Appeal for Saskatchewan), dissent to majority opinion, July 12, 1995.

13. Larry Johnson, personal correspondence, Feb. 7, 1996.

14. Teague Johnson, "My Body Is Not My Enemy," *Vancouver Sun,* Dec. 9, 1994.

15. Teague Johnson, CompuServe, April 4, 1994.

16. Ibid., undated letter.

17. Paul Longmore interview.

18. Larry Johnson, personal correspondence.

19. Rita Marker, *Deadly Compassion* (New York: William Morrow, 1993), p. 44.

20. *Bouvia v. Superior Court* (California Court of Appeals, 1986), California Appellate Report 179, p. 30.

21. Mark O'Brien, interview with author, July 10, 1996.

22. Gregory E. Pence, *Classical Cases in Medical Ethics* (New York: McGraw Hill, 1995).

23. Paul Longmore, "Urging the Handicapped to Die," *Los Angeles Times,* April 25, 1986.

24. Paul Longmore interview.

25. Joseph Shapiro, *No Pity: People with Disabilities Forging a New Civil Rights Movement* (New York: Random House/Times Books, 1993), p. 259.

26. Ibid., 287.

27. K. A. Gerhart, et al., in *Annals of Emergency Medicine* 23 (1994), pp. 807–812.

28. R. Stensman in *Scandinavian Journal of Rehabilitation Medicine* 17 (1985), pp. 87–99.

29. J. R. Bach and M. C. Tilton in *Archives of Physical Medicine and Rehabilitation* 71 (1990), pp. 191–96.

30. Betsy J. Miner, "Messenger Jury Selection to Begin," *Lansing State Journal,* January 10, 1995.

31. Valerie Basheda, "Verdict's Message: Parents Have Rights," *Detroit News,* Feb. 3, 1995.

32. Peter Singer, *Rethinking Life and Death: The Collapse of Our Traditional Ethics* (New York: St. Martin's Press, 1995), pp. 213–14.

33. Lucette Lagnado, "Mercy Living," *Wall Street Journal,* Jan. 10, 1995.

34. Ibid.

35. Mary Voboril, "The Assisted Suicide of Myrna Lebov," *Newsday,* Jan. 16, 1996.

36. "Writer Wanted Relief," *Charleston Daily Mail,* July 8, 1995.

37. Lucette Lagnado, "How Lebov Bared Her Soul to Rabbis of Lincoln Square," *Forward,* Nov. 3, 1996.

38. Lucette Lagnado, "DA Stepping Up Inquiry in Death of Myrna Lebov," *Forward,* July 21, 1995.

39. Beverly Sloane, interview with author, April 19, 1996.

40. George Delury, diary, "Countdown: A Daily Log of Myrna's Mental State and View Toward Death," dated Feb. 27, 1995–July 4, 1995.

41. *Dateline,* NBC, aired Sept. 27, 1996.

42. Ibid.

43. Ibid.

44. Ibid.
45. Ibid.
46. Ibid.
47. *Dateline,* NBC, aired Sept. 27, 1996.
48. George Delury, speech before American Psychiatric Association, New York, N.Y., May 7, 1996.
49. *Charles Grodin Show,* CNBC, aired May 16, 1996.
50. Beverly Sloane interview.
51. *60 Minutes,* "Family Values," CBS, aired Feb. 25, 1996.
52. *In the Matter of Gerald Klooster Sr. ALIP,* Case Summary, File no. 95-01060-GD.
53. Sabin Russell and Henry K. Lee, "Custody Fight Father Hospitalized," *San Francisco Chronicle,* Sept. 25, 1996.
54. Carolyn Jones, "Judge Separates Alzheimer's Patient from Wife," *Oakland Tribune,* Sept. 28, 1996.
55. Dr. Gerald (Chip) Klooster II, interview with author, April 12, 1996.

CHAPTER 8: Commonly Heard Arguments for Euthanasia

1. Dr. Pieter Admiraal, interview with author, Sept. 14, 1995.
2. Rita Marker, interview with author, July 16, 1996.
3. Nat Hentoff, interview with author, July 21, 1996.
4. Ibid.
5. Paul Wilkes, "The Next Pro-Lifers," *New York Times Magazine,* July 21, 1996.
6. Yale Kamisar, "Some Non-Religious Views Against Proposed Mercy Killing Legislation," *Minnesota Law Review* 42, no. 6 (May 1958).
7. Nat Hentoff interview.
8. J. Remmelink et al., *Medical Decisions About the End of Life,* in 2 vols.: *Report of the Committee to Study the Medical Practice Concerning Euthanasia; The Study for the Committee on the Medical Practice Concerning Euthanasia* (The Hague, 1991), Vol. 1, p. 13. Cited hereafter as Remmelink Report I/II.
9. Ibid.
10. Ibid., p. 15.
11. Remmelink Report II, p. 49, Table 6.4.
12. Ibid., p. 50, Table 6.6.
13. Ibid., Table 6.5.
14. Ibid., Table 6.8.
15. Ibid., p. 58, Table 7.2.
16. Ibid., p. 72.
17. I. J. Keown, "The Law and Practice of Euthanasia in the Netherlands," *Law Quarterly Review* 108, no. 16 (1992), pp. 67–68.
18. American Medical Association Council on Ethics and Judicial Affairs, "Opinion 2.20," March 1986, 1992.
19. Ibid.
20. Rita Marker, interview with author.
21. Ibid.
22. "Kids and Pets Are Welcome at Dr. Cicely Saunders's Hospice for the Terminally Ill," *People,* Dec. 22, 1975.
23. Dr. Ira Byock, interview with author, June 18, 1996.
24. Dr. Linda Emanuel, quoted in Wilkes, "Next Pro-Lifers," *New York Times Magazine,* July 21, 1996.

25. Dr. Eric Chevlen, interview with author, July 22, 1996.

26. Ibid.

27. Reuters, "AIDS Pain Similar to Cancer Pain," Aug. 27, 1996.

28. Peter Singer, "Sanctity of Life or Quality of Life?" *Pediatrics* 72, no. 1 (July 1983).

29. Ibid., *Rethinking Life and Death: The Collapse of Our Traditional Ethics* (New York: St. Martin's Press, 1995), p. 220.

30. Scott Judd, book review of *Rethinking Life and Death,* by Peter Singer, *Hemlock Time-Lines,* May–June 1995, p. 10.

31. Yale Kamisar, "Abortion Right Is No Support," *Legal Times,* March 2, 1996.

32. Ibid.

33. Ibid.

34. E. J. Dionne, interview with author, July 24, 1996.

35. National Hospice Organization, "New Findings Address Escalating End-of-Life Debate," press release, Oct. 3, 1996, describing N.H.O.-sponsored public opinion poll conducted by the Gallup Organization of Princeton, N.J.

36. Rita Marker interview.

37. Phyllis Robb, interview with author, Aug. 12, 1996. See also Robb, "The Bitter Lesson of Living Wills," Letters to the Editor, *AMA News,* July 12, 1993.

38. Ibid.

39. David Wasson, " 'No Code" Nightmare," *Yakima Herald-Republic,* March 14, 1993.

40. William F. Stone, interview with author, Aug. 27, 1996.

41. "Rose Kennedy Doing Well After Surgery," *Boston Globe,* July 29, 1984.

42. William F. Stone interview.

43. *In re the Interest of Marjorie E. Nighbert* (Case no. 95-4-PSA, Circuit Court of the First Judicial Circuit of Florida, 1995), Report of Guardian ad Litem, March 23, 1995.

44. William F. Stone interview.

45. Ibid.

46. Ibid.

47. Ibid.

48. Ginny McKibben, "Patient Not Ready to Check Out," *Denver Post,* July 13, 1996.

49. Ibid.

50. Ibid.

51. E. J. Dionne, interview with author, July 22, 1996.

52. Dr. Eric Chevlen interview.

53. Dr. Gary Lee, interview with author, Nov. 30, 1995.

54. Dr. Eric Chevlen interview.

CHAPTER 9:   Hospice or Hemlock: The Choice Is Ours

1. Dr. Robin Bernhoft, interview with author, Aug. 27, 1996.

2. Judith S. Blanchard and Debra D. Seale, "Lessons from the First Year of a State Cancer Pain Initiative," *Journal of Oncology Management* (Nov.–Dec. 1993).

3. "A Guide to Hospice Care," *Harvard Health Letter,* April 1993.

4. Dr. Ira Byock, interview with author, June 18, 1996.

5. Lonny Shavelson, *A Chosen Death: The Dying Confront Assisted Suicide* (New York: Simon & Schuster, 1995).

6. House Subcommittee on the Constitution, testimony of Carlos F. Gomez, M.D., April 29, 1996.

7. Ira Byock, M.D., "Consciously Walking the Fine Line: Thought on a Hospice Response to Assisted Suicide and Euthanasia," *Journal of Palliative Care* 9, no. 3 (Sept. 1993), pp. 25–28.

8. Dr. Gary Lee interview.

9. "A Guide to Hospice Care," *Harvard Health Letter,* April 1993, pp. 9–12.

10. *Charles Grodin Show,* CNBC, aired Aug. 6, 1996.

11. Mark O'Brien, interview with author, Aug. 5, 1996.

12. Ibid.

13. Beth Roney Drennan, interview with author, April 13, 1995, and personal correspondence.

14. Ibid.

15. Ibid.

16. Ibid.

17. Ibid.

18. Ibid.

19. Ibid.

20. Ibid.

21. *Charles Grodin Show.*

22. Dennis Brace, interview with author, June 26, 1996.

23. Ibid.

24. Senate Finance Committee Hearings, "Advance Directives and Care at the End of Life," testimony of Joanne Lynn, M.D., M.A., May 5, 1994.

25. Patrick T. Hill, "Treating the Dying Patient," *Archives of Internal Medicine* (June 1995), p. 23.

26. Ibid., p. 24.

27. Greg A. Saches, M.D., "Improving Care for the Dying: Current Ethical Issues in Aging," *Generations,* Dec. 22, 1994.

28. John Hess, attorney, interview with author, Aug. 12, 1996.

29. Rita Marker, *Deadly Compassion* (New York: William Morrow, 1993), pp. 41–43.

30. Jeff Wong, "Woman Said She Would Seek Kevorkian's Help Days Before Death," Associated Press, July 10, 1996.

31. Dr. Lance K. Stell, interview with author, Sept. 28, 1995.

32. Ibid.

33. Jack Lessenberry, "Kevorkian Goes from Making Waves to Making Barely a Ripple," *New York Times,* Aug. 17, 1996.

34. Dr. Ira R. Byock, interview with author, June 18, 1996.

35. Dr. Maurice Victor, interview with author, Aug. 7, 1996.

36. Ibid.

37. Thomas Lorentzen, interviews with author, June 6 and Aug. 8, 1996.

INDEX

About the Author

WESLEY J. SMITH was born in 1949 in Los Angeles, California, and raised in Alhambra, a Los Angeles suburb. He passed the California Bar examination in 1975, after which he practiced law in the San Fernando Valley.

In 1985, he left the full-time practice of law to pursue a career in consumer advocacy, writing, and the media. His first book was *The Lawyer Book: A Nuts and Bolts Guide to Client Survival* (with an introduction by Ralph Nader), which was followed by *The Doctor Book: A Nuts and Bolts Guide to Patient Power, The Senior Citizens' Handbook: A Nuts and Bolts Guide to More Comfortable Living,* and, in collaboration with Nader, *Winning the Insurance Game, The Frugal Shopper, Collision Course: The Truth About Airline Safety,* and *No Contest: Corporate Lawyers and the Perversion of Justice in America.*

Smith has been an anti-euthanasia activist since 1993. He has appeared regularly on radio and television talk shows to discuss the issue, and his commentaries on the subject have been published in *The New York Times, Newsweek,* the *National Review, The Wall Street Journal, USA Today, Washington Legal Times,* the *San Francisco Chronicle,* the *Detroit Daily News,* and the *San Diego Union Tribune,* among other publications. He is the attorney for the International Anti-Euthanasia Task Force, and is a hospice volunteer.

Smith is also a lecturer and public speaker, and has appeared before professional associations, community groups, political conventions, and educational gatherings across the nation.

He lives in Oakland, California, with his wife, the syndicated political newspaper columnist Debra J. Saunders.